Hanuman
॥ Chalisa ॥

PRAKASH

Reprint 2024

PRAKASH

An imprint of Prakash Books India Pvt. Ltd

113/A, Darya Ganj,
New Delhi-110 002
Email: info@prakashbooks.com/sales@prakashbooks.com

f Fingerprint Publishing
X @FingerprintP
@fingerprintpublishingbooks
www.fingerprintpublishing.com

ISBN: 978 93 9018 347 0

DEDICATION

To a person whom I consider to be a
father figure—Late Dr. Narendra Desai,
whom we also lovingly know as Sri Nathji Prabhu.
He was a prominent industrialist and philanthropist
who impacted many lives. However, for me he
was like a guide and mentor who gave me genuine
appreciation and invaluable suggestions.
Dr. Desai was a life-long student of the Ramayana;
he loved to imbibe deep lessons from the epic,
even when spoken by a 'youngster' like me.
He always encouraged me to write and speak
on the Ramayana.

I dedicate this book on the Hanuman Chalisa
to this special soul, who was a great
devotee of Hanuman.

Introduction

Perhaps the most powerful meditation or the most popular hymn in the land of India is the Hanuman Chalisa. Breaking all barriers of diversity, everyone in India can either recite the Hanuman Chalisa by heart or has at least heard of it. It is so omnipresent that umpteen books have been penned glorifying it. And here I am, with yet another book on the glorious the Hanuman Chalisa, promising more thrills and delights for Hanuman lovers.

I am not a scholar. Nor do I claim perfection in understanding this most powerful prayer. I am simply a devotee of Hanuman and a great admirer of his divine qualities that have attracted millions of hearts. Having said that, this attempt to decode the Hanuman Chalisa is more devotional than scholarly. In this book, I have tried to associate every word of the Chalisa with stories of Hanuman from Valimiki's Ramayana, Tulsidas's Ramacharitramaanas, or the folklore of India in a way that the words come alive and the dohas become fully action-packed, leaving an imprint on the mind. Through various events and anecdotes, we see Hanuman's character weaving into shape. A shape so genuine and lovable that he gets integrated as an indispensable part of our life. At a few instances in the book, you will find a couple of stories repeated. This has been done because the same story can be seen and interpreted in multiple ways, seen through different angles, and each retelling brings something new to the surface.

When an ardent devotee of Hanuman's reads this book, it will serve as a meditation. When a great fan of Hanuman's adventures reads this book, it will serve as a fountain of unheard fun facts about Hanuman. When a story lover reads this book, it will serve as an ocean of sweet and wonderful stories. When a child reads this book, it will serve as a source of a million smiles. When a parent reads this book, it will be a treasure trove of bedtime stories.

The Hanuman Chalisa is amazing when recited, sung, heard, or read. With this book, I have strived to enhance that experience a million times over. If this book does touch a chord in your heart, all I ask from you is a small blessing or a small silent prayer.

Hanuman
‖ Chalisa ‖

shrī guru charana saroja raja,
nija mana mukuru sudhāri।
baranau raghuvara bimala jasu,
jo dāyaku phala chāri॥

buddhihīna tanu jānike,
sumirau pavanakumāra।
bala budhi vidyā dehu mohi
harahu kalesa vikāra॥

jaya hanumāna gnyāna guna sāgara।
jaya kapīsa tihu loka ujāgara॥ 1 ॥

rāma dūta atulita bala dhāmā।
anjani putra pavanasuta nāmā॥ 2 ॥

mahāvīra vikrama bajarangī।
kumati nivāra sumati ke sangī॥ 3 ॥

kanchana barana birāja subesā।
kānana kundala kunchita kesā॥ 4 ॥

hātha bajra au dhvajā birājai।
kādhe mūnja janeū sājai॥ 5 ॥

shankara swayam kesarī nandana।
teja pratāpa mahā jaga bandana॥ 6 ॥

vidyāvāna gunī ati chātura।
rāma kāja karibe ko ātura॥ 7 ॥

prabhu charitra sunibe ko rasiyā।
rāma lakhana sītā mana basiyā॥ 8 ॥

sūkshma rūpa dhari siyahi dikhāvā।
bikata rūpa dhari lanka jarāvā॥ 9 ॥

bhīma rūpa dhari asura sahāre।
rāmachandra ke kāja savāre॥ 10 ॥

lāya sanjīvani lakhana jiyāe।
shrī raghubīra harashi ura lāe॥ 11 ॥

raghupati kīnhī bahut barāī।
tuma mama priya bharatahi sama bhāī॥ 12 ॥

sahasa badana tumharo jasa gāvai।
asa kahi shrīpati kantha lagāvai॥ 13 ॥

sanakādika brahmādi munīsā।
nārada sārada sahita ahīsā॥ 14 ॥

jama kubera dikpāla jahā te।
kabi kobida kahi sakai kahā te॥ 15 ॥

tuma upakāra sugrīvahi kīnhā।
rāma milāya rājapada dīnhā॥ 16 ॥

tumharo mantra bibhīshana mānā।
lankeshvara bhae saba jaga jānā॥ 17 ॥

juga sahasra jojana para bhānū।
līlyo tāhi madhura phala jānū॥ 18 ॥

prabhu mudrikā meli mukha māhī।
jaladhi lāghi gaye acharaja nāhī॥ 19 ॥

durgama kāja jagata ke jete।
sugama anugraha tumhare tete॥ 20 ॥

rāma duāre tuma rakhavāre।
hota na āgnyā binu paisāre॥ 21 ॥

saba sukha lahai tumhārī saranā।
tuma rakshaka kāhū ko daranā॥ 22 ॥

āpana teja samhāro āpai।
tinau loka hāka te kāpai॥ 23 ॥

bhūta pishācha nikata nahi āvai।
mahābīra jaba nāma sunāvai॥ 24 ॥

nāsai roga harai saba pīrā।
japata nirantara hanumata bīrā॥ 25 ॥

sankata te hanumāna chhudāvai।
mana krama bachana dhyāna jo lāvai॥ 26 ॥

saba para rāma tapasvī rājā।
tina ke kāja sakala tuma sājā॥ 27 ॥

aura manoratha jo koī lāvai।
sohi amita jīvana phala pāvai॥ 28 ॥

chāro juga para tāpa tumhārā।
hai parasiddha jagata ujiyyārā॥ 29 ॥

sādhu santa ke tuma rakhavāre।
asura nikandana rāma dulāre॥ 30 ॥

ashta siddhi nau nidhi ke dātā।
asa bara dīnha jānakī mātā॥ 31 ॥

rāma rasāyana tumhare pāsā।
sadā raho raghupati ke dāsā॥ 32 ॥

tumhare bhajana rāma ko pāvai।
janama janama ke dukha bisarāvai॥ 33 ॥

anta kāla raghubara pura jāī।
jahā janma hari bhakta kahāī॥ 34 ॥

aura devatā chitta na dharaī।
hanumata sei sarba sukha karaī॥ 35 ॥

sankata katai mitai saba pīrā।
jo sumirai hanumata balabīrā॥ 36 ॥

jaya jaya jaya hanumāna gosāī।
kripā karahu gurudeva kī nāī॥ 37 ॥

jo shata bāra pātha kara koī।
chhūtahi bandi mahā sukha hoī॥ 38 ॥

jo yaha padhai hanumāna chālīsā।
hoya siddha sākhī gaurīsā॥ 39 ॥

tulasīdāsa sadā hari cherā।
kījai nātha hridaya maha derā॥ 40 ॥

pavantanaya sankata harana mangala mūrati rūpa।
rāma lakhan sītā sahita hridaya basahu sura bhūpa॥

shrī guru charana saroja raja,
nija mana mukuru sudhāri।
baranau raghuvara bimala jasu,
jo dāyaku phala chāri॥

*With the dust of the lotus feet of the Guru,
I cleanse the mirror of my mind and then
I sing the glories of Raghuvara, who bestows
the four-fold fruits of life.*

Blessings invoke auspiciousness. Anything begun with the seeking of blessings becomes most auspicious. Tulsidas begins the Hanuman Chalisa by seeking blessings of Sri Guru. This could mean Sri who is Guru or Guru who is empowered by Sri. Sri refers to Sita, the divine mother who is the essence of the Ramayana. Sita is considered to be the most important Guru in the Ramayana and an epitome of mercy and grace. In her presence, Rama never killed a demon. In fact the worst of the demons who deserved to be killed were forgiven by Mother Sita, beginning with Kakasura. Hanuman learnt so much from Mother Sita during his meeting with her in Lanka. With her blessing, anything was possible. Tulsidas, thus begins the auspicious narration of the Hanuman Chalisa with the divine guru Sita's blessings. Sita is not just a guru but capable of empowering anyone qualified to act as guru. The entire Sri Sampradaya, a bonafide Vaishnava Sampradaya, falls under the disciplic succession of Lakshmidevi who is an expansion of Mother Sita.

The lotus is used extensively in Vedic parlance. This is because the lotus grows in muddy water and yet blooms into a beautiful flower lending purity to its surrounding. Tulsidas refers to the feet of the guru as lotus. However negative the surroundings and circumstances, the guru not only remains unaffected but enlightens the environment.

Tulsidas says that the mirror of my mind has become dirty and contaminated and I am unable to see myself. He asks his guru to give him the dust of his feet to clean it. *Charana saroja raja* refers to the dust from the feet of Sri Guru. How will the dust clean? But divine dust has the power to clean. *Nija mana mukuru sudhāri; he* wants the dust from the lotus feet of his guru to clean his eyes and clean the mirror of the mind in order to see Rama as well as himself.

Taking dust from the feet of the spiritual master also refers to serving Sri Guru with a menial disposition. To love means to serve and to serve means to please. The most important way to serve Sri Guru is to sit at the feet of the spiritual master and hear from him. But what does one hear from Sri Guru?

Baranau raghuvara bimala jasu, which means one hears the glories of the Supreme Lord Rama, the great descendent of the Raghu dynasty. The greatest mercy of the Spiritual master descends from his mouth. Though Tulsidas has written the Hanuman Chalisa, which is technically supposed to be the glorification of Hanuman, but in truth it is the glorification of Lord Rama. Because whatever Hanuman does is to only bring glory and good name to Lord Rama. In every action of Hanuman's, Rama is hidden. Hanuman is most happy when Lord Rama is glorified and Lord Rama is most happy when his devotee Hanuman is glorified. Tulsidas, in glorifying Hanuman, is hoping to attain the mercy of Rama and Sita. The path to enter and understand the master's heart is through understanding and entering the servant's heart.

Raghuvara means a descendent from the lineage of Raghu dynasty. Usually the title is reserved for Rama. However, Tulsidas could also be referring to Hanuman. When Hanuman finds Sita in Lanka, she is overwhelmed with emotions of relief and joy and calls him 'son'. Rama too gets emotional many a times, when Hanuman brings the sanjivani herb to revive Lakshmana, and lovingly calls him 'son'. By referring to Hanuman as Raghuvara, Tulsidas alludes to the high esteem which Rama and Sita had for him.

When one hears the words of Sri Guru glorifying the Supreme Lord or his supreme devotee's activities, one attains perfection of four most important fruits of human life. The exalted commentator on the Hanuman Chalisa, Rambhadracharya, explains that the four goals of human life vary, depending on who you are. For a materialistic devotee, the four goals are dharma, artha, kama, and moksha. For a person seeking liberation, the four goals are salokya mukti, samipya mukti, sayujya mukti, and sarupya mukti. For a person seeking only devotion and nothing else, the four goals are dharma, gyana, yoga, and japa, all centred on cultivation of devotion to the Supreme Lord.

buddhihīna tanu jānike,
sumirau pavanakumāra।
bala budhi vidyā dehu mohi
harahu kalesa vikāra॥

*Knowing my body to be devoid of intelligence,
I remember you, the son of Vāyu.
Grant me strength, intelligence, and knowledge
and remove all my miseries and impurities.*

Tulsidas begins this verse with an attitude of humility. Spiritual life begins with the acceptance that 'I am weak and I need help'. In this acceptance lies the humility that is needed to grow spiritually. Material life makes one proud of even those things that one has not. Spiritual life makes one humble of even those things that one has. Because spiritual life helps one understand that one's strengths are not one's own. If one's strengths are not one's own and we are awarded them by some higher source, then why won't that higher source help us deal with our weaknesses also? That knowledge which makes us receptive to new learnings is the beginning of spiritual life.

Weakness here refers to not physical but spiritual. Spiritual weakness makes one susceptible to temptations of various kinds. When succumbed to, these temptations create miseries and pains. Tulsidas is helping us understand the importance of acceptance of this fact in this doha. He is not just exposing us to our greatest problem but also helping us find a solution for it.

When we accept that we are devoid of spiritual intelligence to deal with our shortcomings, we also simultaneously accept that we need help of someone who is higher in spiritual intelligence. Who is that person who is so evolved in spiritual intelligence and if taken shelter of can uplift us too? Tulsidas introduces Hanuman in that capacity into our lives. He is the one who can give us bala or strength, buddhi or intelligence, and vidya or knowledge, needed to help us deal with our shortcomings.

Rambhadracharya comments on this doha that our shortcomings are not one or two in number but are eleven in all. Tulsidas calls our shortcomings as kalesha and bikara. The word kalesha, according to the Patanjali Yoga Sutra, refers to five types of faults: avidya (mal-perception), asmita (egoism), raga (attachments/indulgences), dwesha (aversions), and abhinnivesa (fears/insecurities). The word bikara refers to six types of vices: Kama (lust/ desires which are born in the mind), krodha (anger which manifests from frustrated desires), lobha (greed which manifests from insatiable desires), moha (illusion which manifests from ignorance), mada (pride which manifests from the ego), and matsarya (envy which manifests from ingratitude).

Dealing with these five types of faults or kaleshas and six types of vices or bikaras is not easy. Together these eleven make one spiritually weak and ignorant. We need strength, intelligence, and knowledge to overcome these eleven impurities that are spiritually weakening us. Tulsidas recommends us to remember Hanuman who, according to him, is the best person who can easily help us overcome these eleven maladies and help us become spiritually strong and connect deeply with the Supreme Lord.

Tulsidas uses an interesting word here, 'tanu', referring to self or body. By using 'tanu', he reiterates the source of his ignorance which is his identification with the physical self. He claims that though one knows there is an inner eternal self, one still identifies himself with the outer changing physical body. He prays to Hanuman to bring about a change in that ignorant state by connecting him to divine and dynamic qualities.

Ramabhadracharya substantiates this even further by telling us why Hanuman is the best choice. Being the eleventh Rudra, Hanuman is the most equipped to help us overcome these eleven flaws. Not only is he the eleventh Rudra, he is also the personification of immense strength, intelligence, and knowledge. The entire the Hanuman Chalisa substantiates how Hanuman is actually the reservoir of unlimited strength, intelligence, and knowledge. When we take shelter of Hanuman, he can easily offer us all of these, thus helping us remove (harau) those deficiencies, and re-establishing us in our constitutional position as eternal servants of Lord Rama.

jaya hanumāna gnyāna guna sāgara।
jaya kapīsa tihu loka ujāgara॥ 1 ॥

Hail Hanuman, an ocean of
knowledge and virtues
The Lord of monkeys who illuminates
the three worlds. (1)

It is said that a fool is recognized the moment he opens his mouth. And a wise man remains unnoticed unless he opens his mouth. Speech reveals the level of your knowledge. Hanuman was such an ocean of knowledge that it was through his speech that Rama realized what a powerhouse Hanuman was! The first sentence of the first doha of the Hanuman Chalisa brings out the profound abundance of knowledge and virtues packed in Hanuman.

When Lord Rama and Lakshmana met Hanuman for the first time on the foothills of the Rishimukha Mountains, Hanuman captured Rama's heart with the first few words he uttered. On hearing only a few words from Hanuman, Rama pulled Lakshmana aside and extolled the glories of Hanuman.

Rama shared with Lakshmana that Hanuman was an ocean of knowledge and virtues. He had yet to meet someone like Hanuman who was as vaakya kushala or a magical weaver of words. Rama estimated that Hanuman must have spent a large quantum of time studying under expert masters. The quality of his speech reflected the quality of his education. Hanuman must have been so highly qualified that Rama couldn't detect a single flaw in either his speech or his body language, which is simply an extension of one's speech.

Rama was convinced that Hanuman had complete mastery over the Vedas. Why? Because mastery over the Vedas manifested itself through expertise in different aspects of communication and self-expression. Mastery over Atharva Veda brings in natural humility that reflects in one's words and gestures. Mastery over Yajur Veda is indicated by lavishness in one's vocabulary and a great retention power conferred by Yajur studies. Mastery over Rig Veda gives one the power of reproducing things verbatim on hearing just once. Mastery over Sama Veda adds a charm, suppleness, and melody to one's voice. Eloquence in speech is strength derived from digested knowledge.

Definitely Hanuman knew vyakrana or grammar to perfection. He was expert in mimamsa as he made no mistake in sentences. He was definitely proficient in tarka or logic, as he made no mistake in the tone in which different words were spoken. While talking, his body was so still that the listener was entirely focused on his speech alone. He knew which words were to be uttered from his palate, which to be uttered from the stomach, and which to be uttered from the nasal passage. The effect of producing sound from different locations created different emotions and had desired effects on the listener at subtle levels.

Rama deciphered all this simply by hearing a few words from Hanuman! In fact, Rama was of the opinion that if a cruel enemy with a raised sword heard Hanuman speak, he would drop his weapons. Hanuman could win hearts just by speaking a few words.

When Hanuman was a small child, he expressed his desire to gain knowledge from the best teacher in the universe. His father Kesari directed him to Surya, the sun god, whom Hanuman had intuitively and spontaneously selected as a storehouse of knowledge that he could devour. When Hanuman approached the sun god for admission into his school, Surya declined him stating lack of place in the classroom as the reason. There were already six million sages occupying the orbiting chariot which was Surya's mobile classroom. But nothing could deter Hanuman. When there is intense eagerness, there can be no obstacle big enough to stop you. Hanuman reasoned with his teacher that he didn't really need a place to sit. All he needed was his permission. Surya, of course, happily gave permission to such an enthusiastic student.

For Hanuman, hearing was the most important part of education. As long as he could hear his teacher, nothing else mattered. Any inconvenience was a price he was willing to pay for the good fortune of hearing from a great preceptor. As the flying school floated around the earth's orbit, Hanuman flew outside the classroom, parallel to them, facing his teacher. Sometimes Hanuman had to fly forward and sometimes backward, depending on the orientation of the chariot. Though faced with constant inconveniences, Hanuman paid rapt attention to the lessons being imparted and absorbed every word like a sponge. The master had no need to repeat a single concept and the student did not forget a single lesson. In a matter of just sixty orbits of the sun, Hanuman had mastered all the Vedas and their auxiliaries. In addition, he had mastered the nine vyakranas or rules of grammar in just a matter of nine days, what would take years for normal students.

But the most amazing aspect of Hanuman was his humility. Although he was amongst the most knowledgeable people in the world, he served Sugriva who possessed not even a fraction of that knowledge.

He served Sugriva simply because his teacher wanted him to do so. To serve someone who is inferior to you in every way requires real humility.

It is often seen that those with vast knowledge tend to become arrogant. They develop a sense of superiority that eclipses humility. But not so with Hanuman. Though he was most erudite even amongst the greatly learned (buddhimatam varistham), his humility stole Rama's heart. Hanuman was not just an embodiment of knowledge but also the embodiment of every virtue, as a result of having digested that knowledge. He was not just gyana sagar or an ocean of knowledge but also guna sagar or an ocean of virtues. *jaya hanumāna gnyāna guna sāgara*

The word kapi means vanara or monkey. When Lord Vishnu was about to incarnate as Lord Rama, he had instructed all devatas to take birth on the earth as vanaras. When he heard of this, Lord Shiva also became extremely eager to appear as a vanara. Lord Shiva explained to his wife Sati that he had been waiting for an opportunity to serve Lord Rama. Since his desire was to serve the Lord who was to appear in a human form, Shiva felt that it would be best to take a form that was less than a human form. Thus a monkey form would be most apt. A human being may hesitate to engage another human in menial service, but a monkey's service would be acceptable unhesitatingly. Thus Lord Shiva chose the form of a monkey to make his contribution to Rama lila. Since he wanted to focus on his service and not be distracted by the presence of his wife, he decided to remain a celibate in that role.

Sati became sad and dejected at not being able to participate and assist her husband in this incarnation. Then she was suddenly struck by a brilliant idea that would satisfy both of them. She proposed to Lord Shiva that she could incarnate as the tail of the monkey that Shiva became. Shiva agreed and thus Hanuman was born who was Rudra and Shakti combined together.

The word kapi also has another underlying meaning. This is in connection with its Sanskrit roots. *Pi* in Sanskrit means to drink and *ka* means joy. So kapi in this connotation means to drink joyfully. But drink what? Kapi refers to Hanuman as the one who joyfully drinks the nectar of Rama katha.

The word kapish is derived from the words kapi and isha, which means king of monkeys. This verse refers to Hanuman as Kapish, the king of monkeys, when he was clearly not the king. When Vali was alive, Vali was the king of monkeys and after his death, Sugriva became the king. Hanuman was not a king but a kingmaker. Whosoever stood by his side, that person became the king. Then why is Hanuman called the king of monkeys?

This is because true leadership is always measured by influence. Vali and Sugriva only sat on the throne, but Hanuman sat in every heart. Sitting on a throne is easy, but to rule hearts is difficult. Not only did he rule over the hearts of every citizen of Kishkinda, he also ruled over the hearts of Sita and Rama. Not only did he rule over the hearts of Sita and Rama, but by their blessings, continues to rule over the hearts of unlimited beings even today. Thus he is rightly addressed as kapish or king of Vanaras. *jaya kapīsa tihu loka ujāgara*

The universe was trembling thanks to Lord Vishnu's pastimes. Because of this, Lord Brahma who was sitting on the lotus and meditating, opened his eyes. The ewer (kamandalu) slipped from his hand. Now this was not an ordinary kamandalu. It held all future events within it. The kamandalu falling meant all the future events stored inside it also fell out. Brahma being alert, gathered all of them meticulously and filled them back in the kamandalu. No harm done, so he thought.

Meanwhile, Indra discovered two galaxies missing

from the universe. He informed Lord Vishnu and the two of them went to Brahma to find the cause behind it. Brahma revealed to them how the kamandalu had fallen from his hand and future events had scattered too. Lord Vishnu requested Lord Brahma to check if anything was missing from there. Searching through, Brahma recalled that a demon named Kaalant had also been stored inside the ewer but was missing now. Kaalant was to be born at the end of Brahma's life, 33 years later. But the mishap had released him much before his time. He had the power to eat all the universes including galaxies, planets, and stars. He could also swallow Adityas, Arun Deva, and celestial chariots belonging to Indra and Surya. His release could create a dangerous situation for one and all.

Lord Vishnu and Lord Brahma wondered what to do. Unfortunately, Lord Shiva was deep in meditation and could not be disturbed. Pushed into a corner, Lord Vishnu remembered Hanuman. Hanuman was one person who could save the world for sure! Lord Vishnu left to meet Hanuman who was at that time an adolescent.

As usual, Lord Vishnu found Hanuman in meditation on his master Lord Rama. Being an emergency, he apprised him of the situation faced by the universe. Things were so bad that Kaalant had even swallowed the Kaal Chakra. Without wasting a minute, Hanuman knew what he had to do and set off in search of Kaalant. All the demigods blessed Hanuman and empowered him to overpower Kaalant. However, Kaalant was not an ordinary demon. He was made of antimatter. When he swallowed matter, it collided with antimatter and both got destroyed. That was the secret of his strength.

Hanuman first tried to persuade him to go back to the kamandalu and come when it was the right time. Kaalant refused point blank. He challenged Hanuman to a duel. During the fight, Hanuman stepped into the Kaal Chakra and got transported to Fairyland. Fairyland was also in chaos. A demon had kidnapped the queen's daughter and all the angels were wallowing in sorrow. Hanuman went to the demon to rescue the damsel in distress. The demon shared his woes with Hanuman about a curse upon him by a vampire. To undo the curse, he needed a special pearl from the queen of angels. The glow of the pearl was sufficient to release him. But the queen had refused to part with her pearl leaving the demon with no option but to kidnap her daughter.

From the queen of angels Hanuman learnt that her pearl was in safe custody in Chal loka, the world of cheats. Hanuman reached there too but the planet had been captured by dwarfs. Hanuman fought the dwarfs and restored Chal loka to its original king who happily gave Hanuman the special pearl. Hanuman dropped the dwarfs to their planets but being in a hurry, he reached the wrong planet which was underwater. He saved the king of that planet too who in turn gave him a compass, a direction indicator. Hanuman used it to come out of the Kaal Chakra and go back to his universe.

Back home, he pursued Kaalant and engaged in another battle with him. Kaalant being antimatter, Hanuman thought of a novel strategy to defeat him. He allowed Kaalant to swallow him. Diving into his stomach, he found all the galaxies and planets that had gone missing. He also found Arun Deva and requested him to rotate the Kaal Chakra in a clockwise direction. Not surprisingly, everything started falling back in its place. Everything but Kaalant who started experiencing severe pain in his abdomen vomited Hanuman out. Lord Vishnu and Lord Brahma then reasoned with Kaalant that if he kept Surya Deva hidden then he would also die before time. Everything should happen in its own time. Kaalant had suffered enough so he understood their logic and agreed to go back into the kamandalu. Before that, he released Surya Deva, the galaxies, planets, and stars and normalcy was restored. Hanuman had saved the world once again. *jaya kapīsa **tihu loka ujāgara***

rāma dūta atulita bala dhāmā।
anjani putra pavanasuta nāmā॥ 2 ॥

*Rama's envoy, a reservoir of unsurpassable power,
Renowned as Anjana's son and 'son of the wind'.* (2)

Early in his childhood, Hanuman's mother Anjana had told him a secret that remained etched in his mind. The moment he met his master, he would have a bone-melting experience. And as predicted, the moment Hanuman came in front of Lord Rama for the first time, the very first glance of his eternal master convinced him that this was his eternal shelter. Every bone in his body had begun to melt.

But what really hit him the hardest was the first question that Lord Rama asked him. Because Hanuman was disguised as a beggar sanyasi, Rama asked him why a beggar was wearing a diamond necklace around his neck. Hanuman was stunned with that question because he had worn that invisible necklace all his life, and it had not been visible to anyone till date. Brahma had gifted it to him in his childhood with a stipulation that it would never be visible to anyone but one. And the one who saw that jewel would be Hanuman's master. So when Rama asked him about that jewel, it was another confirmation that Rama was his eternal master and he was Rama's eternal servant.

However, at that time, Hanuman was Sugriva's servant. And although there was no defect in the speech of Hanuman, he made one mistake in answering Rama. It was a subtle mistake that made Rama step back from developing a relationship immediately with Hanuman.

When Rama asked him to reveal his real identity, Hanuman replied that he was Sugriva's servant. He was right from a practical point of view but from an eternal point of view, the right answer was that he was the servant of Lord Rama. As soon as Hanuman said that he was Sugriva's servant, Rama felt hurt and stepped back allowing Lakshmana to continue the conversation. As soon as Hanuman saw Rama stepping back, he knew he had made a grave mistake in the very first meeting. What was done was done but henceforth Rama would scrutinize thoroughly every action of his. But he hoped that he would win the confidence and favour of Rama once again. Which he did with his sensitivity in understanding subtle nuances in relationships.

When Rama met Sugriva for the first time, Sugriva welcomed him and offered him a seat on the branch of a tree. Sugriva then sat on the same branch with Rama, which sent out a subtle message that he considered himself an equal to Rama. Behaving thoughtlessly, Sugriva did not even offer a seat to Lakshmana who remained standing. Hanuman immediately perceived the awkwardness of the situation, brought a branch of a better tree (sandalwood) and offered it to Lakshmana. While he himself sat on the ground below Lakshmana. With one action, Hanuman accomplished many things. He showed respect to Lakshmana and undid the insult meted out to him by Sugriva. This sensitive approach of Hanuman's impressed Rama and he smiled softly. Thus Hanuman kept gaining the confidence and favour of Rama by displays of sensitivity and such respectful acts. Within four months of the rainy season that Rama spent in Kishkinda, Hanuman managed to win over Rama completely and became a trusted ally. So much so that of the millions of monkeys that were sent out to scout for Sita, Rama chose to give his ring to Hanuman, confident that Hanuman would be the one to find Sita.

Till Hanuman met Sita, he identified himself as Rama doot or messenger of Rama. But after he met her and saw her unalloyed devotion to Rama, Hanuman caught on with her mood and began to call himself Rama das or servant of Rama.

Being Rama doot is to forget one's temporary identities of this world and focus on one's eternal identity as the messenger and servant of Rama. Being a messenger is to take the message of Rama to others who are in need to hear that message. Being a servant is to live a life in alignment with that message. Being a messenger is to do prachar (preach the message). Being a servant is to do aachar (live by the message).

It took Hanuman four months to convert from being Sugriva das (Sugriva's servant) to Rama doot (Rama's messenger) and another two months to convert from being Rama doot to Rama das (Rama's servant). *rāma dūta atulita bala dhāmā*

Kesari and Anjana began their journey towards the Himalayas with little Hanuman. They had been invited to have darshan of Badri Narayana by the disciples of the powerful sage Rishi Vishwambhar. When Rishi Vishwambhar called, no one refused. He wasn't an ordinary sage. He was a powerful maharishi who had taken a lifelong vow of not speaking a single word other than uttering the names of Lord Narayan. He had followed that vow in the most severe way for the last 50 years.

After an arduous journey, the vanara family made it all the way to the peaks of Badrinath. Soon they were standing in the presence of the great sage Vishwambhar who took them for the darshan of Lord Badri Narayana. As soon as baby Hanuman saw the holy deity, he spontaneously and enthusiastically cried out 'Rama', raising his little hands. Kesari immediately corrected his son that it was the deity of Badri Narayana. Just then he heard a hoarse voice that said, "Satyavachan! This is Rama."

No one was able to believe this! The impossible had happened. A 50-year-long-standing-vow had been broken. Sage Vishwambhar had uttered something other than the name of Lord Narayana after such a long time. The disciples gathered around their guru wanting to know the profound reason behind the unexpected aberration. He explained that he had taken the vow because of his worry for protecting the saintly community from harassment at the hands of the demons. At the commencement of this vow, Lord Brahma had prophesized that when the name of Rama is spoken from the mouth of an innocent child, it would herald destruction of the demons. Lord Brahma had further predicted that Lord Rama and Lord Shiva (in the form of Hanuman) would descend for destruction of the negative forces. Sage Vishwambhar declared that this child was none other than Lord Shiva and an abode of strength. In his heart would always reside Lord Rama and together they would destroy the demonic forces.

Being himself an abode of strength (bala dhama) and determination, Hanuman additionally encompasses the strength of Lord Rama who is in his heart. Thus his strength is incomparable or atulita. Thus Hanuman is known as *rāma dūta* **atulita bala dhāmā** ।

There was an extremely beautiful apsara in the heavens, whose name was Punjikasthala. Though born in the heavens and destined for celestial enjoyments, she was not the least bit interested in materialistic pleasures. She was ever absorbed in deeper seeking of the soul and kept herself engaged in austerities, rituals, and worship. One day to please her guru, Brihaspati, she designed a beautiful garland made of rudraksha beads. When she presented it to her master, feeling great joy, he instantly blessed her with motherhood. Only later did he realize his folly. Apsaras in the heavenly realms couldn't have children. But the word of a great sage like Brihaspati could not go wasted either. When he pondered over why he had offered such an unusual blessing to an apsara from the heavens, he concluded this had to be the divine will. Through his mouth had come out prophetic words indicating that Punjikasthala would be the mother of a child empowered by divine will; a child who would be a great instrument of protection and joy for the world.

From that point onwards, Punjikasthala started getting weird dreams. In almost every dream, she envisioned herself as a monkey holding in her arms a beautiful baby monkey that was always smiling. She could never fathom the meaning of these dreams until one fateful day when Durvasa muni walked into heaven. He wanted to perform a particularly difficult fire sacrifice and asked Indra for his able assistance. Indra assigned Punjikasthala as the main assistant to Durvasa muni. She was his obvious choice because of all the apsaras in the heavens, she was the only one who was interested in rituals and austerities. While the rest of her friends frolicked and enjoyed themselves in heavenly bliss, Punjikasthala immersed herself in higher consciousness.

Punjikasthala was thrilled at this opportunity and began to serve Durvasa muni in all earnestness. Durvasa was extremely happy with her services and her ever-enthusiastic presence. However, sometimes in over enthusiasm, she would be more energetic than necessary and that irritated him. One day when she was carrying a pot of water towards the sacrificial arena, she spilled the water all over the place in excitement. That was enough for Durvasa muni to fly into a rage. He had tolerated enough of her antics. He instantly cursed her that since she was jumping around like a monkey, she deserved to become a monkey.

As soon as he pronounced the curse, he came to his senses. What was he doing? Why did he curse her so harshly for a mistake so small? Durvasa was confused about his own bitter action. When Punjikasthala fell at his feet besieging forgiveness for her mistake, Durvasa muni immediately forgave her but his curse was simply an indication of some important future chapter in the course of her life. Though he was unable to lift the curse, he modified it. Even as a monkey in future, she would have the ability to change her form at will. He added that her womb would give birth to a very powerful personality who would bring her great fame and reverence from all over the world.

Years passed and Punjikasthala almost completely forgot about this incident. One day, she happened to be on a joy ride in her plane when she saw a beam of light emanating from earth and shooting up the sky forcing her plane to come to a halt. Out of curiosity, she descended to the source of the beam and found it emanating from a pile of mud. Surprisingly, the pile of mud was in the shape of a monkey. She jumped off her plane and began to dig the pile of mud to ascertain the source of that powerful light. Suddenly, from within that mud emerged a powerful looking sage, shrugging off the mud from his body. He glowed like fire in anger. She had inadvertently disturbed him from his samadhi. She tried to explain how she saw a beam of light that aroused her curiosity and made her dig the mud block. But the sage was in no mood to hear explanations and cursed her that her monkey-like inquisitiveness would make her a monkey. This time Punjikasthala did not get offended or scared of being cursed. She knew that there was a great future waiting for her that was revealing itself in the form of unwanted and unwarranted curses and blessings.

Eventually, true to the curses, she was born as Anjana, to a monkey king named Kunjar. She later married Kesari who was a very powerful monkey chieftain. Though there were ample predictions about the birth of a superhero, there weren't any signs of pregnancy for years. Then both Anjana and Kesari decided to perform tapasya to beget a worthy child. The time when Anjana was performing severe austerities seated on a mountain top in Kishkinda, coincided with completion of the Putrakamesti yajna of Dasharatha maharaj in Ayodhya. A powerful personality ascended from the sacrificial fire and offered a pot of celestial nectar to the king. The king was to divide the nectar amongst his three wives for them to conceive powerful sons. As soon as Dasharatha offered the nectar to Kaushalya, a huge eagle swooped down, grabbed a portion of that nectar and flew away before anyone could react. The bird flew all the way to Kishkinda and dropped that nectar mid-air. The wind god, sensing the divine arrangement, intervened and began to blow the nectar potion towards a particular pre-conceived direction. The nectar eventually landed exactly in the extended palms of Anjana who was meditating intensely on the mountaintop. When she mystically received the nectar drops, she knew this was the grace she had been waiting for. With a prayer of gratitude, Anjana consumed the nectar and instantly became pregnant with the much-awaited superhero. Because he was the son of Anjana (Anjana putra) and the contributed grace of the wind god (Pavana putra) therefore he became known as ***anjani putra pavanasuta nāmā***

mahāvīra vikrama bajarangī।
kumati nivāra sumati ke sangī॥ 3 ॥

Mighty hero, bestowed with courage,
strong as a thunderbolt,
Dispeller of evil thoughts and
companion of the good. (3)

Mahavir. Courage or bravery is not just an external exhibition but more importantly, an internal strength. Whilst most people extend the title of bravery to those who exhibit great heroism on the battlefield, the Vedic scriptures give more importance to those who exhibit bravery in the battle of life. Often it takes greater courage to show bravery in life than on the battlefield. Thus Hanuman is considered as Mahavir not just because he won many external battles, but because he was a hero in the internal battles of life.

One who shows exceptional heroism in a battle is known as Ranveer. One who has the courage to forgive others by exhibiting great compassion is known as Dayaveer. The courage to give away in charity makes one Danaveer. The courage to stay on the path of righteousness in spite of great obstacles makes one Dharmaveer. And one with the courage to renounce attachments is known as Tyagaveer. Each of these subtypes of heroism requires great courage and resolve. Even possessing one of these types of courage is appreciated and worshipped by the world. Then what of one who is simultaneously Ranveer, Dayaveer, Danaveer, Dharmaveer, and Tyagaveer; he is celebrated as Mahavir.

When Hanuman was in Lanka, he fought against the entire Lankan army single-handedly. Ravana sent hordes of demons to eliminate Hanuman. But none of them returned alive. He sent some of his best men including heroes like Jambumali and his own son Akshay Kumar. But all of them ended up in the grave. It takes great courage and self-confidence to stand up against an entire army alone and that too in their own country without any allies. Hanuman was the greatest Ranveer in history. And he fought not for any personal gains but to help others. You will never find a single story of Hanuman where he fought for himself.

Hanuman lived a life of compassion, dedicating himself to serve others through their difficulties. He was an ideal Dayaveer who lived a life of compassion. Even today when we find ourselves hopeless and lost, we turn to Hanuman knowing very well that his compassion is all encompassing and endless. There are many charitable people in this world. But they only give a fragment of their wealth in charity. But one who donates himself is the greatest Danaveer. Hanuman gives himself completely to those who touch his heart by sincerity. Once Hanuman came to the decision that Rama was worth surrendering to, he surrendered completely to Lord Rama, in his mind, body, and words.

Whilst the monkey army was having a discussion about who was going to cross the 800-mile long ocean, Angad claimed that he could easily cross the ocean and reach Lanka but he wasn't sure if he would return. Angad knew about the fatal attractions and temptations in Lanka. He also knew his own limitations and weaknesses in self-control. He doubted if he could resist the temptations in Lanka and come back. Whereas Hanuman not only crossed the 800-mile ocean to reach Lanka but also crossed the ocean of temptations that lay inside Lanka. He was a real Dharmaveer who had the courage to stay on the path of dharma despite great temptations lurking as obstacles to deviate one's focus from higher goals of life.

For a person who is capable, talented, intelligent, and powerful, the greatest challenge is in accepting a subordinate position. For someone who is an expert, fame and adulation follow automatically. There cannot be a greater intoxication than fame. To renounce that fame requires immense inner strength. Giving up other attachments is easy, but only a Tyagaveer can give up attachment to fame. Hanuman was the most powerful and capable person of his era, but he renounced his attachment to fame and followership in order to remain a lifelong follower of Lord Rama.

Hanuman is Mahavir indeed! *mahāvīra vikrama bajarangī*

When Hanuman was a small child, he was powerful but naughty. His energy was not channelized in the right direction. Thus he would use all his intelligence in playing pranks and having fun at the expense of others. He harassed sages who were soft targets for his mischief. Out of great compassion, one harassed sage cursed Hanuman to forget all his strength till he was reminded about them. From that moment, till Rama walked into his life, Hanuman lived a life of ordinariness. Once Rama entered his life, a sense of direction and purpose also found entry. Having found his calling, Hanuman lived life king size but maintained a heart filled with humility. Every single action of Hanuman's was immensely inspiring and impossible to imitate. In every power packed action, there was an element of selflessness and a desire to serve. Whether it was crossing the ocean in one single leap or advising Ravana in his own court or burning the entire city of Lanka or fetching the entire mountain to save Lakshmana. In every action there was heroic sacrifice triggered by selflessness. The word vikram means the one whose actions are mighty. Often, when one is powerful, one tends to become insensitive and self-absorbed. Yes, Hanuman was vikram but always sensitive and selfless.

When Hanuman was an infant, his parents conducted the first grain ceremony. The moment Hanuman ate the first few grains, his appetite got activated. Mother fed him all possible fruits, but nothing could satisfy his hunger. Finally, not wanting to trouble her, Hanuman stopped demanding. But the hunger pangs did not subside, causing a lot of distress to him. One day, as he was tossing and turning in hunger, Narada Muni appeared and offered him some fruits. Even that wasn't enough to satisfy the intense fire in his stomach. Finally, Narada Muni pointed out to the sun. Mistaking the sun to be a big fruit, Hanuman jumped towards it in one leap. Panicking at the sight of a baby monkey zooming towards the sun, the planets began to shift their orbits to stay out of his path. Shukra, Buddha, and Brihaspati planets stepped aside and their sudden change in position caused tremendous disturbance on earth since these planets influence astrological calculations that affect people's lives. When sun god Surya noticed the incoming little bundle of disaster, he yelled out to his friends, Kaal, Varuna, and Agni to protect him. Kaal (destiny or time) was the first to arrive and attack Hanuman. An intense battle ensued. Kaal expanded himself to a huge size and Hanuman instantly matched it by expanding himself. Then Hanuman challenged Kaal. He said expanding is easily done by anyone but shrinking only the great can do. And Hanuman began to shrink himself to a minute particle size. Kaal fell for the ego trap and shrunk himself much more than Hanuman. Hanuman then bounced back to his original size and captured Kaal in his fist. He let Kaal go only when he begged him and promised not to interfere in his matters.

Then came Agni's fiery attack, which could do no harm to the little monkey. Unable to cause any damage, Agni realized that this was none other than a Rudra avatar. He stepped aside only to be replaced with the ice-cold missiles of Varuna. None of them could harm or even disturb Hanuman's progress towards the sun. Kaal, Agni, and Varuna accepted defeat and departed with their heads hung low. Narada Muni smiled from a little distance away. He was happy to see the gods' egos thwarted as they had earlier been making fun of this monkey incarnation of Rudra.

Finally, Hanuman was just inches away from the sun when he saw Rahu approaching it from another direction. Now there were two contenders rushing to swallow the sun. The sun was trapped and fearful. Defeating Rahu with ease, Hanuman menacingly proceeded towards the sun. The sun god, as a last resort, tried to warn Hanuman of the dire consequences of coming closer to him. When Hanuman ignored his warnings, he turned on his heat. The heat became so fiery that the entire universe began to perspire. The residents of earth had no clue why it was suddenly intolerably hot now. Unable to bear the hunger pangs anymore, Hanuman grabbed the sun and gobbled it up. The moment the sun disappeared into the mouth of Hanuman, utter darkness prevailed. The intense heat was replaced with freezing cold.

While this was going on way up in space, back on earth, Ravana under the guidance of Shukracharya, was performing a sacred ceremony that would make him invincible and undefeatable. The completion of the sacrifice had to be timed in such a way that it coincided with the solar eclipse. For years, the guru and disciple had planned this meticulously and strived to carry out every aspect of the elaborate sacrifice to perfection. Just as it was time for the solar eclipse and the time for completion of the sacrifice, the sun suddenly disappeared, much to their dismay. Thus the solar eclipse didn't happen as scheduled and the sacrifice got completed in its absence. Thus the evil plan of Ravana was thwarted unceremoniously.

Just as the whole world was reeling in darkness, Indra appeared on the scene to rescue the sun considering it to be in the purview of his universal responsibilities to ensure that the sun continues to shine offering its heat and light unabated in its orbit. He was mounted on his celebrated elephant carrier, Airavata. Indra lost his head seeing the audacity of little monkey whose mouth was swollen with the sun inside. In his fury, he threw his thunderbolt weapon straight at Hanuman's face. The thunderbolt hit Hanuman squarely on his chin and cracked his jaw. The hit was so intense that Hanuman was pushed backward and fell over unconscious. His mouth opened involuntarily and the sun escaped. Light was restored in the universe . . . but something worse had happened. There was no air to breathe!

Hanuman's injury alerted his father Vayu who caught his falling son and took him into the safety of a cave. Seething in anger at the unjustified attack on his son, he withdrew all air from the world and soon everyone was struggling to breathe. To appease him, all gods headed by Lord Brahma appeared before Vayu and begged forgiveness for his wounded son. They revived the child and conferred upon the child infinite benedictions that made the child powerful, undefeatable, and literally immortal. They offered him immunity from fire, super intelligence, a healing touch and much more. Another boon granted was that his body would become as robust as Indra's thunderbolt, thus giving him the name Bajarangi that literally meant one whose body is robust like a thunderbolt. *mahāvīra vikrama* **bajarangī**

The side on which Hanuman stands never loses. And he always stands firmly on the platform of righteousness. Because he is always on the side of dharma, dharma always is on his side. In his presence, the saintly rejoice and the demonic shudder.

Often, we are surrounded by at least one person that throws negativity and toxicity into our lives. For Sugriva, that person was Vali. Fortunately for Sugriva, Hanuman walked into his life without an invitation. Surya, the sun god, who eventually became Hanuman's guru, sent him to protect and guide Sugriva out of the mess that he was stuck in. Every single day Vali kicked his brother on his head 12 times. Though Sugriva was living in a mountain named Rishimukha on which Vali could not set his foot, due to a curse heaped by Sage Matanga, Vali still managed to attack him through the aerial route without stepping on the mountain. For performing his gayatri, Vali had to jump across to reach the four oceans three times a day. Every time he jumped, he would pass over the Rishimukha Mountain and deliver a kick on his helpless brother's head before proceeding to his next destination.

As soon as Hanuman walked into Sugriva's life, the equation changed. Next time Vali attempted to kick Sugriva on his head, Hanuman caught hold of his feet mid-air. He pulled Vali's feet down in an attempt to make him touch the mountain, which would immediately bring into force Matanga Rishi's curse and end the tyranny of Vali for good. Vali sensing the plan, pleaded and begged Hanuman to let him free, promising to never trouble Sugriva again. Vali learnt an unforgettable lesson and Sugriva experienced relief from pain. He expressed his gratitude towards his newly found protector-cum-guide. Thus, from the moment Hanuman made an entry in Ramayana, he declared to destroy those who support adharma with an evil mind while he stood by those who harbour positive uplifting dharmic thoughts. Thus he is considered destroyer of evil and companion of the good.

kumati nivāra sumati ke sangī

kanchana barana birāja subesā।
kānana kundala kunchita kesā॥ 4 ॥

Golden-coloured and handsomely dressed,
With earrings and curly locks. (4)

When Hanuman was born, his mother Anjana named him Sundar, or beautiful. From an external point of view, the vanara species may not be the most beautiful. But Anjana naming her child Sundar was more because she wanted her child to be internally beautiful. External beauty wanes with time but internal beauty does not.

By virtue of being in proximity of the sun (both during infancy in his attempt to swallow the sun and later in his childhood while he was being educated by Surya who became his teacher), sunshine had a great influence on Hanuman's body. His body had a golden tinge, akin to the sun glow which is known as kanchana barana. That golden tinge only enhanced when he began his journey to the south in search of Mother Sita.

When Lord Rama handed over his ring to Hanuman to show it to Sita as proof of being a messenger of Rama, there was confusion in Hanuman's mind. He began to wonder where to keep that special, invaluable, and extremely potent ring, in the course of his arduous journey. He wanted to keep it in a place that was respectful and yet secure. He definitely could not wear the ring on his finger since it belonged to Lord Rama. That would be arrogance. He couldn't find any place in his clothes that would be safe enough. The long journey and tough encounters on the way would make it impossible to retain it within the folds of his clothes. Especially in a fight or flight situation, when his clothes were sure to get dishevelled. He couldn't tie it on to his sacred thread as it would be too visible and also too susceptible to the risk of falling off or accidentally snapping off the thread during the journey.

He possibly couldn't keep it in his hands as it could fall off during a careless moment or even when he would have to use his hands to climb or fight. Hanuman finally got his answer when he saw the name of Rama inscribed on the ring. There was only one place where the holy name of Lord Rama really belonged. And that was the tongue. The tongue should ideally reverberate the holy names of Rama constantly. Presence of the ring in his mouth was symbolic of the holy name of Lord Rama being constantly on his tongue. Moreover, it would act as a constant reminder to him to absorb his mind in the holy names.

As soon as Hanuman placed the ring in his mouth, his entire body began to radiate a special kind of effulgence. Every pore of his body began to glow with euphoria. The ring illuminated the body of Hanuman in such a way that it dispelled the darkness of the night and more importantly, the darkness of ignorance. Thus Hanuman became the guiding force for the monkey army that scouted the southern region, searching for Sita. This explains his *kanchana barana* or golden-hued body.

When Hanuman entered Ravana's palace in Lanka, he searched all over and finally entered what seemed to be the royal bedroom. In the sea of ordinary beds, Hanuman spotted an opulent stone-studded gigantic golden bed with a white umbrella canopy, bang in the middle of the room. It had a soft sheepskin and silk bedspread, and in place of bedposts were four women waving large silk fans that helped circulate the fragrance from celestial incenses. Fast asleep on the bed amongst hundreds of women was *the* person of interest—the mighty Ravana, the Supremo of Lanka. The bright light from the golden lamps next to the bed lent a golden glow to his lustrous body. Ravana resembled the moon among a sky full of stars.

Hanuman spotted another well-decorated cot with an angelic woman sleeping on it. She seemed to be of divine origin, quite different from the women he had seen thus far in Lanka. He could see a pure and divine aura around her. *Could this be Sita?* Hanuman froze! He immediately began a mental comparison between the woman on the cot and Lord Rama's description of Sita. It was an absolute match. *Finally!* Hanuman was ecstatic having found Sita. He began to prance around kissing his tail, jumping, laughing, and singing. Suddenly he stopped. Something didn't seem quite right. Hanuman regained his composure and now admonished himself for even thinking that she could be Sita. He went over the description and cross-questioned himself on the gross error in his judgment. How could Sita sleep in Ravana's bedroom? How could she sleep so peacefully in the absence of Rama? How could she be so decked up despite being away from Rama? When those connected to Rama never falter, how could he even imagine that his wife would? Even if gods like Indra or Kubera were to come, she wasn't the one to bend, so why would she even succumb to a demon like Ravana? Had she not rejected all the demigods and chosen Lord Rama, so why would she care to accept Ravana? Hanuman was now convinced that it could not be Sita. He resumed his search.

Hanuman intensified his search and walked in and out of all the rooms he could. Everywhere he looked, he saw women in various stages of undressing and sleep. He had to closely observe every woman he came across to ensure none of them was Sita. It was his job to find her from among all the women in Lanka. This was not something the celibate Hanuman wanted to do, but the job had to be done. Hanuman had scoured the entire palace and still not found Sita. He had observed more than 12,000 women, and none happened to be Sita. He began to question the righteousness of having to peep into homes and looking at other people's wives. But his steady and pure mind justified his actions as having been carried out with no impure intent.

He was still not convinced, heavily in conflict about whether this went against his dharma. So he began to chant the name of Rama to calm his disturbed mind. As the names of Rama permeated his being, a state of calmness spread all over his body. Clarity returned. No, I have not come here with the intent of admiring Ravana's women. My goal is to find Sita among the women in Lanka. How can I search for a woman amongst deer? Besides, these women have not spotted me observing them and my mind has been steady and pure throughout this search, thought Hanuman.

Hanuman is said to be *birāja subesā,* splendidly clad

or it could also mean clean clothes. Here the reference is not just to his external clothes. But it is rather to being clothed with the right intentions. There may be many that are clothed wonderfully but their intentions are dirty. Hanuman always clothed himself with the purest intentions, making sure his intentions remained pure by constantly questioning them and always aligning them towards the service of Lord Rama based on the principles of dharma. *kanchana barana birāja subesā*

From the time Narada left Kishkinda, Vali had become miserable. Just when he thought he was the happiest living being alive, the news delivered by Narada destroyed his peace. It was less of news and more of a prophecy. A prophecy that could ruin Vali's name, fame, reputation, and control for good. If the sage's words were to come true, then in a few years, no one in Kishkinda would remember either Vali's name or his rule.

Whilst Vali paced back and forth in great anxiety, a sinister idea struck his evil mind. Wringing his hands, he headed for his chamber to immediately execute the plan that was brewing in his head. The next hour saw him extremely busy implementing what he had envisioned in his mind. He was in know of a secret recipe which he always thought would be useful someday. He grinned at the bowl of piping hot liquid that was in his hands. It was golden brown in hue, like a tasty soup of exotic vegetables. But in truth, it was the most deadly poison. Interestingly, this poison wasn't designed to kill the person who consumed it, but the embryo of the one who consumed it. The amalgam was a combination of five deadly metals melted and then mixed together into a tasty looking gel.

With this most deadly liquid weapon in his hand, Vali walked out of his chamber. Calling his most trusted maid, he handed over the liquid to her with the instruction to feed it to the pregnant Anjana who was a vanara woman and the wife of Kesari, the chief of a section of the vanara army. The maid walked into the bedroom of Anjana and with great confidence, offered the poison to the pregnant lady, assuring her that it was all for the health and accelerated growth of the child within her womb. With gratitude, Anjana accepted the liquid. The maid waited till Anjana had consumed the entire potion. Only when she had herself seen the lady consume the liquid did she leave with the empty vessel.

Vali couldn't contain his happiness at how smoothly his plan had worked out. He was pacing around in excitement, this time waiting for the news of the miscarriage. But nothing came. Maybe the effect will be seen the next day, he concluded. When nothing happened the next day either, Vali was bewildered. Maybe he needed to be more patient. Days passed and still nothing. While Vali kept wondering what had gone wrong, Anjana gave birth to a son. That news came as a shocker for Vali. He ran to the palace of Kesari and Anjana to see the child that was born despite his mother being fed a quantity of poison that could abort a hundred pregnancies. His jaw dropped when he saw the new born!

The vanara child was born with earrings adorning both his ears. But that was not all. Those earrings were made of the five metals that Vali had fed his mother. The metal amalgam had been transformed into beautiful earrings that adorned the child's ears. From then on, the child Hanuman was famous for many qualities, but the one that was really special among those was his mystical earrings. ***kānana kundala*** *kunchita kesā.*

After their victory in the Mahabharata war and winning back their kingdom from the Kauravas, Narada Muni visited the Pandavas and informed them that their father, who now resided in the heavens, was sad. The reason being that he had always wanted to perform the Rajasuya sacrifice during his lifetime on earth but could not do so. Now he desired that his sons fulfil that desire. Yudhishthir decided to take up the mission of performing the Rajasuya yagya immediately, to realize their father's long-standing yearning. In order to perform such an elaborate and complicated sacrifice, they needed the expertise of Rishi Purusha Mriga. The task of finding and getting the elusive sage was given to Bhima.

As Bhima set out to find the sage, Lord Krishna warned him that it was not going to be an easy task. The sage was half deer and half human. Furthermore, the sage was extraordinarily powerful and moved at the speed of mind. If Bhima could not match the speed of the sage, then the sage would finish him off. Now that warning really worried Bhima but he was anyway going ahead with the mission.

When Bhima reached the Himalayan Mountains, he came across Hanuman. Hanuman saw the worried look on Bhima's face and offered to help. On learning of Bhima's difficult task, Hanuman gave him a few strands of hair from his body and asked him to drop one when he needed the sage to slow down. Hanuman explained that as soon as he dropped one strand of his hair, thousands of shivalingas would appear immediately. Knowing the sage well, Hanuman predicted that Purusha Mriga would not move ahead without aptly worshipping each shivalinga carefully. That would give Bhima ample time to cover a considerable distance.

In great excitement, Bhima finally reached the sage and invited him to perform the Rajasuya yagya. The sage warned Bhima that there was a pre-condition. He would follow Bhima and if he managed to catch him, then he would devour him. However, if Bhima reached the palace before the sage, then he would perform the yagya there. Agreeing to the condition, Bhima took off at great speed. Every time the sage got closer, Bhima dropped a strand of hair given to him by Hanuman and thousands of shivalingas would sprout all over the place. While Rishi Purusha Mriga busied himself worshipping the shivalingas, Bhima would dash ahead.

Outwitting the sage in this way, Bhima managed to reach the doors of the palace of Hastinapur. He had almost entered the palace with one foot inside and was about to place the second foot in when Rishi Purusha Mriga caught his second leg. Now he claimed that Bhima hadn't reached inside the palace completely and therefore, he had won. But when Yudhishthir and Krishna walked in, the sage stepped back and allowed the just Yudhishthir to make the decision. Yudhishthir analysed the facts and concluded that since Bhima's entire body and one leg was already inside, the sage only deserved to devour the second leg of Bhima, sparing Bhima's body. The sage was very impressed with Yudhishthir's sense of justice and decided to forgive Bhima. He also offered to perform the yagya on behalf of Yudhishthir. Bhima silently offered a prayer to Hanuman's curly hair, each of which had unlimited powers and were as potent as thousands of shivalingas.

*kānana kundala **kunchita kesā***

hātha bajra au dhvajā birājai।
kādhe mūnja janeū sājai॥ 5 ॥

*Your hands hold a divine mace and
a victory banner,
A sacred thread of munja grass
adorns your shoulder.* (5)

Mother Anjana had to return to her celestial abode a few
years after she gave birth to Hanuman as the stipulated
duration of her curse was completed. Hanuman
desperately wanted his mother back. Aware that his
mother has gone to the heavens, Hanuman proceeded to
Swargaloka to try to get his mother back. Meanwhile,
Kesari was also despondent on seeing his wife missing
from his palace. When he realized that their son Hanuman
had ventured out to get his mother back, Kesari decided
to try something from his side too. He approached a
powerful sage named Matanga Rishi to help him. After
many requests, Matanga Rishi began a yagya that would
transport Kesari into the heavens through yogic means.

Meanwhile, Hanuman had reached the heavens
where he met Urvashi. She explained to him that it

was impossible to take his mother back, who by then had acquired her original form as Punjakasthali. But Hanuman would hear nothing of that so Urvashi suggested that the only person who could help him was Durvasa Muni who had cursed her to begin with. Hanuman immediately set out to meet Durvasa Muni who was held captive in Yakshaloka.

The king of Yakshaloka was a great friend of Ravana's and Kubera's bitter enemy. He was always eyeing Kubera's position, aspiring to be the treasurer of the demigods. With the help of Yaksharaj, Ravana had planned kidnapping Durvasa Muni knowing well that Hanuman would be coming there for him. The plan was to eliminate Hanuman when he reached Yakshaloka. But exactly the opposite happened. Instead of Yaksharaj capturing Hanuman, Hanuman captured him. The release of Durvasa Muni from the clutches of the Yakshas brought great fame to Hanuman in the heavenly realms. Not only were the demigods grateful but even the powerful Saptarishis expressed their gratitude. Durvasa Muni was so grateful to Hanuman that he agreed to allow Punjakasthali to return with him in vanara form as Anjana.

Indra himself decided to accompany Hanuman and his mother on their return journey to Kishkinda on the earthly realms. While the three of them were on their way, they were attacked by a demon named Vidyutsura who was sent by Ravana. He was one of the most powerful demons at Ravana's disposal. Indra advised Hanuman to proceed ahead with his mother while he would take care of that demon. But Hanuman was in no mood of turning his back on a good fight. Moreover, it was his moral duty to stand by Indra during a crisis. Vidyutsura attacked Indra faster than anticipated and as a result Indra's weapon slipped off his hand. The extremely alert Hanuman jumped to grab the vajra weapon. Vidyutsura turned around to face Hanuman who had by now steadied himself for a fight while his entire rakshasa army attacked Indra.

While Indra busied himself destroying the Rakshasa army, Hanuman jumped high to land himself on Vidyutsura's shoulders. With a single swift move of his right hand, Hanuman slit Vidyutsura's throat with the razor-sharp thunderbolt weapon. In a short while, all that was left of the demons was a pile of bodies. Hanuman held out the vajra to return it to Indra. When Indra extended his hand to take it back, a loud celestial announcement boomed declaring that the vajra now belonged to Hanuman who had saved Swargaloka from the demons and Indra should let him keep it. Indra gladly gifted the thunderbolt weapon to Hanuman along with a victory flag and blessed him to be ever victorious in every battle in life. Indra also declared that from that day Hanuman would be known as Vajradhari (the carrier of vajra weapon) and Dhvajadhari (the heralder of the victory flag). *hātha bajra au dhvajā birājai*

The literal translation is that Hanuman carries the vajra and a dhvaja in his hands. Vajra means thunderbolt, a weapon of Lord Indra, and dhvaja means flag. Vajra and dhvaja also refer to lines on the palm of Hanuman's hands rather than just physical objects which he carried. Lines of vajra and dhvaja on his palms signify immense power and fame respectively. Hanuman's palms predicted great power and fame in his life. *hātha bajra au dhvajā birājai*

During their exile, the Pandavas travelled through many forests and met many sages. These were times of great sadness, having lost all their wealth and being greatly insulted. During such despondent times, the Pandava brothers sought wisdom from sages to help them deal with their pain. The sages narrated various histories about kings in the past who had dealt with challenges in life with dignity. One such time, Arjuna conversed with the great sage Markendeya who was blessed with longevity. Markendeya Rishi narrated the story of Lord

Rama and how he took the help of an army of monkeys to build a bridge across the ocean to rescue his wife from the demon king Ravana.

While the story of Rama's struggle and determination helped Arjuna, a doubt plagued him. Though he didn't ask Markendeya Rishi, he kept mulling over it. Later, when he was standing next to a lake, pondering about his doubt as to why Rama being such a powerful archer needed to use an army of monkeys to build a bridge which could have easily been made using arrows, an old monkey came and stood next to him. As if continuing the trail of Arjuna's thoughts, the monkey said that it would have been impossible for a bridge of arrows to withstand the weight of an army of monkeys. Arjuna begged to differ and argued that an expert archer could achieve any goal with his arrows. In fact, he boasted, that even a small time archer like himself could achieve that feat easily.

The old monkey dared Arjuna to build a bridge of arrows across the lake that could handle his own frail weight. Within a minute, Arjuna created a bridge of arrows. He challenged that if this bridge collapsed with the monkey's weight, he would end his life. The monkey didn't even bother to step on it, but only dropped his tail on it and the bridge collapsed.

The old monkey urged Arjuna to try again with

greater focus. Arjuna made a sturdier bridge and this time it stood the weight of the monkey. But when the monkey reached the middle, it collapsed. Disappointed, Arjuna was ready to end his life. Just then, an old brahmana appeared and stopped him from jumping into a pyre. He told the two of them that any conflict between two people needed a neutral witness. The brahmana agreed to become the witness if they tried once more.

Yet again, Arjuna created a bridge with greater concentration. The monkey walked on it but nothing happened. He jumped on it and still nothing happened. The old monkey gave up his disguise and took on his original form of Hanuman. Expanding himself to a massive size, he began to jump on the bridge, still nothing happened. Both of them were shocked. How could the bridge take so much weight? Then it dawned on them that the old brahmana was none other than their worshipable Lord. Arjuna saw him as Krishna and Hanuman saw him as Rama. Both fell at the Lord's feet promising never to be proud of their powers.

The Lord then blessed both his devotees and expressed his desire that they both unite for the upcoming war against the Kauravas. The Lord instructed Hanuman to sit on the flag of Arjuna's chariot. The presence of Hanuman on Arjuna's flag would herald auspiciousness and serve as a declaration of their imminent victory.

Since Hanuman was the one who held the victory flag of Lord Rama in the war against Ravana, his presence on the flag of Arjuna would indicate certain victory.

Hanuman sits on the flag of the chariot of every devotee of the Lord, signalling their victory against illusory forces. Thus Hanuman is *dhvaja viraje,* one who sits on the victory flag or the one who upholds the victory flag.

The practice of keeping Hanuman on war chariot was set by Lord Sri Rama during the war in Treta yuga, when Indra sent a chariot to Sri Rama. Sri Rama circumambulated the chariot to honour it, and then got Hanuman seated along the banner post as his own personal assistant as well as an alternative war chariot (as an emergency provision). ***hātha bajra au dhvajā birājai***

Most people stop learning beyond school. But Hanuman considered himself an eternal student. As many opportunities as he got to learn from great teachers, he grabbed them eagerly. Every teacher that walked into his life taught him different skills. And he learnt each skill to perfection and thus became multi-talented.

First he was placed under the tutelage of Angavahan

Rishi. After a short while of learning there, his father Kesari felt that he would do better if he was given greater exposure and after consultation with the wind god, chose to send Hanuman to learn from Surya dev, the sun god. While he was under Surya's tutelage, Lord Rama was under the tutelage of Sage Vashishta. One day something interesting happened. Hanuman was learning archery on the sun planet and Rama was learning archery on earth in the ashram of Vashishta. Hanuman shot an arrow towards the earth and Rama shot an arrow skywards. Both arrows collided in mid-air and created a tumultuous sound that reverberated all over the universe. This was their first connection through the medium of learning.

Hanuman then shifted to the tutelage of Narada Muni to gain music skills. Narada Muni taught him singing and playing musical instruments. Hanuman became so proficient at everything he learnt that even his teachers were highly impressed with him. To test his learning, once Narada Muni asked him to sing a particular song. Hanuman sang it so melodiously that it melted Narada Muni's heart. Mesmerized by Hanuman, Narada Muni closed his eyes and did not even realize when his veena (stringed instrument) fell off his hands onto the ground. Amazingly, Hanuman's singing did not just have this effect on sentient beings but also on inanimate objects like stones and rocks. Hard stones melted in the ecstasy of the song. Narada Muni's veena also happened to fall on one of those melted stones.

When Hanuman stopped singing, everything assumed its original shape and the melted stones regained their rigidity. Unfortunately, the veena got stuck in the now rigid stone. Narada Muni requested Hanuman to sing again to get his veena released. Hanuman refused to comply and ran all over the place. The helpless Narada Muni ran behind, trying to catch the naughty boy. After running around considerably, Hanuman returned to the original spot and sang. Soon the veena was released and in Narada Muni's hands again. When he asked Hanuman why he'd troubled him, Hanuman gave a very interesting answer. He disclosed that he wanted the dust of the feet of his guru to fall all over the place and sanctify it. This was Hanuman's style of making that happen.

Janeu, a sacred thread worn by brahmanas, represents knowledge of Vedic scriptures. Wearing the sacred thread is an indicator of being a student. Hanuman remained an eternal student, always absorbed in hearing and learning from many teachers. Thus a sacred thread always dons his shoulders, declaring his eternal role as a student who is always eager to learn. *kādhe mūnja janeū sājai*

The janeu on Hanuman's shoulder also implies that

Hanuman was well-versed in scriptures, because the sacred thread ceremony initiates a person into formal study of Vedic literature. Once Rama himself had explained the secrets of Brahma Vidya to Hanuman. Sri Rama Rahasya Upanishad states that great sages and seers like Sanak, Sanandan, Sanatan, and Sanat Kumar had learnt the hidden secrets of Rama Tattva from Hanuman. Other sages like Prahlad were his disciples. *Janeu saaje* describes the thread as Hanuman's ornament that was his wealth of knowledge. **kādhe mūnja janeū sājai**

shankara swayam kesarī nandana।
teja pratāpa mahā jaga bandana॥ 6 ॥

As Lord Shiva's son and Kesari's joy,
Your effulgent power shines
throughout the universe. (6)

Enough was enough! Ravana had crossed all limits of decency and the most powerful gods in creation were unable to handle the atrocities of Ravana. Imagine the king of the heavens cutting vegetables in Ravana's kitchen! Even death personified feared him! After long discussions they decided to visit Lord Shiva in Kailash. Not that they expected him to sympathize knowing well that Ravana was one of Lord Shiva's greatest devotee. But they were in for a great surprise when they found Lord Shiva equally furious with him.

How was it possible that the Lord was furious with his own devotee? Lord Shiva gave them some shocking facts. He explained that Ravana had undertaken severe austerities to please him. In spite of such intense tapasya when Shiva did not make an appearance, Ravana began to chop off his heads and offer them into the sacrificial fire to appease the Lord. He had offered nine heads and he was now offering the tenth one into the fire. Unable to bear the gruesome sight of a headless Ravana, Lord Shiva appeared in front of him ready to fulfil his desires. Ravana asked him for two boons at that point. But the boons were like two bombs that Ravana threw at Lord Shiva. He asked for the atma linga, which was a special form of Shivalinga and he asked for Lord Shiva's wife Parvati. Lord Shiva was flabbergasted. He had dared to ask for his wife! But having given his word, he had to send Parvati with him. Of course, Lord Vishnu intervened and tricked Ravana, thus getting Parvati back from him. But the impact of the trauma was deep and it had deeply displeased the eleventh Rudra. Ravana had managed to appease ten of the eleven Rudra forms of Lord Shiva but the eleventh Rudra was incensed. Shiva promised the demigods that the eleventh Rudra would appear in the form of vanara named Hanuman and prove to be the instrument of destruction of Ravana.

While the gods returned happy with this news, Lord Shiva called upon Vayu, the wind god, and handed over his energy to him. Shiva instructed Vayu to place his effulgent energy into the womb of Anjana, a vanara woman, at an appropriate time. Vayu placed the powerful seed on a special metal leaf that could handle the potent energy. He then handed it over to the Saptarishis for safe keeping till the right time arrived.

Meanwhile, Anjana was meditating in a cave way up in the mountains. While she was absorbed in meditation, someone else was meditating on her beauty. A demon named Shambasadhana had been smitten by lust and been eyeing her for the last few days. When he approached her, Anjana panicked and ran away to escape from his clutches. She somehow reached a village of powerful sages. When she told them her predicament of being followed by a demon, the sages replied that the only person who could protect her was the vanara chieftain Kesari. And what a coincidence! As soon as they mentioned his name, Kesari arrived. Soon a terrible battle ensued between Shambasadhana and Kesari. Both were so powerful and skilled that none was able to get an upper edge. Then Shambasadhana began to change forms. Taking on the shape of a giant elephant, he attacked Kesari. Kesari in turn, reduced his size dramatically and continued the onslaught. He perched himself on the head of the giant elephant and began pounding his head with his fists. Shambasadhana was bleeding profusely but there was no sign of him tiring or slowing down.

As Kesari began to worry, Anjana prayed for divine help which came as a vision—the only way the demon could be killed was by using his own blood. He was immune to everything except that. She dipped an arrow into the demon's blood that was spilt all over. Holding the arrow in one hand, she grabbed a bow with the other, darted towards Kesari and threw both in his direction. Kesari lunged forward and caught both in mid-air, understanding her intention. He turned around, knocked the arrow onto the bow and shot it, all in one motion. As Kesari landed on the ground, the arrow shot ahead, penetrated the demon's body, killing him at once.

The sages who watched this brave act, complimented Kesari and Anjana and blessed them profusely. They declared that providence had willed them to come together. In fact, they predicted, that the child born through this marriage would be an incarnation of Lord Shiva himself and the cause of destruction of demonic forces. Thus, with blessings from the great sages, Kesari and Anjana happily entered a marriage alliance.

Despite so many predictions and blessings heaped upon them, the vanara couple could not beget a child. They decided to visit Matanga Rishi and seek his blessings. It was a long and arduous journey through forests and mountains, which they undertook barefoot. Anjana additionally vowed to cover this entire journey without a single break. Kesari tried to dissuade her but gave in seeing her determination and decided to do his best to help her. As they began walking, thorns and pebbles greeted their path and soon their feet were sore with blisters, gashes, and cuts. Nonetheless, their determination was so strong that they continued walking.

Meanwhile, Ravana's spies gave him a full report of the prediction of the sages and the worrisome child that was to be born and predicted to be the cause of future trouble for him. He decided to nip the problem even before it bud by sending Mayavi demon to prevent the vanara couple from completing their journey. Taking the form of a dangerous looking buffalo, Mayavi came and obstructed their path. Anjana was least concerned about the balloonic demon. She kept walking, much to the shock of Kesari, straight into the powerful demon ahead. He rushed ahead and managed to push the demon out of her way just in time. With this first-hand experience with Kesari, Mayavi realized there was no chance of winning against this mighty vanara and fled to save his life.

Finally the exhausted couple managed to reach the ashram of Matanga Rishi. Anjana's legs were totally bruised and bleeding. As soon as she sat down to examine them, a sweet little child came running and tended to her wounds very gently. The child was so beautiful that Anjana was spell-bound. Even Matanga Rishi was awestruck. He had never seen such a beautiful boy anywhere in the vicinity of the ashram. Only when he observed minutely, did he realize that the child was none other than Lord Shiva himself who had come to serve his future mother. After serving Anjana for a while, the child disappeared.

Hurrying back to Kailash, Lord Shiva shared with Parvati his ecstatic experience of serving his mother. Back in the ashram, Matanga Rishi offered Anjana his blessings and also gave her the Shiva mantra. When she began to chant the Shiva mantra, Vayu got his signal that it was time to deposit the energy of Lord Shiva. Taking the Shiva energy from the Saptarishis, Vayu reached Anjana and placed the potency in her womb. From that moment onwards Anjana became as effulgent as the sun. Kesari understood that a divine child had entered her womb.

When Ravana heard this news, he panicked and immediately got in touch with his friend Vali to warn him of the danger that was coming from Anjana's womb. Initially Vali did not consider the unborn child of Anjana's to be a threat. But when Ravana reminded him about the mighty exploits of Kesari, Vali feared that Kesari's to-be-born child might excel him in warfare and strength. To keep Kesari under subjugation was almost impossible. And if his son was born stronger, then definitely there was a great chance of Vali losing his throne. Coaxed and instigated by Ravana, Vali agreed to find a way out. In order to assist Vali, Ravana handed over a mystical arrow; an arrow that could be aimed at the grossest or the subtlest of targets and would never miss its mark.

Vali then invited Anjana and Kesari to his palace under the pretext of celebration ceremony of his coronation as the king of Kishkinda. They couldn't refuse the invite and joined the celebrations. Vali was a perfect host and with his gracious hospitality he made them feel comfortable in the palace guest house. In the middle of the night when the whole of Kishkinda was sleeping, Vali released the mystical arrow aiming it at the embryo of the sleeping Anjana. The arrow whizzed past the palace corridors, entered the sleeping Anjana's room and penetrated her womb to destroy the child within. In great agony and pain, Anjana screamed out for help. Kesari reached out to his wife and realized that a mystical weapon had attacked his wife and was destroying the foetus. Nothing was visible externally but he knew the existence of such mystical weapons that worked on the power of mantras and did not miss their aim.

Feeling immense pain and helplessness, Anjana began to chant the Shiva mantra. As soon as she began chanting, Lord Shiva instantly made an appearance and neutralised the effect of the arrow. He then went on to revive the child and blessed it to be immune from all sorts of attacks from external forces. Relieved that their child was saved and shaken up by the whole ordeal, Kesari and Anjana fled from the palace in the middle of the night to reach the safety of their own territory.

Eventually, the child that was born was an incarnation of Shiva himself, *Shankara suvana*; or in some places it is mentioned as *Shankara svayam*. The child was also the son of Kesari and thus is called *Kesari nandana*. Of course, he is also the son of the wind god and thus is known as *Pavana suta* also. But more than that, he is the darling child of Lord Rama and is known as *Rama dulare*. How can one person be the child of so many people? Hanuman is connected to all these personalities at various levels.

A person exists at three levels, the spiritual, the life breath, and the physical body. At the deepest level of the spirit, Hanuman was an expansion of Lord Shiva. His physical body was born in Anjana's womb through Kesari, thus he is physically the son of Kesari. But since the energy of Shiva was transported through the medium of the wind, the life air that flows in his body is a contribution of the Pavana and thus he is Pavana suta.

shankara swayam kesarī nandana

۸

After Lord Rama vanquished Ravana and installed Vibhishan as the king of Lanka, He requested Hanuman to share this good news with Mother Sita who was held captive in Ashok Vatika. Hanuman reached Ashok Vatika immediately to deliver the good news. Sita was thrilled to see him yet again after a month. In great details, Hanuman shared the war happenings with Mother Sita and culminated his narration by revealing the news of the death of Ravana, the victory of Rama, and the establishment of Vibhishana as the king of Lanka. Sita was overjoyed. Eleven torturous months had ended with this news. She was so happy with Hanuman that she wanted to reward him suitably. But alas, she had nothing in her possession at that time. The only thing she could give him then were her heartfelt blessings. There was nothing in the three worlds that could match the news that Hanuman had just given her.

With gratitude and joy, Sita blessed Hanuman that the day on which he had given her the news would become a day more special than other days of the week. He would be glorified and worshipped on this day forever, all over the universe. She further blessed Hanuman that all virtues would reside in his heart and Lord Rama would always shower his mercy on him.

Hanuman became renowned in all the three worlds by the blessings of Mother Sita and the grace of Lord Rama. By utilizing his talent, strength, skills, and by exhibiting exemplary attitude in the right consciousness, Hanuman forever established a kingdom in the hearts of Sita and Rama and ruled there forever. Seated on this high throne as a king of their hearts, he rules the hearts of devotees of the Lord spread over the three worlds.

His lustre and brilliance is immediately recognized and praised by all who come into contact with him. By the blessings of Mother Sita, the whole world worships the brilliance and power of Hanuman. *teja pratāpa mahā jaga bandana*

vidyāvāna gunī ati chātura।
rāma kāja karibe ko ātura॥ 7 ॥

Supremely learned, virtuous and intelligent,
Ever eager to serve Rama. (7)

One of the most prominent aspects of Hanuman is his illustrious and supreme wisdom. In Ramcharitmanas, Tulsidas described him as made of pure intelligence and the foremost amongst men of wisdom. In Sri Rama Raksha Stotra, he is described as the wisest of the wise.

In another version, Hanuman is said to be so intelligent that he was able to learn the entire Vedas in a mere fortnight. The sun god, however, was reluctant at the thought of his favourite pupil leaving. So he repeatedly made Hanuman forget what he had learnt so that the lessons were dragged on and on for many months. Hanuman pleased him so much by his simplicity and devotion that he let him go and bestowed him a boon that henceforth those who invoked Hanuman's name would never forget their lessons! ***vidyāvāna gunī ati chātura***

Yamaraj hurried towards Rama's camp to give him a piece of news that had really shaken him up.

Ravana's evil brain had cooked up a way to defeat Rama's army in a sure shot way. He had organized recitation of the Chandi Stotra, completing which would give him iron-clad immunity from any defeat. The news sent a jitter down the monkey army. The mere mention of Chandi Stotra gave them visions of impending doom. However, Rama huddled into a meeting with Vibhishana and other advisors to chart out their course of action. After lot of discussions, Rama called Hanuman and gave his final verdict, "I give you full freedom to go to Lanka and do whatever is needed to stop this ritual from being completed. Use any tactic you like, just stop it somehow."

Hanuman got really excited with this seva; it was more like a fun project. He had open instructions to do what he liked. His brain was already in overdrive, thinking of creative ways to foil Ravana's plans. He laughed to himself just thinking about what all he could do. Soon he was in Ravana's palace disguised as a fly. He quickly figured out where the ceremony was happening and evaluated the scene. He couldn't believe what he saw. Brihaspati, the guru of demigods, was the chief priest leading the recitation. Why would he help Ravana? But then he saw the security guards pointing their lances at him. It was only under duress that

Brihaspati was helping Ravana. Hanuman was ready for action. He quickly went near Brihaspati and began deleting important words and lines so that Brihaspati would skip important lines. But to his horror, Brihaspati was hardly referring to the texts because he was reciting from memory. Hanuman came up with another plan. He morphed into a huge atrocious looking monster and appeared in front of him. As soon as Brihaspati's vision fell on him, he shrieked. He dropped everything and ran for his life. Hanuman quickly changed into the shape of a fly before the guards could see his monstrous form. With Brihaspati shrieking like a mad man, there was no way the ritual could continue.

But Ravana was not one to give up. He decided to start another fire sacrifice to appease Goddess Chandi. He gathered his best brahmanas and started the ceremony within no time. Although they were falling short of brahmanas, they had to manage. Soon a young brahmana came asking to be of assistance. The older brahmanas were only too happy to get more assistance. The young brahmana was enthusiastic and energetic. He helped them sincerely and without any mistakes. The delighted brahmanas blessed him with a boon to which the brahmana replied, the best boon is to get more seva. The brahmanas were now totally floored by his dedication and insisted on granting him a wish. Hesitatingly, the young man asked them to replace two alphabets in the hymns. Instead of 'ha' they should pronounce 'ka'. He assured them that this small change will greatly benefit their master Ravana, The young man was hoping that they were not learned enough to know what this change meant. Only an exalted Vedic scholar would realize the significance. Luckily, the brahmanas readily agreed, seeing nothing wrong with the substitution.

Jaya tvam devi chamunde
Jaya bhutartha kaarini

Instead of saying haarini they said kaarini!

Little did they know the catastrophic effects of the change! The goddess, instead of being pleased, was absolutely enraged. With her fiery eyes, she burnt everything in the vicinity. How dare they evoke her anger! She would show them how angry she could get. The sacrifice was a total failure producing the opposite of expected results. The brahmanas fled from there to save their lives while the young man smiled as he came back to his original form. Hanuman. He was glad he knew the significance of the Sanskrit verses and could make the exact change in letters by tricking the learned brahmanas. *vidyāvāna gunī ati chātura*

Mission accomplished, he flew back to his own camp.

Hanuman used his bookish knowledge in the most practical manner according to time, place, and circumstance. He was extremely clever and flexible in the application of knowledge while keeping the essence and goal in mind. The result was that he always managed to achieve what he set out to achieve and that too in the most unique ways.

When there is eagerness, there is opportunity. When one is very eager to do something, nature arranges more of that opportunity. Rama kaj means working for the pleasure of Rama. This is called seva or the spirit of service. Hanuman was always eager to serve Rama.
rāma kāja karibe ko ātura

When Lord Rama returned to Ayodhya with Mother Sita and Lakshmana, the entire Vanara army accompanied them and witnessed the spectacle of the coronation of Sita and Rama as queen and king of Ayodhya. A few days passed and the monkeys had begun to settle down in the Ayodhyan culture. They really liked being in Ayodhya and of course, they were blissful in the divine company of Lord Rama. Rama called all of them for a meeting in which he instructed them to return to their homes in Kishkinda and continue performing Rama kaj. They were shocked at his instruction. First of all, they did not want to return home. For them, Ayodhya was home now. Secondly, they were confused as to how they could perform Rama kaj in Kishkinda. Technically speaking, they could engage in Rama kaj or serving Rama if they continued to live in Ayodhya. But if they went back to Kishkinda they would only be able to perform kaam kaj or mundane work.

When they asked Rama, he explained to them that prior to them meeting him, whatever they were doing in Kishkinda was kaam kaj or mundane work. But after they connected with Rama, they belonged to him and their mind, body, and words belonged to Rama now. Thus their kingdom, houses, and even families were Rama's property. So whatever they did there, technically, was their service to Rama only. Rama explained that before they saw their family and property as belonging to them, but now they can see that their family and property actually belonged to Rama and thus they ought to take care of them with that consciousness. By taking care of their families and taking care of the affairs of the kingdom of Kishkinda with a higher and purer consciousness, they would be doing Rama kaj or service to Lord Rama. With this understanding, all the vanaras agreed to return to their kingdoms.

Each vanara returned to Kishkinda after bidding farewell to Rama, except Angad and Hanuman. Angad fell at the feet of Rama begging him to allow him to stay back in Ayodhya. Since he had no family, unmarried that he was, he was ready to do any menial service in Ayodhya. Rama embraced him and insisted that Angad return to Kishkinda. With Rama firm about his decision, Angad reluctantly returned to Kishkinda. Rama denied Angad's plea of staying back in Ayodhya for two reasons. When Angad asked for any menial service, it showed his attitude towards service, that he categorized service as low and high. The moment you categorize service, it shows that you don't deserve service. The second reason was that when Angad expressed that he didn't have family in Kishkinda, it meant that he feared Sugriva. So his motivation to stay back was not love for Rama but fear of Sugriva. Rama knew Sugriva very well and realized that Angad's fear was baseless and would be allayed once he reached home.

The only person Rama did not ask to return was Hanuman. He didn't ask Hanuman to leave and Hanuman didn't need permission to stay. There was an unspoken agreement and pact between the two. It was an agreement of the heart. Hanuman had no existence without Rama and Rama could not bear to live without seeing Hanuman constantly. Hanuman's greatest satisfaction was to constantly serve Rama in every possible way. *rāma kāja karibe ko ātura*

prabhu charitra sunibe ko rasiyā।
rāma lakhana sītā mana basiyā॥ 8 ॥

You crave to hear about the Lord,
Rama, Lakshmana, Mother Sita dwell in you. (8)

Before the vanara army left in search for Sita, Rama
met each one of them. This news that Rama wanted to
meet them came as a complete surprise to the vanaras
who were used to a king who hardly looked at them and
treated them as commodity. As the army lined up to meet
Rama one by one, there was an air of excitement. The
vanaras kept peeping ahead to see the heart-warming
exchanges between Rama and their own kith and kin
from their ranks. His patting them, encouraging them,
and thanking them was so heart touching. They had
never seen any leader do anything as kind as this. Their
desire to go till the end of the earth to serve Rama's goal
intensified. For each monkey who stood facing Rama, it
was a life melting experience. The most sublime feeling
in their life. Rama respectfully looked into their eyes
and expressed his gratitude for taking so much risk and
putting in so much effort to find his beloved Sita. For the

few moments they spent with Rama, they felt they could surrender their entire life in serving him.

But while Rama interacted with them, his eyes searched for someone else. At the end of the long winding queue stood Hanuman. Rama's face visibly relaxed as soon as he saw Hanuman. Rama continued meeting all the monkeys while patiently waiting for Hanuman's turn. Finally, when Hanuman was in front of Rama, Rama decided to test him. He first asked him where he had disappeared to all this while. Hanuman rather than replying to that question, immediately fell at the feet of Rama and held them tightly. Holding his shoulders, Rama tried to pick him up, but Hanuman held on tightly to his feet. Rama was surprised at this odd behaviour. Hanuman then said, "My dear Lord, let me remain in this position forever. As long as my hands are at your feet, your hands will be on my shoulders. As long as I take shelter of you, you will continue to empower me. The moment I leave your feet, you will leave my shoulders. Your touch and blessings are the source of my strength and abilities. All my life I have been waiting to serve my eternal master and finally I have the opportunity."

Rama was in a light mood and he said, "You are talking about blessings. But you have come so late, right at the end, I have no blessings left to offer you. Since all my blessings are exhausted, what can I offer you now?"

Hanuman replied in an instant, taking the liberty of being a tad cheeky, "You may have given away the big things you have, my Lord, but you definitely still possess a small but powerful blessing. To some, you may have given knowledge of the scriptures as blessing, to others you may have given wisdom or guidance or power or fame or even wealth, but I am not looking at such big things as blessings. I am only interested in the smallest thing in your possession. Please give me that as a blessing and I will be truly happy."

Rama was utterly confused at the puzzling request. He wanted to test Hanuman but the tables had turned and it was Hanuman testing him now. He asked him, "What is it that I haven't given away yet as a blessing? What is the smallest thing I have?" Hanuman was thrilled to have confused the Lord. The look of confusion on the Lord's face was priceless.

Hanuman continued speaking with a smile on his face, "My dear Lord, when you had met Lord Parashuram, you had told him that the smallest thing in your possession was your name Rama. I want that. Please give me your name as a gift and blessing. Though it's small, but that little word contains the strength of the entire universe in it."

Rama was deeply touched. Hanuman's devotion and his wisdom were very special. He had managed to create a deep impact in the heart of the Lord. With tears in his eyes, Lord Rama embraced Hanuman. The deal was done. From that moment onwards, Hanuman owned Rama's name. With great relish, he would chant the holy name of Lord Rama and would listen to it chanted by anyone else with equal relish. He never lost a chance to chant and hear Rama naam and Rama katha with great relish. *prabhu charitra sunibe ko rasiyā*

From Hanuman, we learn to establish the presence of God in our hearts. Our hearts are filled with darkness, because we have not given permission to light to enter. Light can also enter through windows. The Lord can enter through our ears if we engage in hearing about Him.

Hanuman was always interested in listening to the Ramayana, and in this way, the Divine is always established in his own heart. Hanuman's great qualities were his Wisdom, Strength, and Devotion, which resided firmly in his heart as Rama, Lakshmana, and Sita.

Much later, when Rama became the king of Ayodhya, something really interesting happened. Seeing the Lord settled and living happily in the company of Mother Sita, Lord Shiva and Parvati decided to pay a visit to Ayodhya. Once the welcome formalities were completed, Mother Sita invited the visiting couple for lunch. While everyone had assembled for lunch, Lord

Shiva noticed that Hanuman was missing. He asked Rama his whereabouts. With a smile Rama told him to check in the gardens. Surely Hanuman would be there. Lord Shiva's eagerness to see Hanuman far exceeded his desire to eat the meal. He and Parvati stepped out into the garden to find Hanuman. There they heard a very unique sound that sounded like someone snoring. As they walked towards the source of the sound, they were amazed to see that it was Hanuman, sleeping peacefully under a mango tree, oblivious to the world, and snoring away. But what amazed them most was the sound of the snore. For from the snore emanated the holy name of Rama. Rama's name was so much ingrained in Hanuman's psyche and consciousness that even his snore was emanating Rama naam.

While Shiva's gaze was fixed on Hanuman, Parvati pointed out towards the tree under which Hanuman was resting. Something magical was happening there. Every leaf on that tree was swaying in sync with the vibrations of the holy name of Rama. Lord Shiva saw this as the most divine sankirtan of the holy names of His worshipable Lord Rama. In great happiness, he himself began to dance, chanting the names of Rama. Seeing her husband enter an ecstatic trance, Parvati also joined in the singing and dancing. With the divine couple dancing enthusiastically and chanting the names of Rama, the gandharvas, kinnaras, and apsaras from the heavenly realms also joined in, filling the atmosphere with divine music and singing.

Back at the palace, Sita was anxious her guests hadn't returned from the garden. She sent Lakshmana to get them back for lunch. Lakshmana quickly walked into the garden to see the enthusiastic surprise that was in store for him. The mood in the garden was so festive and surcharged with devotion that Lakshmana couldn't resist participating in the dancing and singing of the holy names. When Lakshmana did not return, Sita sent Bharata and then Shatrughana but neither of them returned with the guests. They had all joined in the kirtan festival! Exasperated, Sita herself went to look for them, along with Rama. When she walked into the garden, she was totally fascinated to see the dancing and singing festival going on in full swing. In the midst of all this hullabaloo, Hanuman was blissfully sleeping under the mango tree and Rama's names was vibrating from his sweet snoring.

Sita and Rama were overwhelmed by his devotion. Walking up to Hanuman, Rama gently sat beside him and touched his head with great love. As soon as Rama touched him, Hanuman woke up. Lord Shiva, who was so inspired with Hanuman's devotion, glorified him endlessly. Hanuman became red with embarrassment, being glorified in front of his master. Sensing his discomfort, Sita invited everyone for lunch.

As soon as everyone was seated, Sita began to serve lunch. She noticed that, as usual, Hanuman was not sitting but had busied himself with some service. Today, she forced him to sit along with the guests. Initially, Hanuman was embarrassed to be sitting along with Rama for lunch. He always preferred to eat the remnants of Rama's food. But once he began eating, he got so enthusiastic that he gobbled down crazy quantities of food. Nothing seemed to satisfy him. No matter how much Sita served, he kept eating more and more. He kept looking for more and more food. Everyone was surprised at Hanuman's appetite. Then Sita realized how she could quench Hanuman's insatiable hunger.

She placed a tulasi leaf with the name of Rama written on it. As soon as Hanuman ate the leaf, his hunger vanished miraculously. Lord Shiva and Parvati were so amazed and pleased with Hanuman's devotion. They blessed him with a boon that his devotion for Rama would be glorified across centuries, that the devotees of Lord Rama would know him as Sankat Mochan or the destroyer of troubles and that his love for Rama's holy names and Rama's pastimes would grow unlimitedly.
prabhu charitra sunibe ko rasiyā

After Sita and Rama's coronation ceremony, they called upon all those great personalities who had sacrificed so much for their sake. Each one was given valuable gifts as significant tokens of appreciation for their timely help. Though they felt that nothing could be considered worthy enough a gift to those who had assisted them in the time of their greatest need. When it came to Hanuman, both Sita and Rama were at a loss for words as well as ideas for what would be a suitable gift. They owed their lives to him. When his name was called, Hanuman walked ahead looking very indifferent.

Sita and Rama began to describe in great details about how Hanuman had entered into both their lives as a saviour. They glorified his intelligence, sensitivity, expertise, determination, strength, and compassion. The citizens of Ayodhya were astounded at the way their king and queen were glorifying a vanara. They hadn't heard any past king glorify their subjects in such an elaborate way. After speaking at length, Sita wanted to offer him some gift. She stood up and did something uncharacteristic of a queen. She removed a beautiful diamond necklace from her own neck and held it out for Hanuman. There was pin drop silence in the court. That act meant a lot!

Hanuman took the necklace from her hand. He turned it around and looked at it from all directions. There was something missing. He turned it around yet again to be doubly sure. Again it was missing. Now he held the big diamond that was hanging in the centre and plucked it off. There was a big gasp in the courtroom. Hanuman had just destroyed the queen's gift. He was now turning around the diamond and suddenly took it to his mouth and placed it between his teeth. With great strength he bit into it and it cracked into two. He observed the two halves and then discarded them carelessly. Then he began to break apart every stone in that necklace, observe carefully, and throw it away with disappointment. Finally he threw the complete necklace onto the floor. It was of no use to him.

This monkey-like behaviour had outraged the entire courtroom. Voices were rising. People began to question Hanuman's disrespectful act vociferously. How could he be so arrogant to dismantle a royal gift and that too in front of the royal couple in a full courtroom? In explanation to all the questions being raised, Hanuman simply said that he was only looking for Rama and Sita in the gems. Since he could not find them inside or outside in any of the stones, he threw away the necklace. Giggles could be heard from different quarters. The monkey was trying to find Rama and Sita inside the diamonds. While many were giggling, some began to pass sarcastic comments to chide Hanuman. One of them said, "If Hanuman was looking for Rama Sita everywhere, he should first be looking to see if they exist in his own heart. There was no point in looking for them everywhere else, if they didn't exist in his own heart."

The next moment, screams were heard all over the courtroom. Blood had spilled everywhere. Hanuman stood in the middle of the court with his chest torn, exposing his heart. Inside there was an effulgent and beautiful image of Sita and Rama. They were eternally enshrined within Hanuman's heart forever. Not only did they reside in his heart but he too resided in their hearts. *rāma lakhana sītā mana basiyā*

One day Rama and Sita had a friendly argument as to which of them got greater devotion from Hanuman. They asked him outright but smart Hanuman managed to get out of the sticky situation by saying that he was devoted to both of them equally. Sita promptly asked him to get a glass of water since she was dying of thirst. Rama immediately countered by feigning to faint due to heat and begged Hanuman to fan him. They both waited expectantly to find out which request would be attended to first. But Hanuman expanded both his arms and fetched water with one hand and fanned Rama with the other. This pacified both his divine masters.

sūkshma rūpa dhari siyahi dikhāvā।
bikata rūpa dhari lanka jarāvā॥ 9 ॥

In a tiny form you appeared before Sita,
In a terrifying form you burnt Lanka. (9)

In his journey to Lanka, Hanuman assumed a diminutive form as many as seven times. And it was in this tiny form that he made contact with Sita.

After a long and arduous search through the island of Lanka, Hanuman finally reached Ashok Vatika gardens. That was the only place he had not yet scanned. Considering this to be Ravana's favourite garden, Hanuman thought this could be an ideal place to hold Sita captive. Ravana may have probably wanted to invoke the romantic side in Sita by hosting her in a scenic and extremely beautiful garden with beautiful flowering trees and sweetly chirping birds. Since Hanuman had kept his eyes and ears wide open, he knew quite a few secrets of Lanka by now. With great hope, Hanuman hopped into the garden. Taking a very tiny form, he scaled the wall of the garden and leaped onto a tree inside. From tree to tree he traversed across the garden. Since there was a dense array of trees, there was no way anyone could spot him in his tiny little form. He had assumed that tiny monkey form for two prominent reasons. One, of course, was to remain discreet and invisible to the demonesses, 700 of whom were guarding Ashok Vatika. The second was more personal. This was the first time Hanuman would come in front of Mother Sita. Rama had become his spiritual father and naturally Sita was his eternal mother. When Hanuman met her for the first time, he wanted her to address him as 'son'. His logic was that if he appeared small in size, it would awaken Sita's motherly affection towards him.

As he scouted around the garden, he reached the central section, which was also the most beautiful part of the garden. Right in the middle was a huge Simshupa tree. Under that huge tree was a raised platform on which sat, morosely, an extremely beautiful lady in simple attire. Looking at her aroused great feelings of reverence and respect in Hanuman's heart. Without any tangible proof, Hanuman instantly knew that this was Sita indeed. He was so excited to have finally found Sita that he wanted to jump right in front of her and talk to her about Rama. But he contained his excitement when he saw the hordes of rakshasis strolling around keeping a close watch on her. He decided to wait for an appropriate moment when he could get a private audience with her.

A few hours later, in the wee hours of the night, Ravana walked into the garden with great pomp along with his entourage of women carrying eclectic gifts. In the middle of the night, though in the midst of so many beautiful women, Ravana had remembered Sita and come to pay her a visit. For the last ten months he had been trying unsuccessfully to convince her to forget Rama and marry him instead. But Sita hadn't paid heed to his courting and attempts to coax her into submission. This was yet another failed attempt. Sita insulted him once again and Ravana could no longer bear it. He almost assaulted her physically, restrained only by his wife Mandodari. He stormed out in a huff, giving her a warning to submit within two months or be ready to face death.

As soon as Ravana left, the rakshasis ganged around Sita and abused her verbally for her foolishness in not submitting to Ravana. Hanuman wanted to jump down and punch those hooligans on their faces. But he restrained himself considering that he wouldn't be able to talk to Sita if he did that. In addition it could also happen that Sita may even consider him to be Ravana or one of his allies disguised as a messenger of Rama. While Hanuman in his tiny form was seething in anger seated on the branch of a tree above Sita, something very interesting happened.

A demoness called Trijata walked towards the others and began to share her nightmare with them. She had a vision of a monkey coming into Lanka and destroying it. She saw the whole city go up in flames and the wild monkey destroying everything including the king's palace. The only person the monkey seemed to be interested in was Sita. She further said that if the rakshasis ill-behaved with Sita, then surely Sita wouldn't protect them from any upcoming danger. This scared the rakshasis who then left Sita alone and began drinking liquor in sheer frustration. Eventually all of them fell asleep. This was the chance that Hanuman was waiting for. Just as he was about to jump down in front of Sita, he saw something shocking. Sita had tied her hair into a noose and was about to hang herself from the branch of the very tree on which he was stationed. He panicked and almost fell down. He realized that Sita was in too delicate a frame of mind to accept a stranger monkey as a messenger of Rama's. She wouldn't even want to hear him out before giving up on her life. Thus he chose to do something else. Something he had great faith in. He decided to narrate Rama Katha, the story of Lord Rama.

As soon as the first words of Rama Katha escaped from his mouth, Sita's heart skipped a beat. She immediately connected to his melodious divine voice. Someone was here who loved Rama as dearly as she did.

She withdrew the noose and relaxed. When Hanuman saw the effect his narration had on Sita, he continued enthusiastically. Keeping himself hidden behind a leaf, he narrated the entire story of Rama to the attentive Sita. Several times during the narration, Sita tried to find the narrator but couldn't as he was carefully concealed behind a leaf. Finally when Hanuman felt it was the right time, he jumped down in front of Sita. When Sita saw such a cute little monkey, her motherly affection surfaced. As Hanuman had desired, she called him son. That address made Hanuman smile blissfully. *sūkshma rūpa dhari siyahi dikhāvā*

He told Sita that he would take her back to Rama. Sita almost giggled at his proposal. How could a tiny monkey claim to take her back? She didn't want to be insensitive by showing that she doubted his capacity, but she still needed clarity. So she asked him whether all monkeys were similar in size in Rama's army. The intelligent Hanuman immediately smelled the doubt in her voice. The next instant, he expanded in size. He kept expanding till he was much taller and much bigger than the tree under which she sat. Now Sita was thoroughly confused. First he appeared so small and now he was so huge. She asked Hanuman what his original size was. Was he small, was he big, or was he medium-sized?

Hanuman gave a brilliant answer that showed his

humility. He replied that he was originally small and insignificant but in the service of Lord Rama, he could take up any size and any responsibility. By the grace of Lord Rama, there was nothing that he couldn't achieve and there was no obstacle that he couldn't cross. Sita was so happy to hear that answer. This was the essence of devotion. After a long and deep conversation with Mother Sita, Hanuman decided to do something, which he considered equally important. Create new history in Lanka! Do something that was historical and impactful!

He began to wreak havoc in Ashok Vatika. Every single thing that was standing at night was broken and dismantled by morning. When the demonesses woke up after a long slumber, they saw the once beautiful garden of Lanka was nothing but a disaster. Soon thousands of soldiers were rushing towards the garden to figure out what had happened. When the demonesses saw a monkey emerge from the midst of that wreckage, they immediately panicked. Trijata's dream was coming true after all. They ran helter-skelter while the foolish soldiers ran towards the monkey for a head-on collision. Soon thousands of dead soldiers lay scattered here and there. All day Ravana kept sending his soldiers and all day Hanuman kept destroying every single demon that came by. Soon some of Ravana's most powerful men were dead including his own son Akshay Kumar.

Having no choice left, Ravana sent Indrajit with the instruction to capture the arrogant monkey alive. Indrajit soon managed to bind Hanuman with the Brahma pasha. Though Hanuman had a boon that no weapon would work on him and Brahma had himself given him immunity from the Brahma pasha, Hanuman wilfully got bound. This had to do with the execution of the second part of his mission. He wanted his visit to serve as a warning to Ravana. Something that Ravana would remember forever. When he was dragged into the courtroom, Hanuman gave Ravana fine advice, which of course, did not even enter into the ears of the proud demon. Ravana wanted to kill the mischievous monkey, but Vibhishan convinced him that a messenger should not be killed. Then Ravana chose to set his tail on fire.

Miles of cloth soaked in gallons of oil was brought, to be tied and spread on his tail. Mystically, Hanuman's tail kept growing. Soon all the cloth and all the oil in Lanka was over. As soon as his tail was lit with fire, Hanuman simply freed himself from the ropes that bound him and jumped out of the courtroom. Once outside the building, he expanded himself and jumped around burning all the houses and structures in Lanka. Soon the whole city was a blazing inferno. *bikata rūpa dhari lanka jarāvā*

In the midst of chaos in Lanka with the fire

raging intensely, Hanuman was disappointed to see that it suddenly began to rain all over Lanka. More specifically, it was pouring over the sections of Lanka that were burning. Hanuman was very upset with the rain god, Indra, for having done that. He had taken so much effort to burn the city and here was the rain god undoing everything. When he summoned the rain god and complained, instead of offering a justification, Indra simply smiled. He told Hanuman to look carefully; he wasn't showering water, rather he was showering inflammable oils so that the city would burn harder. Ravana had tortured the gods enough and this was Indra's first chance to retaliate.

After all the adventure, when Hanuman returned to Lord Rama and shared the details of his actions in Lanka, Rama had a very fundamental doubt. He asked Hanuman why did he burn the city when he was only sent as a messenger to deliver a message to Sita. Hanuman explained that it wasn't his idea but rather Rama's own idea which he simply executed. Rama was confused, how it could be his idea when he wasn't even present in Lanka at that time. Hanuman explained to the Lord that though he wasn't physically present, as paramatma he was very much present in the heart of Ravana. It was he who had implanted the idea in Ravana's mind to burn the tail of Hanuman rather than injure it in any other way. It was Rama who had predicted this would happen as a dream in the mind of Trijata. As soon as Hanuman had heard the dream he was quite sure that this was Rama's desire. But he wanted to be doubly sure that it was indeed Rama that wanted Lanka to be burnt. The only way he could ensure that it wasn't the trick of his mind but actually the will of the Lord was by allowing himself to be bound and being helpless to take any decision on his own. Thus he agreed to be bound by Indrajit's Brahma pasha. Hearing Hanuman's logical explanation, there was nothing that Rama could do except applaud him silently. Hanuman was not just an expert in deeds but an expert in his words too.

bhīma rūpa dhari asura sahāre।
rāmachandra ke kāja savāre॥ 10 ॥

In a dreadful form you vanquished demons,
And collaborated in Ramachandra's work. (10)

Bhima was for once highly confused. He had no idea who he had encountered! This was the first time in his life he felt utterly powerless. And it wasn't the easiest feeling to live with. It all began that wonderful morning when Bhima had the best experience of his life. Interestingly, the best experience and the most embarrassing experience of his life happened on the same day. Almost as if nature was trying to balance the good and the bad.

That morning, as he was taking a stroll by the river, he saw the most beautiful sight ever. As if the rainbow was hanging upside down having transformed itself into a smile. His wife Draupadi was the most beautiful person he had ever seen in his life. But that morning she appeared almost like a goddess from some higher realm, smiling brilliantly. She was glowing like never before. When he reached closer, he realized that the radiance was sponsored by a golden lotus flower she held in her hand. It was not just golden but a 1000-petalled lotus flower. Bhima had never seen anything like this before and from the look of excitement and joy on Draupadi's face, he could understand that neither had she.

When Bhima sat down next to her admiring that flower, Draupadi made a request. A request that caused a flutter of joy in Bhima's heart. She asked him to get more such flowers for her. Bhima leapt up in excitement. This was the first time in so many years of their marriage that Draupadi had made any request whatsoever. He was eager to fulfil her desire. Reasoning that the 1000-petalled lotus had floated down the river, Bhima began following the trail of the river backwards. He had never been this excited in his life. He really wanted to make Draupadi happy. He was even daydreaming of how happy she would be when he returned with the many golden lotuses. There was a bounce in his gait. Soon he began to blow his conch shell, expressing his happiness to the world.

Of course, the world did not exactly appreciate the blasé display of his happiness. The terrible sound of the conch rattled through the forest, startling the birds and animals in the vicinity. Oblivious to the effect he was causing on the living beings, Bhima kept marching ahead along the river. Suddenly the earth below his feet quaked. He almost lost his balance and fell. He stopped smiling when he realized that the source of the quake wasn't natural but rather created. He had heard a thump distinctly. It felt as if someone had stomped the ground and artificially created the tremors. The warrior instincts of Bhima took over considering it to be a provocation to challenge his strength. His pursuit for the mystical golden flower suddenly became secondary and his inquisitiveness to find the source of the tremor became primary. He walked stealthily towards the direction from which the tremor had originated. Before he reached, another more powerful thud was heard and a more intense tremor was experienced. Now this was a serious matter. Bhima began walking cautiously towards the source of the quakes.

Just when he was almost there, he saw something on the ground that was unbelievable. Sprawled on the middle of his path was something that looked like a thick rope. When he saw carefully, it was actually a thick tail. His eyes followed the tail and found that it belonged to a really huge elderly monkey resting under a tree. Bhima had never seen a monkey so huge. Approaching the monkey respectfully, he requested him to move his tail so that he wouldn't have to step over it. The monkey lazily replied that he was too exhausted to even open his eyes, then what to speak of putting such a huge effort in shifting his tail. He casually told Bhima to take care of the tail shifting business himself. Bhima was really irritated with the attitude of the old monkey. But because he had other pressing matters to take care of, he didn't want to get into any discussion here. Plus who would want to quarrel with such a weak elderly person? Setting aside his anger, Bhima gently touched the tail of the frail monkey in order to set it aside. Somehow the tail was heavier than he expected. First he had just used two fingers to pick it up, but now he used his entire hand to lift up the tail. Interestingly the tail refused to budge. He now used both his hands. No matter how much energy he put in, the tail would not budge. It almost felt as if it was stuck to the ground. Bhima was flabbergasted. What was the point in having the strength of 10,000 elephants when he couldn't lift the tail of an ordinary monkey and that too an elderly one? He summoned all his strength and, taking a deep breath, once again tried to lift the tail. As he was pulling with all his might, he suddenly lost his grip and fell.

Right in front of his eyes, the tail rose in the air slightly and thumped onto the ground. The power with which the tail hit the ground created tremors that spread in all directions shattering the earth's tectonic plates. Bhima was bewildered at the power exhibited by an ordinary looking monkey. He realized that this couldn't possibly be an ordinary monkey. This had to be some divine being in disguise. With folded hands, he approached the elderly being. In great supplication, he begged forgiveness for being arrogant and for displaying his puny strength. He requested the powerful personality to reveal who he really was and bless him. The elderly monkey smiled and in the next moment in place of that old monkey stood Hanuman, the powerful servant and messenger of Lord Rama and the hero of the Rama Ravana war in Lanka.

Bhima was absolutely thrilled to see his worshipable master and source of his inspiration right in front of his eyes. Falling at the feet of Hanuman, he surrendered himself completely. Pleased with his sincerity, Hanuman picked up and embraced Bhima. It was a happy reunion of two brothers who were both sons of Vayu, the wind god. Both of them spent many hours together happily recounting the adventures of their lives and sharing notes.

Hanuman was dejected with the sorry state of the Pandavas and promised to help Bhima in the upcoming war. He tutored Bhima in the art of mace fighting and wrestling. He also promised him that during the war, he would be present on Arjuna's flag and would add to the intensity of Bhima's war cries by adding his own voice. Thus even before the enemy approached Bhima, his heart would be shattered hearing the terrible war cries. Thus half the fight could be won by simply scaring the enemy. *bhīma rūpa dhari asura sahāre*

When one approaches God, the question is not what can He do for you but what can you do for Him. Hanuman personifies this attitude. There is absolutely no story of Hanuman's life where he gains anything or does things for his own pleasure or benefit. His life was a life of sacrifice. His life was a life of service. The primary and single-pointed focus of Hanuman's life was to enthusiastically serve Rama and his devotees, to the best of his capacity. Every mission of Rama's, was carried out so wonderfully by Hanuman. *rāmachandra ke kāja savāre*

The first service of Hanuman was to unite Sugriva with Rama. Knowing very well that both Sugriva and Rama needed each other, Hanuman spoke to both parties individually and convinced them to collaborate to achieve their goals and solve each other's problems. In fact, understanding that Sugriva's monkey mind is unpredictable and may change anytime, he sealed their friendship by making them take vows of friendship and dedication in a fire sacrifice. Eventually when the right time came, he inspired Sugriva to mobilize the entire monkey army. Regularly following up with him and pushing him into timely action, Hanuman made sure that the massive vanara army arrived at the right time.

Not only did he inspire Sugriva to send millions of vanaras around the globe, but he himself went on the search expedition in the southern direction. He did not just believe in delegating work, he believed in getting involved personally in every mission of Lord Rama's. He was not just an expert in organizing, but also in working at ground level. During the entire search operation, he kept everyone motivated and focused. Everyone has a tendency to forget why we do what we do. People tend to focus on the activity and forget the intention behind any action. Hanuman kept the whole army focused on the fact that this was Rama's mission and as long as they remembered that, Rama's grace would flow through them.

Of the millions of monkeys who left to find Sita, Hanuman was the one who actually found her. He left no stone unturned in doing so. He jumped across an ocean, fought with demons, searched the length and breadth of an entire country alone, risked his life by entering an enemy zone single-handedly, and resisted sensory temptation in the golden city. But all this was worth it when he finally saw Sita. By finding Sita and giving her

Rama's message, he successfully completed a job that was most dear to Rama and of course a crucial need in the given situation. By giving Sita Rama's message, he gave her hope and by giving Rama Sita's message, he gave him hope. Thus, he united Sita and Rama through hope.

A good servant is one who not only does the task given to him, but accomplishes several others along the way. Hanuman was only given the task of finding Sita and conveying Rama's message to her. But along with that, he accomplished much more. He conducted a complete survey of Lanka, assessing its strengths and weaknesses, studied Ravana's army, understood the entire layout of Lanka, and finally gave Ravana a warning he would remember forever. Moreover, he even identified a potential friend in Lanka in the form of Vibhishan. Hanuman, in fact, recommended him to Rama when he arrived asking for shelter. This connection became the most crucial link that turned the tide during the war.

Hanuman also played a key role in building the 80-mile wide and 800-mile long bridge of stones in just five days. He carried huge boulders, rocks, and even mountains from far and wide to ensure that the engineers were never short in supply of stones to build the bridge. During the war, Hanuman saved the lives of everyone, including Rama and Lakshmana, several times when unconquerable mystic weapons were used. Hanuman was Rama's most powerful instrument during the entire war, probably destroying more enemies than all monkeys put together. He not only helped Rama win the war with his physical strength but also helped strategize with his intellectual strength. Several times during the war, Hanuman jeopardized the yagyas of Ravana that could potentially make him immortal.

Finally, the most important way Hanuman served Rama was by reuniting him with Sita at the end of the war. Not only that, he reunited Bharata and Rama after the war as well. When Rama returned to Ayodhya, he sent all the monkeys back to their kingdom in Kishkinda while he kept Hanuman with him. Hanuman meant everything to Rama. He was a messenger, a minister, a friend, a servant, an advisor, a war commander, and even served as a vehicle for Rama when needed. Whatever Hanuman did, he did with complete faith, risking his life. He never gave any excuse and fulfilled his commitments, no matter what the price. Food and sleep were of no consequence to him till his mission was completed. For him, the mission of Lord Rama was always first and foremost.

He was the best of brahmanas. When needed, he became the best of kshatriyas to wield weapons in a war.

He was the best of vaisyas because a vaisya gives loans and puts people under his debt; he put Rama Himself under his debt. And sudra dharma being seva, who could follow it better than Hanuman? He completed every mission of Lord Rama, in whichever varna that was needed of him, as an exemplary brahmana, kshatriya, vaisya as well as sudra. *rāmachandra ke kāja savāre*

lāya sanjīvani lakhana jiyāe।
shrī raghubīra harashi ura lāe॥ 11 ॥

You brought the life-saving herb
Sanjivani and revived Lakshmana
And Raghuvira joyfully embraced
you close to his heart. (11)

No one knew where the arrows were coming from. No one knew who was shooting them. That was the state when Indrajit entered the battlefield. He was not just powerful, he was skilled; and not just skilled, he was cunningly deceptive. Fighting with Indrajit wasn't as easy as fighting with all the other demons of Ravana's army. With the ease with which he shot arrows, the monkeys knew they stood no chance. In fact it wasn't just the ease, it was also the speed with which he operated. Most of the times the monkeys didn't even realize where the arrows were coming from until they were too close to them. This was because Indrajit operated in an invisible mode. He had the mystical ability to keep himself hidden for substantial periods of time. From the moment Indrajit entered the fight arena, the morale of the monkey army was low but it reached an all-time low when one of Indrajit's arrows found its mark on Lakshmana's chest. This wasn't an ordinary arrow. It was an arrow bestowed on him by none other than Lord Brahma. The celestial arrow rendered Lakshmana unconscious. Seeing one of the brothers fall, a huge uproar went through the monkey army bringing them on the verge of panic.

With the fall of Lakshmana, the orderliness in the monkey army was lost and they all began to scatter in different directions. Some to save their lives, some losing hope, some towards Lakshmana in great anxiety and many in search of Rama or some other hero they could gain support from. Taking advantage of the panic mode, Indrajit struck intensely and slaughtered the confused monkeys by the thousands. Meanwhile, Jambavan reached the scene. He had been informed about the fall of Lakshmana. As soon as he spotted the fallen hero, his first question was, "Is Hanuman alive?"

Jambavan knew that there was only one person who mattered the most in times of crisis and that was Hanuman. Jambavan had such confidence in Hanuman's abilities that as long as Hanuman was alive then surely, he felt, hope was alive. When Hanuman was brought into the scene, he was in tears seeing Lakshmana helplessly unconscious. But the aura of confidence around Jambavan gave him an assurance that there was a way out of this mess. Jambavan took Hanuman aside and shared with him an action plan. He gave him the names of four herbs that were only available in the Himalayan Mountains. Jambavan explained the names of each herb and its medicinal properties. The first was mrta-sanjivani, which could restore a dead man to life. The second was sailya-karani, which could extract embedded weapons and quickly heal wounds. The third was suvarna-karani, which restored the body colour to its original texture. And finally, samdhani, which could unite fractured bones and severed limbs. Absorbing Jambavan's instructions, Hanuman made his leap towards the Northern realms. Getting the herbs wasn't the issue, getting it in time was. Hanuman knew that such impossible time-bound activities were more complex than impossible activities. He had to get the herbs before sunrise the next day, else the sun wouldn't rise for Lakshmana ever.

As Hanuman took off with great speed by the aerial route towards the Himalayan mountains, he saw something on the way that caught his attention. In the middle of a forest situated on a hill, was a charming hermitage, outside of which were a couple of sages performing a fire sacrifice with great intensity. Something compelled Hanuman to descend and meet the sages. Of course, one of the reasons for his descent was personal and another professional. On the personal front, the reason was his thirst. He hadn't had a chance to drink water for days together during the battle. He desperately needed some water now and there was a glistening river flowing next to the hermitage. The second reason was that he had to reconfirm his route. Jambavan had given him the name Dronachal, the specific area in the Himalayan ranges where the herbs were to be obtained. Surely these sages would know if he was flying in the right direction.

Even before Hanuman could say a word, one of the sages began to speak. He declared himself to be a seer of past, present, and future. He could see that Hanuman had come to seek the sanjivani set of herbs from the Himalayas to revive Lakshmana. He asked Hanuman not to worry and predicted that surely Rama would win the war against Ravana. In fact he asked Hanuman to have a quick bath in the river and return so that he could bless him with divine vision that would help him identify the herbs amidst the plethora of herbs that grew there. To Hanuman, something felt not right. Whilst on one hand this sage seemed to be glorifying Rama, on the other hand he was profusely indulging in self-praise. With this doubt, Hanuman began to walk towards the river to quench his thirst. While he was bent low cupping water in his right palm with the intention of drinking it, a crocodile attacked him. Not wanting to waste time, Hanuman continued drinking water with his right hand and dispassionately fighting the crocodile with his left hand. In a few minutes he was done with both. The crocodile was dead and his thirst was quenched. In place of the crocodile now stood a beautiful apsara who thanked him for liberating her from a curse and warned him about the fake sage he had just met. He was in fact a demon named Kalanemi who had been sent by Ravana to delay him from getting the life-saving herbs on time.

Armed with this new knowledge, Hanuman walked towards the hermitage. There was a look of surprise on the sage. How did he manage to outlive the crocodile? Anyway, he had another idea in store still. He called Hanuman closer to offer him the mantra that would impart divine vision to find the herbs readily. Hanuman came close by and instead of hearing him, punched him straight on his face. The punch was so intense that the demon disguised as a sage died instantly. Before falling, he automatically let go of his disguise and came back to his original demonic form to breathe his last. That being accomplished, Hanuman leaped towards his destination.

When he arrived on the Dronachal Mountains, a bigger, more complex challenge awaited him. There were millions of herbs on the mountain. In fact, the entire mountain was filled with herbs. And to make matters worse, there was very little difference between them, if at all. How on earth was he to decipher which were the four herbs that Jambavan wanted him to procure? He racked his brains for a while trying first logically and then intuitively to come to the right conclusions. That's when he realized that this process wasn't going to work and the risk he was taking of carrying back the wrong herbs was immense. It was then that he arrived at a very dynamic and unusual conclusion. Surely the herbs were on this mountain itself. What if he carried the entire mountain, then there was no risk of not getting the right herbs! He did something that was literally impossible for ordinary people to even fathom. He picked up the entire Dronachal Mountain effortlessly. Holding it on his right palm, he took a leap heading towards the southern regions. What a scene it was! A huge mountain flying in the air, held at its base by Hanuman, who himself had taken a huge form to be able to support the huge mountain.

Hanuman was determined to get back on time and save the life of Lakshmana. As per his calculations, he had sufficient time to make it back much before the scheduled time span. Just as he was getting proud of his timing, something hit him very hard on the chest. He found himself being dragged downwards at a great pace.

He had lost control over his flight and some mystical force was now dragging him down. He landed with a thud on the ground and the mountain slid away from his grip, parking itself on an open ground close by. Hanuman caught his balance and shook his head to stabilize himself after the fall. He looked around and realized that he was at the outskirts of a bustling city. Though this place was not too far from the city, it had a typical rural atmosphere that vibrated peace. Suddenly he saw someone walk towards him. He was shocked to see that the person he was gazing at had an uncanny resemblance to Lord Rama. Carrying a formidable bow in his hand, the mysterious person walked up to him with a serious look on his face. He asked him who he was and why he was passing over Ayodhya carrying such a huge mountain. The mention of the word Ayodhya brought clarity to Hanuman. Instantly he knew that this person was none other than Bharata, Lord Rama's brother.

Hanuman immediately bowed down with great respect and introduced himself to be the servant of Lord Rama. Bharata was extremely pleased to meet an associate of his brother's, whom he hadn't met for 13 long years now. Bharata began asking Hanuman innumerable questions about his brothers and their whereabouts. Hanuman explained to him that he didn't have enough time to answer his questions now as Lakshmana's life was in danger and he had to immediately return with the mountain before it was too late. Bharata understood Hanuman's predicament over the lack of time. Even then there was something that Bharata wanted Hanuman to do before he left. And that was to convey the news of Lakshmana's fall to Sumitra, the mother of Lakshmana. The soft-hearted Bharata could never muster enough courage to convey bad news to anyone. He felt that he had already hurt everyone enough in Ayodhya, simply by taking birth as the son of Keikeyi. So he literally dragged Hanuman to Ayodhya to Sumitra's palace.

When Hanuman conveyed the news to Sumitra, her reaction stunned him. Instead of crying at the loss and the possible death of her son, she had a totally different approach towards it. She told Hanuman that no matter what happens to her son, service to Lord Rama must never stop under any circumstances. If one son was dead, Sumitra told Hanuman, he could take her second son Shatrughana along with him to serve Lord Rama in place of Lakshmana. Hanuman was amazed at her reaction. What a family it was! Lakshmana and his mother both lived in a mood of sacrifice. Both were ready to sacrifice anything for service to Lord Rama. He had never seen such dedication in his life. Promising Sumitra that her son would be safe and that the service to Lord Rama would continue unobstructed, Hanuman walked out of Ayodhya. Picking up the Dronachal Mountain, he shot up the sky, moving southwards with renewed enthusiasm and determination.

When the silhouette of Hanuman carrying the massive mountain on the palm of his hands appeared in the sky, the entire monkey army broke out into applause and happy cries. Their hero had come back. His superheroic actions continued to amaze them. He had gone to bring some herbs and here he was returning with a mountain. As soon as Hanuman neared the battlefield, the fragrances of the various herbs wafted heavily in the air. As soon as the fragrance hit the nostrils of Lakshmana, he gained consciousness. *Lāya sanjīvani lakhana jiyāe*

Not just Lakshmana, but all the monkeys who were slain on the battlefield woke up as if from a deep slumber. What was a cause of celebration in the monkey army became the cause of frustration in the rakshasa army. This was because Ravana had disposed off the bodies of dead demons into the ocean just so that the enemies would never get to estimate his losses and would always be clueless as to how much of his army was still alive in the safety of the palace. What seemed to be a master strategy till now seemed foolish on seeing the revival of all the dead monkeys.

Rama, seeing his brother back to life, was overjoyed.

With great love he embraced his brother. Hanuman knew what place Lakshmana had in Rama's life. When one's hand fetches a glass of water, one does not thank the hand. Neither does the hand expect any gratitude, because it is not a separate identity. Lakshmana was that hand of Rama, an integral part of Rama, non-different from him.

Rama was so happy to regain his association. How could he reciprocate sufficiently for everything Hanuman had done and was doing for him? *Shrī raghubīra harashi ura lāe.*

raghupati kīnhī bahut barāī।
tuma mama priya bharatahi sama bhāī॥ 12 ॥

The descendent of Raghu dynasty praised you,
'You are as dear to Me as My brother, Bharat'. (12)

Ayodhya was decorated with great pomp during
Hema's svayamvara ceremony, the daughter of Kusha,
and granddaughter of Rama. Rama's joy knew no
bounds seeing his granddaughter about to get married.
But calamity struck in the form of a prince named
Chitragandha, the son of King Ugrabahu, the king
of Avanti. Chitragandha kidnapped the bride right in
front of a full assembly by releasing a Mohanastra
that mesmerized everyone into a temporary swoon.
Even before anyone had the chance to gather their wits
together, Chitragandha had disappeared. On coming
back to their senses, the most powerful warriors of
Lord Rama's army were in hot pursuit of Chitragandha.
With great zeal, the young prince routed the entire
Ayodhyan army. Using the Vayavastra, he created a
tornado effect and soon hundreds of soldiers were
flying in air and thrown across the battlefield. Seeing

the army in disarray, Lava stepped in to be at the helm of affairs.

Just about the same time, King Ugrabahu too made his entry. The fight went to another level with that. By the power of his mighty arrows, Ugrabahu rendered Lava weaponless and very soon Lava was left unconscious on the battleground. With Lava unconscious, the entire Ayodhyan army broke into panic mode, unsure of their next move. Kusha stepped in and took control of the situation. Within a short time, both rogue father and son were held captive. Next, Kusha turned his attention to his unconscious brother. The matter was escalated to Lord Rama who in a surprise move freed his friend Ugrabahu from captivity and embraced him warmly. To reward Kusha for his bravery, Rama offered him a celestial bracelet that was gifted to him by Agastya Muni. Kusha was very pleased to receive that gift from his father.

As soon as he wore that bracelet, his effulgence increased manifold. Immediately Kusha wanted to know more about the source of the bracelet. Agastya Muni who happened to be there too, explained that he received that bracelet from Varuna, the ocean god, in return for a favour he had offered. Long time ago, a horde of demons had taken shelter on the ocean bed. No matter how much Indra tried to locate them, they remained untraceable in the vast expanse of the ocean. But when Agastya Muni drank up the entire ocean water, they were exposed and eventually slaughtered by the gods. Agastya returned the waters of the ocean through another channel and thus the ocean was restored. As a token of gratitude, the ocean god offered the sage this priceless bracelet as a gift. Agastya gifted it to Rama and Rama in turn gifted it to Kusha as a mark of appreciation for his valour.

But the question regarding the revival of Lava remained. Agastya Muni immediately suggested that Hanuman be sent to procure the mrta-sanjivani herb from the ashram of Mudgal Rishi. When Hanuman expressed his surprise at the availability of the herb in such close proximity, Agastya explained that when Garuda was carrying the celestial nectar, a few drops had fallen which resulted in the growth of the magical herb there too. Soon Hanuman returned with the mrta-sanjivani herbs, which he had learned by now to recognize very well. As soon as the herbs arrived, Lava woke up from his unconscious state. Rama was so thankful to Hanuman for helping revive Lava that he offered him another bracelet as a token of appreciation. Glorifying Hanuman as if he had numerous mouths, Rama embraced him. He declared to the world that the one and only solution he always had for any crisis was Hanuman. Lord of the Raghu dynasty derived great pleasure in glorifying Hanuman. *raghupati kīnhī bahut barāī.*

Just before the war in Lanka, Rama had a grave discussion with the monkey army. This was immediately after accepting Vibhishan into their folds. He revealed to them that if anyone came with the thought of surrendering his life in service to Rama, Rama would immediately accept him without any consideration of qualification or disqualification. Even if Ravana came, he would give him shelter, overlooking all his misdeeds. The monkeys were really impressed with Rama's mood of compassion and acceptance. They realized in hindsight, that anyone who had taken Rama's shelter had gained a kingdom. Sugriva took shelter, he gained Kishkinda. Bharata took shelter, he gained Ayodhya. Vibhishan took shelter, he gained Lanka even before the war began.

But alas, now that Rama had offered the sovereignty of Lanka to Vibhishan, what would he do if Ravana took shelter of him at this point?

Rama's instant reply was that he would make him the king of Ayodhya. Then what about Bharata, the monkeys inquired. Rama said that he would make Bharata the king of Vaikuntha. Then what about Rama himself, the monkeys questioned. Rama said, "I will move around the three kingdoms, Ayodhya, Lanka, and Vaikuntha and serve all of them."

At that point, Rama's attention turned towards Hanuman. Hanuman had been one of the most surrendered souls and yet he had been deprived of a position or kingdom. Feeling really sorry about that, Rama asked Hanuman, "O' Hanuman, everyone who took shelter of me has received a kingdom from me, but I haven't been able to give you a suitable gift. All those who have achieved the fortune, have achieved it due to your grace and yet you yourself haven't received anything. I really wish to bless you and earnestly fulfil your desires."

Hanuman smiled broadly. What was the secret behind that smile? He confided to Rama that while others whom he favoured had gained kingship over only one kingdom, he had gained kingship over two kingdoms. Rama was pleasantly surprised to hear that and so were all the monkeys. How did Hanuman manage to gain kingship over not one but two kingdoms without anyone being aware of it?

When asked by Rama which two kingdoms did he have sovereignty over, Hanuman bent low and touched his head at Lord Rama's two lotus feet and declared that he was fortunate enough to have received kingship over these two kingdoms. Hanuman considered Lord Rama's lotus feet to be supreme treasures and everything else including material kingdoms to be insignificant and worthless pursuits. For him, these two treasures were worth more than one worthless kingdom. Rama was so elated with Hanuman's loving reply that he embraced him with great love and appreciated his dedication and service attitude. *raghupati kīnhī bahut barāī*

One time, Rama was so pleased with Hanuman's service that he spontaneously declared that he loved Hanuman twice as much as Lakshmana. Immediately after saying that, he became thoughtful and asked Hanuman how he felt about that comment. Was Hanuman happy hearing that? Hanuman replied with a smile that his comment simply meant that Lakshmana was dearer to him than anyone else in the world. Rama was surprised. How could that be? He had explicitly declared that Hanuman was twice as much dearer to him than Lakshmana. That being the case, how could it mean that it was Lakshmana who was dearer to him than anyone else? Hanuman clarified that in common parlance, great love is expressed by saying that "I love you more than my life." But Rama did not say that but instead told Hanuman that he loved him more than Lakshmana. Logically this meant that for Rama Lakshmana was his life. Because Rama considered Lakshmana to be his very life, he compared Hanuman to him. In this way Hanuman concluded that Rama loved Lakshmana more than him because Lakshmana was a more integral part of him like life itself.

Rama was very impressed with Hanuman's keen sense of logic and his deep observation of psychology. Now that Hanuman had shared his thoughts on his comment, he turned to Lakshmana to find out what his thoughts were. Rama was sure that the possessive Lakshmana would have felt bad that Rama loved Hanuman twice as much as him. Lakshmana surprised Rama by saying that he totally agreed with Rama. Hanuman was indeed twice better than him. When Rama asked for an explanation, Lakshmana gave two logical reasons to substantiate his conclusion.

The first explanation Lakshmana gave to substantiate how Hanuman was much better than him was with regards to Mother Sita. He explained that he knew Sita for 25 years but in spite of knowing her for so long he had not managed to gain her trust. In fact, she doubted his intentions even after such a long relationship. But Hanuman hardly knew her for a few minutes yet he managed to gain her complete trust and faith. What Lakshmana could not do in 25 years, Hanuman had managed to do in just a few minutes and thus was far better than Lakshmana.

The second explanation Lakshmana gave to validate his point was much deeper from the perspective of his eternal role in his service to the Lord. The eternal role of Lakshmana in his spiritual capacity was as

Anantashesha, the divine snake bed of Lord Vishnu. As Anantashesha, his service was carrying Lord Vishnu on his back. But Hanuman not only carried Rama on his back but also carried Lakshmana along. Thus Hanuman was twice better than Lakshmana even from the point of view of the amount of service he renders.

Rama was even more impressed with Lakshmana's explanation. These two great personalities, instead of feeling insecure, had the humility and maturity to focus on the good qualities of the other and not on their own greatness. This is what really attracted Rama to both Hanuman and Lakshmana. Though Hanuman wasn't born in Suryavanshi family, he had become such an integral part of Lord Rama's family that he was literally inseparable. Rama considered him as one of his brothers.

Though Rama compared Lakshmana to Hanuman, he also said that he was like Bharata for him. It's interesting to understand why Rama mentions Bharata and not Lakshmana. Simply because although Lakshmana was physically near Rama all the time, Bharata was on Rama's mind all the time. Since Bharata was serving from a distance, he occupied Rama's mind even more than Lakshmana. Both the brothers loved Rama dearly and Rama loved both of them dearly. But even then Bharata was the one who had to go through so much insult, misunderstanding, pain, separation, and thus drew out the deepest possible love from Rama's heart. So when Rama declared Hanuman as his brother, he declared him to be his brother equivalent to Bharata. He was as dear a brother to him as Bharata. *tuma mama priya bharatahi sama bhāī*

One fine day, Rama and the three brothers were walking along with their fifth brother Hanuman in the gardens of Ayodhya. After a long walk, Rama felt tired and decided to rest in the garden itself under the shade of a huge tree. As soon as Rama expressed his desire, everyone looked towards Hanuman expecting him to make necessary arrangements for Rama's comforts. But Hanuman turned around and kept looking at the sky. With Hanuman so unresponsive, Lakshmana himself spread a sheet for Rama on the grass and sat near his head, gently placing it on his lap. Then Bharata looked at Hanuman expecting him to take some action at least now. But Hanuman seemed indifferent to what was going on. He was busy watching the birds and smiling to himself. Bharata immediately sat at the feet of Rama, placing his lotus feet on his thighs, to massage them gently. Then Shatrughana turned towards Hanuman expecting him to render some service. But Hanuman was still too busy, playing as he was with the squirrels now. Shatrughana sat down and began to massage Rama's arms. As soon as the three brothers got busy in different services to Rama, Hanuman immediately ran only to return in a short while with a peacock fan. With great enthusiasm, he used it to fan all the four brothers. The cool refreshing breeze brought great comfort to all four. That is when the brothers understood Hanuman's mood and intention. His mood was that why should he render service to Rama alone when he could grab the opportunity to render service to all four brothers whom he revered. No wonder Rama considered him as dear as his loving brothers! *tuma mama priya bharatahi sama bhāī*

sahasa badana tumharo jasa gāvai।
asa kahi shrīpati kantha lagāvai॥ 13 ॥

*The thousand-hooded snake will
always sing your fame
And Rama embraced you again and
again after saying this.* (13)

With the death of Samsadan, the immediate danger
was taken care of. But unknown to Kesari and Anjana,
danger now loomed over their son, Hanuman. Samsadan
had a son, Vrikshasura. When he heard about his father's
death, he vowed to take revenge. He waited patiently for
the right time and when Hanuman was born, he decided
that killing the enemy's child would be appropriate
revenge for the death of his father.

Vrikshasura, as the name suggests, had a boon of
taking the form a tree. In the form of a tree, he would
be free to kill Hanuman and still be above all suspicion.
Additionally, he had the special skill of catching the
enemy by his shadow. Using both his boons, he would
surely succeed in taking his revenge.

One day Hanuman expanded himself to cover the entire sky. That was a good opportunity for Vrikshasura to catch his shadow. The shadow was huge enough to be within the stationary tree's grasp. He quickly latched on to it and started pulling it towards him. As he dragged the shadow, Hanuman felt a force pulling him against his wish. He quickly called out to his father Kesari, who began to pull him back. Hanuman was being pulled from both directions and it was getting difficult for him to bear the pain on both sides of his body. He finally did something to escape this attack. He reduced his size manifold. As soon as he did that, the shadow also shrunk and Vrikshasura had to let go of it. He could not hold on to a shadow that was out of his reach.

Relieved to be his normal self again, Hanuman decided to teach Vrikshasura a lesson. He surveyed the area from where he was getting pulled and recognized the demon tree. But the problem was that the moment he approached the tree, the demon would catch his shadow and devour him. If only he could stop the demon from eating him somehow. Hanuman decided to defeat the demon with his speed. He picked up a big stone and ran towards the demon, giving the demon no chance to react. Before the demon could even realize what was going on, how Hanuman came so close to him, Hanuman had thrust the stone in his mouth with lightning speed.

The stone in his mouth would not allow the demon to devour anything else. But Hanuman had miscalculated the demon's size. The stone was not enough to stop the tree from devouring Hanuman. The tree, regaining his senses, caught hold of Hanuman's shadow and in went Hanuman right into his mouth.

Meanwhile, Hanuman's tail had tied itself around the tree, providing a pause in the demon's plan of eating him. As the tree tried harder, the tail uprooted the tree further. The more he pulled Hanuman, more he himself got uprooted. Finally, the entire tree toppled over and fell on the ground, releasing Hanuman from his grip. And that was the end of Vrikshasura. His father had died at the hands of Kesari and the son had died by the tail of Kesari's son.

It is believed that the demon was killed not by Hanuman, but by Hanuman's tail. So does that make the tail a different entity? Hanuman had observed very early in life that unlike other monkeys, his tail did not obey him. Other monkeys always had their tails under their control. Whereas Hanuman's tail did exactly what it wanted to do. All his friends made fun of him because he could not even control his own tail. That was the height of uselessness for a monkey, they mocked. He enquired from his father why his tail was so disobedient. His father gave him valuable advice. He said that a monkey should always respect his tail. Make friends with it. From that day, Hanuman began to worship his tail and also referred to it as his Sakha. And he was happily surprised and relieved when the tail soon began to respond to his thoughts. Why did Hanuman's tail behave as it did? Why did it have a mind of its own? That's because his tail was actually Parvati herself. Not wanting to be left alone, she had come along with her husband Lord Shiva on earth when incarnated as Hanuman.

After killing many dangerous demons, the entire world, including the thousand-hooded Anantashesha sings Hanuman's glories. *sahasa badana tumharo jasa gāvai*

Ravana was jittery. He was afraid that Hanuman's mighty power would sound his death knell. Many demons had already lost their lives in trying to kill Hanuman. Every move Ravana made had failed. Now it was Chakrasura's turn to enter Kesari's kingdom and attack Hanuman. However, Hanuman's fearful parents had put Hanuman under house arrest, refusing to let him go out to play. Their beloved child had already survived many attacks and they did not want to take any more risks. So Hanuman remained confined to his house.

Chakrasura, the whirlwind demon, entered the vanara kingdom, creating havoc and destruction. As luck would have it, Kesari was out for an urgent meeting and little Hanuman was alone for some time. Hanuman quietly escaped from the house, inquisitive to see what the demon was up to. As soon as Chakrasura saw Hanuman, he quickly captured him in a whirlwind motion. The more Hanuman tried to escape, the more stuck he got, going deeper and deeper into the storm.

Hanuman's brain then started to work overtime. He noticed that the whirlwind did not enter any pit when the demon went over it. He also observed that the direction in which the demon moved was clockwise. He instantly had an idea. He began rotating anti-clockwise, which helped him get unstuck and he moved lower and lower till he could jump into a pit. He leapt into a pit as soon as the demon went over it. Finally, Hanuman, the intelligent baby, was free from the demon's captivity.

Having lost Hanuman, the demon wandered all over, in search of him. Unfortunately for him, he encountered Hanuman's friend. This friend had a damru (drum) given to him by Hanuman. Hanuman had received this toy from Vriksharaj, the vanara father of Sugriva and Vali. It was a magical one especially made to save Hanuman from any disaster. Hanuman had instructed his friend to play the damru whenever he was in trouble. Sensing trouble from Chakrasura, the vanara child began to play the damru.

The strange sound of the damru was unbearable for Chakrasura. The shrill sound pierced his ears and sabotaged his brain functioning. So much so that he couldn't even think straight. He yelled at the monkey to stop playing but all in vain. The sound continued and Chakrasura was on the verge of fainting.

Meanwhile, Hanuman also joined his friend and with his added power, the volume of the sound doubled and then tripled. It was so horrific that the entire jungle was reeling under anxiety. Hanuman flew closer to Chakrasura's ears and played it right outside his ears. Chakrasura could not handle the torture anymore. He simply collapsed in pain. Writhing on the ground, he died slowly and painfully.

Hanuman is so powerful for various reasons. He is an incarnation of Shiva. He is the son of Kesari and Anjana and of the wind god. He has been blessed many times over by all demigods. Rama and Sita have blessed him. He is so powerful that his name is also enough to save one from all possible calamities and to frighten away negative elements. Everyone including the thousand-hooded Anantashesha sings his glories. *sahasa badana tumharo jasa gāvai*

෴

There are three times that Rama expressed his gratitude to Hanuman by embracing him. First was when Hanuman returned from Lanka after finding Sita's whereabouts. Rama, who had been so dejected in Sita's absence, suddenly came alive when Hanuman declared—Found Sita I! Hanuman had then fallen at Rama's feet and Rama had tried to lift him up to embrace him which Hanuman resisted. Rama tried again and again but Hanuman would not budge. Finally Rama said, "I want you to leave my feet and come closer to my heart. Why are you differentiating between my feet and heart by resisting? Only ordinary people differentiate between good and bad, not a gyani like you." And the quick-witted Hanuman shot back, "My Lord, if there is no difference between your feet and heart, then let me stay at your feet."

The second time Rama embraced Hanuman with tears of gratitude flowing from his eyes, was after Lakshmana was revived by Hanuman's efforts. He said to Hanuman, "Our relationship is forever. You have accepted that I am Brahma and the world knows that you are a Brahmachari, so Brahma and Brahmachari's relation is forever." The word Brahmachari means that the one who is endlessly remembering Brahma, who is moving towards Brahma only.

And third time was after the war with Ravana. Pleased with Hanuman's heroics in the war, Rama wanted to grant him a boon. Hanuman was so thrilled with Rama's loving embrace that he said he never wanted to leave this body that had been purified by Rama's touch. And Rama then gave him the boon of being immortal so he could spread the glories of the holy name. *asa kahi shrīpati kantha lagāvai*

sanakādika brahmādi munīsā।
nārada sārada sahita ahīsā॥ 14 ॥

Sanak and the great sages, Lord Brahma,
and the holy saints,
Along with Narada, Sarasvati,
and the King of Serpents. (14)

Right since childhood, Hanuman was helplessly attracted to saints. They appeared to him as loving and gentle as his father. But though he loved being around them, as a child he had no idea how he could benefit from their company. Little Hanuman could never understand why they were angry with him when he was simply imitating them in meditation. Nor could he understand why they got annoyed when he sat on their laps during yagya. They looked so fatherly that their lap was the best place to cuddle. Though his intention was to associate with them lovingly, he did not realize he ended up harassing them.

While most people stay away from sages fearing their wrath, Hanuman ventured close to them without any fear whatsoever. He had so much power rippling through his muscles, but no knowledge of how best to channelize it. Unfortunately for the sages, he found them as the best associates. Without being welcomed, he invited himself to their hermitages and harassed them beyond limits. When he saw the sages meditating, he would run up to them and pull their beards. When he saw them bathing in the river, he would swim inside the water and pull their legs. Sometimes he would make huge holes in their clothes while they bathed. At other times, he would hang their clothes on the topmost branches of trees, making it impossible for them to retrieve them. When the sages came out of the river, freshly bathed, he would fill up his mouth with water and spray it on them, making it necessary for them to go back and bathe again. As soon as they came out after another bath, Hanuman would spit on them yet again. He would catch hold of one sage and harass him for hours and hours together, repeating this act in a loop.

He would love to enter a hermitage in the middle of a serious discussion by the sages. Then climb a tree under which the sages sat and jump on the branches. Invariably, the branches would crack under his weight and come crashing on to the ground, right on top of the sages, causing them to reel in shock. Though the sages hated him for his mischief, they also couldn't help feeling great love for the little monkey child. He somehow tugged at their hearts in a way they just could not comprehend. There was one particular sage that he harassed the most, beyond his tolerance capacity. His name was Trinabandhu. One early morning when the sage was leaving his house to answer nature's call, he got the biggest shock of his life. As soon as he opened his door, a tiger roared at him. Someone had tied a tiger at his doorstep. He just couldn't step out of his house through the front door now. But his tummy was churning and he had to go out to answer nature's call, which was getting more intense by the minute. He opened the back door to rush out. He got a much bigger shock, as outside the back door was tied a wild elephant with massive tusks. He couldn't fathom who had done this. Who had the strength and the guts to manhandle these wild beasts and tie them to his door posts? Just as he was struggling with the turmoil in his body and mind, he looked through the window of his house and spotted a little monkey boy rolling on the ground, laughing away at his predicament. What was an intense suffering for him was a hilarious joke for Hanuman!

This prank was the straw that broke the camel's back. The sage couldn't handle it anymore and he hurled a curse at Hanuman. Though it was a curse, it was actually aimed at saving Hanuman from any further damage and curses. He cursed that the monkey child would forget all his powers till someone reminded him of them. Even when the sage was cursing Hanuman, he could feel immense love for him. There was no anger but just compassion and a fatherly feeling of protecting him from messing around with more powerful sages who could potentially get really angry and curse him to condemnation. ***sanakādika*** *brahmādi munīsā*

This was the day Hanuman decided to step away from the outer world and focus on his inner world. He wanted some private time for himself. While he was seated on the edge of a cliff, meditating deeply on Lord Rama, he felt a nudge on his shoulders. Just when he was getting deeper into his meditation, someone was disturbing him. He opened his eyes and turned around to find out who it was. He was surprised to see Vali, the prince of Kishkinda, standing with a wicked grin on his face. He signalled Hanuman for a fight. But Hanuman was in the mood of praying and not fighting. Realizing that he was disinterested, Vali began to heap insults on Hanuman. Hanuman ignored his insults and humbly requested him to chant the holy names of Rama. Instead of heeding Hanuman's advice, Vali fired a volley of abuses for Rama. That really drove Hanuman mad; he immediately got up and accepted Vali's challenge. They mutually decided to fight a duel the next morning that would be witnessed by the whole kingdom.

The next morning as Hanuman was making his way to the wrestling arena, Lord Brahma appeared and made a request. He appealed to Hanuman to use only one-tenth of his energy in the fight against Vali. If he used anymore of his strength, Vali would surely die. Acceding to Brahmaji's request, Hanuman made his way into the wrestling arena. Vali, with great pride in his heart, used the mystic jewel necklace that he had in his possession to suck half the energy of Hanuman. But to his horror, he was unable to handle even half of Hanuman's energy. His veins burst open and he began to bleed all over. He felt that he was going to blow up. At that crucial moment, Lord Brahma appeared and instructed Vali to immediately release the energy he had sucked in and run away from the wrestling arena. Realizing his condition was critical, Vali released the energy and staggered away from the presence of Hanuman.

A little distance away, Vali collapsed and fainted. When he regained consciousness, he found Lord Brahma seated in front of him. Vali asked him why he was unable to absorb the power of Hanuman. Lord Brahma explained that although Hanuman was operating at one-tenth his regular power under his instructions, it was still too much for him because Hanuman was an incarnation of Lord Shiva. As an incarnation, his powers were unlimitedly greater than that of Vali who was ultimately an ordinary living entity with ordinary powers. Glorifying the greatness of Hanuman, Lord Brahma explained to Vali how Hanuman had been blessed profusely by every god in existence, including him. *sanakādika* **brahmādi** *munīsā*

Hanuman's favourite childhood pastime was to play with tigers. He always chose the most dangerous ones to play with because he found the regular tigers very boring. Pouncing on the tigers effortlessly, Hanuman took great pleasure in doing that. The tigers would usually tire out after being pounced upon and pounded with Hanuman's extraordinary energy. They had no option but to surrender and give Hanuman a free ride to any destination of his choice.

When Hanuman was on one such joy ride, a strange looking hunter approached him, dressed in tiger skin and adorned with a necklace of tiger claws. Little Hanuman smiled at the hunter. The hunter asked him if he wasn't afraid of hunters who could potentially be monkey catchers. Hanuman declared boldly that he was afraid of no one. Impressed with his fearless attitude, the hunter offered to teach Hanuman many novel skills. Hanuman's interest was aroused and he took the hunter to meet his parents. When Kesari and Anjana saw the rustic hunter, they were horrified at the idea of leaving their adorable child with the hunter for long durations. Moreover, what could a wild nomad teach their child? But to add to their misery, Hanuman was very keen on having him as his guru.

When Kesari called him uncultured, the hunter challenged him to a duel. As soon as the fight began, Kesari was flat on the ground. No matter how much he tried, the hunter floored him in seconds. Anjana had seen Kesari engage in numerous fights with powerful demons, but he had never been defeated so effortlessly. She closed her eyes and meditated on the Lord within her heart and when she opened her eyes, she found the same Lord Shiva standing in front of her in the dress of a hunter. Immediately plucking some flowers, she walked up to the hunter and offered the flowers at his feet and offered her respects to him. Imitating his mother, Hanuman also gathered some flowers and offered them at the lotus feet of Lord Shiva, his new teacher. Kesari, having understood his folly, followed suit and begged forgiveness for his transgression.

As soon as Lord Shiva was officially accepted to tutor Hanuman, he touched the child's tongue with his ring and magically, the child began to recite eloquent prayers in praise of the Lord. Shiva then whispered the secret pranava mantra into the child's right ear and thus Hanuman became a fully enlightened being. Lord Shiva then told Hanuman that very soon Goddess Saraswati, the goddess of learning, would bestow unlimited intelligence upon him, and would facilitate proficiency in music when the right time came.

In due course of time, Hanuman's intelligence and learning capabilities grew to an unbelievable proportion. He desired to learn anything and everything possible. When the right age came, Goddess Saraswati inspired Narada Muni to visit Kishkinda. As soon as Hanuman heard Narada sing and play his veena, he was inspired to learn singing and playing musical instruments. The eagerness of Hanuman incited Narada to teach him immediately all his musical skills and everything he knew about music. Soon Hanuman was an expert singer, composer, percussionist, flutist, and player of all possible musical instruments.

After a while, Narada decided to test his student. He requested Hanuman to sing his favourite song in the best possible way. Hanuman sat down obediently and immediately began to sing in the most beautiful manner. His voice itself was so melodious that Narada could hardly believe that it was just recently that he had become his student. The astounding impact of Hanuman's singing was not only visible on Narada, but on all aspects of creation. In fact, all moving entities froze in joy and all non-moving entities began to move and flow. Narada too was stunned and frozen like a statue, completely immersed in the singing of his disciple. The stones began to melt and flow. Hanuman was completely oblivious to the impact of his singing on the world around him. He continued singing with great intensity and absorption. Meanwhile, Narada was so absorbed that he lost all connection with the material world and his veena slipped off his hand and fell into a puddle. It was a puddle of melted rock created by Hanuman's intense singing and the veena fell right into it. In a short while, when Hanuman stopped singing and came out of his concentration, the melted stones began to harden once again and the stunned Narada recovered his movement. As soon as Narada returned to external consciousness, he noticed that his veena had fallen down. He bent to pick it up only to realize that it was stuck in the re-hardened rock.

Grasping the fact that the rock had first melted due to Hanuman's singing and then hardened once he stopped singing, Narada requested Hanuman to sing once again, only to release his veena. When Narada made that request, Hanuman sported a naughty smile on his face. He flatly refused to sing again. Narada was flabbergasted at Hanuman's blatant refusal. How could he refuse to sing? This was the only veena Narada had. It was his only possession. He loved it dearly. He began to beg Hanuman to sing. Contrary to expectation, Hanuman began to walk away from Narada and then ran away from the scene. Narada had no option but to chase Hanuman who was running all over the city of Kishkinda. It was a comical sight what with Hanuman running and Narada chasing. Finally Hanuman got back to the exact spot where they had begun. Narada caught up with him panting heavily. Hanuman then sang, abiding by his guru's request. Sure enough, the rock melted and the veena was released.

Once he got his veena back, Narada had only one question in his mind. Why did Hanuman make him run so much if he was finally going to sing and release the veena? Hanuman answered with a sweet smile that he wanted the dust of the lotus feet of his guru Narada Muni to fall all over the land of Kishkinda. He could find no other way to do it other than making him run all over. Narada was spellbound by that answer. What an unconventional way of showing his devotion and dedication to his guru! Narada was highly impressed with Hanuman's humility and creative thinking. *nārada sārada sahita ahīsā*

jama kubera dikpāla jahā te।
kabi kobida kahi sakai kahā te॥ 15 ॥

Yama, Kubera, and the guardians of the quadrants,
Poets and scholars—none can truly express
your infinite glories. (15)

Even before Hanuman had a chance to regain his
balance or even his breath, he got a tight kick on his
back and began to topple over. His warrior instincts
took over instantly and he leaped. There was no rest in
a warrior's life. He hadn't even recovered from his long
arduous travel to Lanka and here was a new challenge.
One moment he was fallen on the ground and in the
next he was standing on his feet. Steadying his arms
ahead of him, ready for a duel with his unseen enemy.
He could only see a thick mist in front of him. Whoever
or whatever had kicked him was hiding behind that
mist.

Suddenly a very scary looking personality came
into view. Hanuman relaxed. "O' Mrityudev! O' god of
death! I can't believe it's you! Why would you be on
Ravana's island? And why would you kick me?"

The ice-cold stare disappeared suddenly and was replaced by a look of recognition. "O' son of Vayu! O' Pavana Putra! What have I done? Please forgive me for inadvertently kicking a gentle soul like you. I know very well that I myself had given you a boon that you wouldn't ever be touched by death. But what can I do! I am now a helpless prisoner. I no longer have the freedom to do what I want. Ravana has chained me on this mountain with the shackle of Rudra mantras and has instructed me to kill anyone who dares to step on this mountain. No matter how much I try, I am unable to break free from this bondage."

One touch by Hanuman and the shackles of Rudra mantras fell off and Yama was free once again. Hanuman was extremely impressed by Ravana's foresight and strategy. Profusely thanking Hanuman, Yama blessed him. He was so grateful to his saviour that he blessed him with fearlessness. In fact he told Hanuman that anyone who remembers him would never have to be afraid of death. Yama will personally protect whoever follows Hanuman. *jama kubera dikpāla jahā te*

This happened on the eve of the most obnoxious episode of Ravana ransacking the palace of his stepbrother

Kubera. It wasn't just enough for Ravana to forcibly take over Kubera's kingdom Lanka, he also couldn't tolerate Kubera being settled in his newly acquired place in the vicinity of Kailash mountains, offered by none other than Lord Shiva himself. Because Kubera was carrying out such an important role on behalf of the gods, being their treasurer, Lord Shiva felt that he deserved a decent residence. Especially after Ravana kicked him out unceremoniously from his own kingdom Lanka that had also been offered to him by the gods.

Seeing his brother resettled unsettled Ravana; again he made a surprise attack on Kubera. He forcibly took away everything valuable from Kubera's kingdom and his followers carried away the rest. Of all the things he acquired, the most prized possession was the Pushpak Vimana. He had an eye on it right from the time their father, the powerful Sage Vishrawas, had given it to Kubera.

So far watching the world from afar and from high up in the air had only been a dream. Now it was about to come true. Ravana stepped into the Pushpak Vimana with his uncle Maricha and an aide, Prahasta, to make an aerial tour of the Kailash Mountain, to turn his dream into a reality.

Whilst they were in the middle of their first joy ride, the plane began to slow down over the Kailash Mountain.

Both Ravana and Maricha had no idea how to handle a fully automated plane. As the uncle-nephew team was trying to make sense of it all, a unique creature with a robust torso and pillar-like arms emerged from behind the peaks of Kailash. One hand wielding a spear and the other placed on the hip, the creature's posture was certainly aggressive. His daunting personality seemed menacing and his booming voice sounded authoritative, just as loud as the rumbling clouds atop the mountains. "This is a restricted area. Ordinary mortals, rakshasas, gandharvas and even devas are not permitted here without the sanction of Shiva, the lord of this area."

Ravana was very agitated with the obstruction, much like a child prevented from entering the kitchen to steal sweets. But something about the creature's demeanour tickled his funny bone. Although right in the middle of a warlike situation, Ravana began giggling impetuously, much to the surprise of all. He tried to muffle his giggles with his hand, but this impudence did not go unnoticed by the daunting warrior from Kailash.

"You mock me because my face resembles a monkey's? Your pride will soon be vanquished in the most humiliating way, you haughty fool!" scowled Nandishwar, the loyal bull mount of Lord Shiva. "Very soon a monkey will destroy your Lanka. He will burn your city and deface your people. You will be able to do nothing but watch everything you are proud of burn. He will bring hordes of monkeys and annihilate your entire race. When you are on your death bed, you will remember this costly snigger. Then you will cry, and the monkeys will laugh. I could kill you this instant, but then it will not be a shameful enough death. I want you to die feeling helpless, watching everything you value demolished right before your eyes." *jama **kubera** dikpāla jahā te*

Just as Hanuman was about to move forward towards the city of Lanka, he heard something. He had just saved Yama and was now moving towards his mission of finding Sita. There, he heard it again! It was a very feeble voice. But Hanuman's keen ears didn't miss it. As he stepped in that direction, the voice became louder, clearer. It was coming from a cave on the mountain. He ran towards the cave not knowing what to expect. But there was a sense of desperation in that voice. It almost seemed to be begging. The scene that greeted him as soon as he stepped into the cave shocked him.

Hanging from the ceiling of the cave was someone who had been mercilessly hung upside down with his face closely staring at the wall. His hands and legs were tied in such a way that he couldn't even turn or make a move in any direction.

"Please help me!" was all he could say in that dire condition.

Yet another prisoner of Ravana's! Taking off the chains that were hooked to the ceiling, Hanuman carefully brought that suffering personality down. Once down, Hanuman turned him around and got the first glance at his face. He was utterly shocked to see that it was Shanidev. The one whose infamous stare reduced people to nothingness was here himself reduced to nothingness. Now it all made sense. Being an astrological scholar, Ravana knew the power of Shani's stare. He knew that Shani glanced favourably at an individual for two and half years and unfavourably for the next two and half years. Timing his visit to Shani's abode during the time when astrologically Shani had been favouring Ravana, he had imprisoned him to ensure that he didn't stare at him at all in the future. So that there was no question of unfavourable glances. Ravana wanted to ensure that Shani didn't glance unfavourably at not just him but at anyone in Lanka and even at anything in Lanka. Thus blocking him in a cave on the edge of Lanka, he had tied him up in such a way that he could only stare at the wall of the cave and nothing else.

Shani expressed his gratitude to Hanuman for

rescuing him after months of torture. Shani blessed him that anyone who remembers Hanuman would never be affected by miseries caused by Shani's glance. Devatas like Shani and even Indra, important personalities in the universal administration, are eternally grateful to Hanuman. *jama kubera* **dikpāla jahā te**

At one point Ravana decided to attack the heavens directly along with his son Meghanada. News of the attack of the invincible father-son duo spread far and wide forcing the demigods to scurry for safety. Indra tried his best for protection from Lord Vishnu, but strangely, this time the lord had other priorities, which left Indra broken-hearted.

The war had begun at a frenetic pace. Indra took on Ravana headlong as Jayanta, Indra's son, attacked Meghanada. During this point in the war, it seemed as if Indra would be the victor, especially when he strategically engaged his army to surround Ravana and capture him alive. But right then Meghanada resorted to the art of samadhi, Lord Shiva's gift to him. Soon Jayanta swooned against his chariot and was carried off the battlefield by his men, to be safely hidden in the ocean bed. Assuming his son dead, Indra went ballistic with rage and launched a full-throttle attack on Ravana with his explosive thunderbolt. Ravana fell unconscious, unable to withstand the power of the bolt.

Everything seemed perfectly aligned for Indra's victory. And then, everything froze! A cold eeriness enveloped the atmosphere. Indra could move only his eyes. What had just happened? Why did his body freeze? The army looked at him for orders as he helplessly looked back at them. Indra hoped that they would understand and forgive him, while they hoped he would speak and save them. Without his directions, his army was mercilessly chopped to death right in front of him, as helpless tears rolled down his cheeks. Soon a pair of muscular hands seized his shoulders in a crocodile grip and his body was back in motion. But he was now tied up with ropes. Meghanada's magic had worked yet again. Hanging his head in defeat, Indra was hauled into the Pushpak Vimana and disgracefully tied to the flag post. With their leader captured alive, the demigods who saw no more sense in continuing the fight, dropped their weapons. They, too, were rounded up and pushed into the magical air chariot. At last all the universal directors were under Ravana's control!

Meghanada got a new name, Indrajit, after that but Indra got a gift of a magical prison cell in which he was locked in. It wasn't like a regular prison but a prison that was blocked with magical spells from all sides. It was impossible for anyone to enter or exit. When Hanuman made his entry into Lanka, Narada appeared in front of him and gave him the whereabouts of Indra and requested him to release the king of heavens. Hanuman swiftly killed the watchmen who were guarding the prison and disabled the spells that were blocking the cell. Setting Indra free from the prison, Hanuman destroyed the prison cell itself. Indra was so indebted to Hanuman that he blessed him profusely and departed immediately, not wanting to be caught once again. *jama kubera* **dikpāla jahā te**

Lord Rama had a big heart and ruled with great magnanimity. One day he was invited to be the guest of a Gandharva king along with Sita and his brothers. The king worshipped Lord Rama with great reverence and they sat down for lunch. The royal kitchen was a beehive of activity, preparing food fit for God himself. But before they could begin to eat, they were interrupted by some brahmanas. They had reached the Gandharva king's palace looking for Lord Rama. On hearing about their arrival, Rama left the feast untouched and went to welcome them himself. He brought them in and gave them a reverential welcome. He then invited the brahmanas to first have lunch. The brahmanas were not sure what they should do. They had come to ask their king for charity and lunch was not on their agenda. Some of them were keen to speak to Lord Rama before partaking in the lunch offering. Others wanted to go along with whatever Lord Rama said, knowing well that they would not be disappointed either way. Sensing their reluctance and confusion, Rama said, "O' brahmanas, I know what is on your mind. I will surely give you a kingdom that you have come seeking. In fact, you could have just sent your disciples for it. Why did all of you take so much trouble? I declare that the kingdom of Brahmapur now yours. Please eat first."

Rama asked Lakshmana to call the royal sculptor to get a stone and inscribe Rama's order and his seal on it as a legally valid notification. It was the kingdom's law for travellers and kings governed by Rama, to carry with them a letter bearing Rama's stamp. Rama wanted his stamp engraved on a big shila and given to the brahmanas as proof of his charity to them.

The happy brahmanas now had no problem in eating. They even requested Rama to finish his meal, which had been served but left unattended. They were not in any anxiety or hurry now to complete the formalities. Rama had assured them of his intentions. But Rama could not eat. He said, "I will honour the food only when the entire process is completed to your satisfaction. It is necessary to complete an act of charity because wealth, intentions, and life are all uncertain and highly unpredictable. You never know when Yama, the god of death, may come. Therefore, always finish the task at hand. Scriptures say that one should leave a hundred tasks at hand to eat one's food, a thousand tasks to bathe, a lakh of tasks to chant the holy names. One crore obstacles are said to be seen in the course of Gita recitation, ten crore obstacles in the course of bathing in Ganges and hundred crore obstacles while donating charity. Hence, charitable acts should be accomplished as soon as possible. One's consciousness changes significantly before and after eating food. This is my humble opinion. So please allow me to complete the process of donating the kingdom unto you after which I will sit for lunch."

Soon, a 9-feet long stone arrived from the river Gandaki. The royal sculptors then carved the message on it which read, "I, the scion of Suryavansha and the Lord of the Seven islands, Maharaj Dasharatha's son, Shri Ramachandra happily give the kingdom of Brahmapur to the brahmanas in charity. Till the sun shines, will my name exist, till my name exists will the winds continue to blow and till then will this charity remain valid. I request the kings succeeding me to protect this boon."

Next Lord Rama asked Hanuman to engrave his royal seal to validate the message.

Hanuman eagerly engraved Lord Ram's insignia on the stone. Brahmapur was renamed Ramnathpur. Shri Rama donated wealth equal to the weight of the shila to the brahmanas and asked Hanuman to assist the brahmanas in carrying the shila to Ramnathpur. Having completed the task at hand, Rama and the brahmanas accepted their food. The brahmanas and Hanuman then went back to Ramnathpur on the Pushpaka airplane.

Many generations of brahmanas lived peacefully in their kingdom, singing glories of Lord Rama. No one disturbed them for many centuries. But once the brahmanas went into a crisis, facing great danger from kings who wanted to take over their kingdom. In panic, the brahmanas submerged Lord Rama's shila under a lake, in an attempt to prevent it from being destroyed. Little did they know that this act would endanger them further. It so happened that the next time they were attacked, the king asked them to show proof of their ownership. But they had submerged the proof under a lake. The angry king gave them one month's notice to produce the proof before him or they would be killed. The hapless brahmanas broke down the dams surrounding the lake hoping that the water from the lake would drain out to reveal the shila. However, nothing like that happened. The water level remained as it was. Refusing to budge. One month passed and there was no sign of the shila. The brahmanas now had no option but to get ready for their last moments in life. They consoled their grieving family members, distributed charity, bathed in the lake to purify themselves and stood facing the north to embrace their death, praying, "O' Rama, the charity we asked from you has become the very cause of our death. The wealth that you gave our ancestors is now exhausted. The wicked king will kill us and snatch away our kingdom—"

"Aaaaaaaarrghhh!" The brahmanas' prayers were interrupted by a roaring sound which seemed to be coming from a nearby Hanuman temple. Hanuman, in his deity form, had come alive. The brahmanas were astounded to see his gargantuan form in front of them. He had long hands, yellowish hair and was now old. Hanuman said, "O' brahmanas, there is no need of giving up your life. Just chant the name of Lord Rama." And he dived into the lake, retrieving the shila effortlessly in one stroke.

The elated brahmanas dragged the huge shila to the baffled king. Hanuman then caught hold of the shocked king, dragged him to the lake and crucified him as a punishment for harassing the brahmanas. He even killed the king's soldiers when they tried to intervene by merely lashing out at his tail. He then named the lake as Hritaparshmana Lake and directed the brahmanas to bury the shila in a cave and continue to remember Lord Rama. With this, Hanuman merged back into his deity form having saved Sri Rama's promise to his devotees.

kabi kobida kahi sakai kahā te

tuma upakāra sugrīvahi kīnhā।
rāma milāya rājapada dīnhā॥ 16 ॥

You rendered Sugriva a great favour,
Connecting him to Lord Rama
and making him king. (16)

In Treta yuga, the Supreme Lord helped Surya's son,
Sugriva, and killed Indra's son, Vali. But in Dwapar
yuga, he helped Indra's son, Arjuna, and killed Surya's
son, Karna. Was there any hidden significance behind
this change in order with the change in yuga? Was he
trying to balance it out? Though to the external vision
it may seem to be a balancing act, but the real reason is
much deeper than this understanding. In Dwapar yuga,
Arjuna was humble and Karna was egoistic. In Treta
yuga Sugriva was humble while Vali was full of pride.

So who does the Supreme Lord help? He helps the
one who has no pride. One who is devoid of the 'me'
mind-set gets God's grace. God does not like pride; his
nature is to destroy it. Sugriva was weak physically and
he was definitely weak in his character and he had no
courage; but his only plus point was that he had no pride.

Pridelessness was his only qualification. One cannot demand grace. When and how it will come no one can tell. But if we get saintly association, our weakness can become an asset in getting the grace of the Supreme Lord. This is where Hanuman comes into the picture in Sugriva's life. Hanuman was that saintly person who united Sugriva with God. Hanuman led Sugriva to God through the path of mercy and not effort.

In this world, there are three categories of people— materialists, sadhakas (those pursuing the path of spiritual perfection), and siddhas (those who have perfected the path of spirituality). The materialists are least likely to reach God. Sugriva is one such materialist. Hanuman, the exact opposite of Sugriva, is a prime example of a siddha who has reached perfection. Hanuman's character has so many strengths and Sugriva's character has so many weaknesses. But Sugriva, who more or less falls in the materialist category, still attained God. If it weren't for the perfect Hanuman, the imperfect Sugriva wouldn't have met Rama.

The mind is known as Tripurasur because it lives in three cities of desire, anger, and greed. Greed can be counteracted by giving charity. But charity leads to pride. After giving charity, one desires to be praised and recognized for it and wants respect in return. And knowledge means absence of desire for respect.

When Hanuman completed his education with Surya, he wanted to offer guru dakshina, which is a form of charity. The charity that Surya sought was not wealth but a promise. He wanted Hanuman to promise him that he would take care of his son Sugriva and serve him. Hanuman immediately made that promise and from then on stood beside Sugriva through thick and thin. Though he offered charity, Hanuman had no desire to be recognized or respected for that charity and he had no pride of being a giver. Thus he proved that he had gained complete knowledge from his guru Surya. Because knowledge means absence of desire for respect.

Not only did Hanuman serve Sugriva, but he also made him respectable in the eyes of Rama and in the eyes of the world. From Sugriva's example we learn that it is not by our own sadhana and efforts that we attract God's grace but by God's mercy that comes through the grace of the saintly people. Sugriva received God's grace without any sadhana or effort. To such an extent that Sugriva is constantly thinking of Rama and Rama is constantly thinking of Sugriva. That makes Sugriva extremely respectable. This perhaps is the greatest help Hanuman rendered Sugriva. *tuma upakāra sugrīvahi kīnhā*

Hanuman's entry in the Ramayana is to give hope to others. This is his role even in today's times. Giving hope to others.

"Do not worry! There is no fear on this mountain!" These were Hanuman's first words to Sugriva and his assistants who hid on the Rishimukha Mountain due to Vali's fear. In fact these were his first words in the Ramayana. He entered into the Ramayana and in this world to give hope, assurance, and confidence to everyone. When Sugriva and his assistants saw Hanuman, they smiled through their fears.

Every inch of Hanuman's body was chiselled with rippling muscles that indicated years and years of disciplined lifestyle. He wore a yellow silken garment on his lower half and his upper torso was bare except for the golden ornaments that decorated his broad and deep chest. With a set of armlets and bracelets embracing his arms, he looked powerful and regal.

Hanuman assured the scared vanaras, "There is no fear of Vali on this mountain anymore. As long as we are by your side and the curse of Matanga Rishi favours you, there can be no danger for you on this mountain from Vali."

With that assurance Sugriva turned in the direction of the problem he had recently perceived. He had spotted two humans making their way towards them and he was afraid they had been sent by Vali to kill him.

"Look at their lengthy arms. Look at their broad eyes. Look at their bows and arrows. Just one look at these two beings instils fear in me. Vali has surely drafted these two divine-looking handsome human beings to ensure my death. Hanuman, if my premonition is true then there is no one that can save me and there is no place that is safe for me to feel safe in."

Following Sugriva's gaze, Hanuman walked forward towards the edge of the cliff and carefully looked down at the two handsome human beings that were walking by the edges of the Pampa Sarovar heading towards the Rishimukha Mountain. From his vantage point, Hanuman could immediately decipher a few facts about these two stunning personalities. They appeared to be the most virtuous people that Hanuman had ever glanced upon. In fact, their brilliant lustre gave them godly looks. Were they in reality gods in human form? But such divine beings wouldn't engage in immoral acts.

Walking back towards the shaken Sugriva, Hanuman revealed his observations. "O' Sugriva, look at the two of them carefully. They seem to be oceans of mercy. They don't seem to be indulging in acts of violence for their own sadistic pleasure or to facilitate anyone else's adharmic whims. It appears that their weapons are meant for protecting the weak. O' Sugriva, there is no fear from them."

Sugriva thought of a plan that he revealed to Hanuman. "Hanuman, I can't rely on intuition anymore. When my life is at stake, I need clear proof before making any conclusions. I want you to use your guise-changing ability to ascertain the intentions of these personalities. I specifically want you to take the form of a genuine wandering sanyasi. Any dharmatma cannot possibly hide his intentions from a saintly soul. Use your expertise in analysing human psychology through behavioural sciences to decode their minds."

Hanuman immediately took the form of a sanyasi and left to find the identity of the two strangers. In the short conversation that followed, Hanuman could easily understand that the two were not enemies but friends. But in that short conversation, Rama understood that Hanuman couldn't be a sanyasi nor could he be any ordinary entity. The first impression of Hanuman on Rama was intense. Rama was very highly impressed hearing the flawless speech of Hanuman's from which he got a glimpse into his character and mind-set. "If this is the quality of a servant, what must be the quality of the master?" Rama whispered into Lakshmana's ears while looking at Hanuman with great admiration. "Just by meeting Hanuman, I am thoroughly convinced that Sugriva is the right person to help us find Sita."

As soon as Rama declared that Lakshmana agreed

too. He expressed their eagerness to connect with Sugriva to Hanuman. Hanuman's face lit up with great joy. More than joy it was a hope that Sugriva would soon be liberated from his bondage.

"It is actually Sugriva who is fortunate to have your refuge. In fact, Sugriva should have come himself and sought your shelter rather than you having to go to him. But now Sugriva is tired of life. If the patient cannot go to the doctor then the doctor has to go to the patient, " saying this Hanuman bent down on one knee. Folding his hands in front of the brothers, he made a request. "Please allow me the fortune of carrying the two of you on my back to meet Sugriva who lives on top of the invincible Rishimukha Mountain." One who is capable can reach God himself but if one is incapable, then God goes to him.

Soon both the brothers, seated on Hanuman's broad shoulders, were cruising up the lofty stone mountain. Hanuman was nimble and agile as any other monkey. He made sure that the two brothers weren't inconvenienced too much and were comfortably seated on his shoulders. He carried them up the mountain where Sugriva was.

When Rama met Sugriva, he declared that he saw all nine limbs of bhakti in Sugriva simply because he had the association of the saintly Hanuman. Sugriva had a simple heart. He was so simple that he had no hesitation in telling Rama all his shortfalls. He could have easily covered his faults but he frankly narrated to Rama how he had been running from Vali like a coward. He admitted all his failures and his weaknesses. The ability to admit one's weakness is actually the sign of one's inner strength, humility, and simplicity. The word Sugriva means neck. A humble person always stands with his neck bent. A special feature of Sugriva was his humility. Sugriva had many capabilities as well as weaknesses but Hanuman channelized those capabilities in the right direction. One should know one's capabilities and incapabilities. Some people after knowing their inabilities become dejected and so disappointed with life that they commit suicide. But after knowing your inabilities, if you search for your abilities then that knowledge is worthwhile. Most often when we focus heavily on our inabilities, we lose sight of our abilities. That is when we need a guide to step into our life. Hanuman helped Sugriva look beyond his inabilities and look towards Rama. Hanuman was the link between Bhagawan (God) and Bhakta (devotee).

Once Rama and Sugriva shook hands and mutually agreed to help one another, Hanuman lit a fire to seal the friendship between them. Both wood and fire need each other to burn. Both represent the dharma of friendship. But Rama says more important than the wood and fire is the person who brings them together. Even if there is wood and fire but without vayu or air the two cannot burn together. So if Pavanputra (son of air god) Hanuman was missing then there would be no friendship between Rama and Sugriva. *Rāma milāya rājapada dīnhā*

Lakshmana asked Rama why he chose Sugriva and not Vali to find Sita. Rama laughed at Lakshmana's assumption that Vali was stronger. Sugriva had two unique strengths. One was that he was fast in running. Because of that neither Vali nor pride could catch him. Second was that he was very resourceful. He had found out that he could stay on Rishimukha Mountain, which was out of bounds for Vali. These two strengths were the right qualities to find Sita.

Finding Sita through Hanuman would not have been a miracle. Miracle lies in making a person like Sugriva, a sadhaka, to find Sita (bhakti). To highlight the incapacity of Sugriva, Shabri takes his name. And the last certificate is given by Hanuman. Sugriva's life is full of deficiencies, which he presents to Hanuman. Then the saintly Hanuman brings Rama into his life and unites him with God. Finding Sita is a process. First knowledge of God should dawn which then facilitates bhakti. Sugriva takes help of Hanuman to get this transcendental knowledge. And Hanuman is faith personified. This implies that we need intelligence to learn about material knowledge but faith to acquire knowledge of God.

However, after Rama killed Vali and made Sugriva the king of Kishkinda, he immersed himself in worldly pleasures. Once in a while he would remember God but his mind would say that there's no time limit given so what's the hurry. God had not given a time frame to find Sita. This is also an excuse people give, what is the hurry to practice bhakti. In fact, they tell youngsters also that they should not take up bhakti in young age. Do it later. They assume death will wait till they are ready. If we knew our time of death then we could allot a certain time for bhakti. But not knowing when death will come, we are only fooling ourselves.

Meanwhile, Hanuman reminds Sugriva about the promise he gave to Rama. He gave such a Rama katha that the clouds of desires covering Ramachandra from Sugriva got scattered. Hanuman being the son of the wind god could scatter the clouds. He asked Sugriva if he knew what happened to the arrow that Rama used to kill Vali. Sugriva said that it went back to Rama because Rama does not let anybody leave Him; He calls everyone back. Hanuman rejected it; this logic was not right for this situation. Hanuman told him that the arrow was back with Rama because he had vowed that if Sugriva forgot his promise then he would use the same arrow on him. As soon as Sugriva heard this, he began to tremble. The clouds of lust were scattered and the moon of Ramachandra started rising. Sugriva ran back to Rama and rendered his service of assembling the monkey army to find Sita. Thus in every step in Sugriva's life Hanuman was present. He not only helped him connect with Rama, but he also helped him gain a kingdom. But when he was lost in the pleasures of the kingdom, Hanuman helped him gain back Rama. *tuma upakāra sugrīvahi kīnhā I rāma milāya rājapada dīnhā*

tumharo mantra bibhīshana mānā।
lankeshvara bhae saba jaga jānā॥ 17 ॥

*Vibhishana accepted your advice,
And became the king of Lanka, this the
whole world knows.* (17)

Hanuman was in Lanka searching for Sita. He was
searching for her not inside the houses but inside the
temples because where there was Sita, that place was
naturally a temple. Expecting Sita in every place,
Hanuman considered every house in Lanka to be a
temple. He did not find her in the temple of Ravana.
Ravana's palace was also a temple because full-scale
worship happened there! Who did Ravana worship?
He worshipped his body the most because he wanted
to live in this body eternally, be immortal. In fact, all
the citizens of Lanka worshipped their body. No wonder
then that Hanuman referred to the houses in Lanka as
temples. They had a choice to worship God or worship
their bodies. They chose the latter. Materialistic people
keep their bodies in the centre of their life. Every demon
of Lanka, from an ordinary citizen to Ravana, believed

that sense gratification and enjoyment were the ultimate goals of life. The only exception to this was Vibhishan. He lived not in a temple where the body was worshipped but in a house where God was.

Hanuman was delighted to hear sounds of chanting of the holy name coming from this house. He decided to find out who it was. Vibhishan welcomed Hanuman as he heard Hanuman saying 'Jai Sri Rama'. When asked who he was, Hanuman introduced himself in an unlikely manner. He did not say, "I am Pavanputra Hanuman. I swallowed the sun as a baby." Instead, he introduced himself as servant of Lord Rama. And after that he began a mini Rama katha, glorifying his divine master.

But Vibhishan still did not know who his visitor was. He again asked him to tell his name. Hanuman then gave his name reluctantly. "I am Hanuman, but please do not chant my name. The only name worth chanting is Rama's."

Hanuman realized how difficult it must be for Vibhishan, Ravana's brother, to live in Lanka amongst demons. Vibhishan described to him the hazards of being a devotee amongst demons. He performed his sadhana in hiding, fearing fatal repercussions if caught. His brother Ravana usually turned a blind eye to him but if anyone complained then there would be stern action taken against him. He was constantly walking on a tightrope.

"Why don't you leave Lanka and take shelter of Lord Rama?" asked Hanuman.

"How can I," sighed Vibhishan, "leave my brother? After all he is my brother. Lanka is my home."

Vibhishan's face showed genuine remorse, trapped in a demonic birthplace with no route to escape.

Hanuman explained to him gently, "It all depends on who you think you are. What is your 'swa dharma'? If you think you are Ravana's brother, then your dharma is to stay in Lanka and be his advisor. Then you can fulfil your duties at a physical level, your bodily relationships. If you think you are my brother, belonging to the family of Rama and Sita, then your dharma is spiritual, which means you can leave Lanka and take Rama's shelter. Dharma is always dynamic, never static. It changes with the understanding of who you really are."

Hanuman's words of wisdom overwhelmed Vibhishan. He promised Hanuman he would think over it and take the next step. After Hanuman departed, Vibhishan had another visitor. It was Ravana, his brother, the king of Lanka. His arrival always meant only one thing, some sort of trouble. Ravana came barging inside Vibhishan's palace and roared in anger. "Vibhishana, because of you I have to constantly face embarrassment. You are a blot on our esteemed Rakshasa dynasty."

"What did I do?" asked a baffled Vibhishan.

"What did you do?" spat Ravana. "Whatever you do is unforgivable. You are constantly chanting Rama, God's name. Which demon does that? Why are you hell bent on behaving like heavenly citizens instead of a true demon?"

"Oh!" said a relieved Vibhishan. "Is that it? I can explain that. I'm not chanting God's name. I'm actually chanting your name. 'Ra' is short for Ravana, my venerable older brother, and 'Ma' is short for Mandodari, my reverent sister-in-law. I am constantly chanting your names. Since chanting Ravana Mandodari becomes quite long and time consuming, I have invented a short form of it Ra-Ma. Simple!"

Hearing these words, Ravana's anger immediately melted. From a roaring, fiery wild animal he turned into a smiling, loving domestic pet.

"Is that how you feel about me?" He couldn't stop grinning with the respect Vibhishan had bestowed upon him. His chest puffed up more than ever and his voice was now sugar coated.

"I want you and every citizen of Lanka to fill their walls with 'RaMa'. Every wall should carry my name. And every citizen of Lanka should begin chanting Rama from today. That's my order." Pleased with himself, he returned to his palace. *tumharo mantra bibhīshana mānā*।

One day in the court of Lanka, there was a discussion on how to handle the tricky situation of Sita's obstinacy. Ravana's ministers could never go against him or speak against him so they suggested forcing Sita into submission. This is what Ravana liked, flatterers. Yes men. He did not have any well-wisher who could tell the truth. Except Vibhishan, who had never approved of Ravana's evil actions. But by kidnapping Sita, Ravana had gone too far. Vibhishan had to figure out what he should do now. Speak up or shut up. If he spoke up, Ravana would in all probability kick him out of the kingdom. If he shut up, he would continue with his life of opulence.

He had to choose between a life of opulence and a life of satisfaction. A life of compromise or a life of focus. A life of show or a life of substance. A life of exploitation or a life of sacrifice. A life of vices or a life of values. It was a question of security versus uncertainty. If only he could tolerate Ravana, he would have everything. Hanuman's words rang in his ears. "If you think you are Ravana's brother, then your dharma is to stay in Lanka and be his advisor. Then you can fulfil your duties at a physical level, your bodily relationships. If you think you are my brother, belonging to the family of Rama and

Sita, then your dharma is spiritual, which means you can leave Lanka and take Rama's shelter."

Vibhishan had clarity now. Hanuman's words made perfect sense. He knew what he had to do. He would go with his spiritual dharma, the ultimate dharma. ***tumharo mantra bibhīshana mānā***

He gave Ravana a piece of his mind, "Please leave Sita. It is a sin to kidnap another's wife and force yourself on her. It does not befit a king to behave in this manner."

But Ravana was blind with lust. He kicked Vibhishan out of his court and out of Lanka. With that kick, Ravana kicked out Rajya Lakshmi (the goddess of kingship) also. And with that kick Vibhishan found the greatest opulence—the lotus feet of Rama. Although insulted, Vibhishan left the assembly feeling great exhilaration. He believed that this attack of Ravana's foot would lead him to another pair of feet that would bring him great joy. Had he not felt the hard feet of Ravana, how would he have experienced the soft feet of Rama?

Most people experience happiness only when things are going as per their expectations. This is a materialistic mind set. To experience happiness even when things are going wrong, is a spiritual mind set, a sadhaka's mind set. A spiritualist or a devotee is happy even in unfavourable conditions. Vibhishan was happy even though he had been chucked out of Lanka. He was happy to be seeking shelter of Rama. *tumharo mantra bibhīshana mānā*

What is surrender? Surrender is understood in two parts. One is akincanatvam. Which means to surrender with hands folded. The folded hands indicate humility. It implies everything belongs to God and nothing belongs to me and thus I have nothing to give. And second part of surrender is ananyam gatim. This means I have nowhere else to go other than your shelter. Sometimes, people offer obeisance with their legs crossed locking each other, which indicates that my legs are tied and I cannot go anywhere else now.

Vibhishan, along with his four trusted friends, left Lanka and flew over the ocean to reach Rama's camp. He informed the guards of the vanara army that he had come seeking shelter of Rama. Seeing Vibhishan beg with folded hands, the monkeys dashed inside to deliver the startling message. They themselves were shocked with Vibhishan's arrival.

When the monkeys gave Rama the message, he was with Sugriva, Hanuman, and few other trusted friends. He looked at others to know their opinion. Rama always sought their opinion before he made any decision. Sugriva was not keen on the enemy's brother joining their camp. He said candidly, "O' Lord, it is unwise to let the enemy enter our camp. He may open all our military secrets. How can we trust someone who is betraying his own brother?" The other vanaras too agreed with their king's analysis. When Sugriva saw Rama was not convinced, he said, "You are not a very good judge of people either, so please send him away." Hearing this, both Rama and Hanuman smiled because Sugriva was himself such a bad judge of people. Sugriva had mistaken Rama and Lakshmana to be Vali's spies.

Next Rama turned to Hanuman for his opinion. "What do you say, Hanuman? Both Sugriva and I trust your opinion so we will do as you say."

Hanuman recalled his experience with Vibhishan in Lanka. He narrated to them how Vibhishan was the only pious person in the whole of Lanka, chanting God's names against all odds. Despite constant threat from Ravana and other demons. And how his was the only sane voice that had prevented Ravana from killing Hanuman.

"In my opinion, Vibhishan is genuine. He should be given shelter."

Rama's eyes lit up with Hanuman's words. Rama recalled his encounter in Panchvati with Surpanakha, Vibhishan's sister. She had criticized Vibhishan saying he had no qualities of rakshasas. Being a pious person, he was the black sheep of their family. Surpanakha had given vivid examples of Vibhishan's unwarranted pious behaviour. When all the siblings had done penance to please Brahma, Vibhishan had asked not for immortality or name or fame but for dharma to be always present in his life. This had shocked all his siblings. Rama reflected that despite the association of demons like Ravana and others that Lanka was full of, Vibhishan had still managed to retain his purity. That was definitely commendable. And he had also saved Hanuman's life. When Ravana had ordered him to be killed, it was Vibhishan who had come to his rescue arguing that a messenger is innocent and should not be killed. Ravana had then reversed his order of killing and set fire to his tail. Vibhishan's act of kindness had not gone unnoticed by Rama. As far as Rama was concerned, Vibhishan, by this single act, had become qualified for his shelter. Any kindness that we do, makes us attractive in Rama's eyes.

Rama said, "I will give shelter to Vibhishan. My dharma is to accept in my fold anyone who comes to me. No one is ever turned back." He asked the monkeys to allow Vibhishan in. As soon as Vibhishan entered, they all stood up and Rama said, "Lankesh, you are welcome here. You are my fifth brother from now."

Vibhishan turned red as a beetroot when he heard Rama addressing him as Lankesh. He was embarrassed that his deep-rooted desire had become obvious to Rama. But Vibhishan's embarrassment caused Rama a lot more embarrassment. Because there was no need for Vibhishan to turn red since Rama was only giving him what was rightly his. Rama arranged for a fire sacrifice for coronation and Vibhishan was immediately crowned as the king of Lanka. Much before the war was fought, much before Ravana was killed, Vibhishan became the king of Lanka. *lankeshvara bhae saba jaga jānā*

Rama always knew how to build bridges. Whether it was difference of opinions, difference in behaviour, or difference in feelings, Rama removed all differences by building bridges and joining people.

The next step for the vanara army was to cross the vast expanse of ocean. Vibhishan suggested that Rama pray to the ocean god and take his help to cross. Lakshmana, however, believed in action. He did not want to wait for the ocean god to come and help. Lakshmana advised Rama, "Only the weak stand and wait and do nothing. Just shoot your arrows and make way to cross."

Lakshmana and Vibhishan were poles apart. One was Rama's younger brother while the other was the enemy's younger brother. One loved his brother to death while the other had not an iota of love for his brother. One believed in action while the other believed in mercy.

Rama had to cross not just the vast ocean but also the vast expanse of differences between the two. Who would he listen to? He didn't want to take sides. He wanted to unite them. He was an expert in finding the essence of unity even in the midst of differences. The common theme between the two was that they both loved Rama. And the common goal was to cross the ocean.

Vibhishan did not expect Rama to take his advice when Lakshmana was so openly not in favour. His face fell in anticipation of being rejected. But Rama said, "Yes, Vibhishan, we will try what you say." Vibhishan became ecstatic. Then Rama said, "Lakshmana, we will have to use your method also." And with his body language he conveyed to Lakshmana that he valued his opinion. For three days, they tried Vibhishan's suggestion and the next day, they tried Lakshmana's suggestion and in this way Rama succeeded in maintaining unity by building bridges between hearts.

juga sahasra jojana para bhānū।
līlyo tāhi madhura phala jānū॥ 18 ॥

Though the sun is thousands of miles away,
You swallowed it, thinking it a tasty fruit. (18)

juga sahasra jojana para bhānū refers to the distance
between the earth and the sun.

1 Yuga is 12000 years
1 Sahasra is 1000 years
1 Yojan is 8 miles
Yuga x Sahasra x Yojan = par Bhanu (to the Sun)
12000 x 1000 x 8 = 96000000 miles
1 mile is 1.6 km
So, 96000000 x 1.6 = 153600000 km

This is the exact round figure distance of earth from
Sun when the earth is farthest.

When Hanuman was an infant, his parents conducted
the first grain ceremony. The moment Hanuman ate the
first few grains, his appetite got activated. His mother
fed him all possible fruits, but nothing could satisfy his
hunger. Finally not wanting to trouble her, Hanuman

stopped demanding. But the hunger pangs did not subside, causing a lot of distress to him. One day, as he was tossing and turning in hunger, Narada Muni appeared to him and offered him some fruits. Even that wasn't enough to satisfy the intense fire in his stomach. Finally, Narada Muni pointed out to the sun. Mistaking the sun to be a big fruit, Hanuman jumped towards it in one leap. *līlyo tāhi madhura phala jānū*

Knowledge can be gained only if you possess the eagerness to gain it. Hanuman was a reservoir of so much knowledge that it even impressed Rama because he had that eagerness for it. Hunger for knowledge is akin to hunger for food. When you are really hungry, you desperately search for food that will satisfy your hunger. Hanuman was an extremely hungry child. But his hunger was not like the hunger of regular babies. His was an intellectual hunger. The hunger for understanding the deeper truths of life. While the story of baby Hanuman jumping to gobble up the sun is often seen as the hunger of the belly, great acharyas consider that to be the hunger of the heart to gain knowledge. The sun represents light of knowledge. When Hanuman jumped towards the sun and swallowed it up, symbolically it represented his eagerness to gain infinite knowledge.

❧

At one point during the war, a catastrophe struck Rama's army when Ravana struck Lakshmana with the Shela weapon, which was created by Mayadanava. Ravana had planned the attack well. He shot the weapon much after sun set knowing full well that the effect of the weapon was connected to the movement of the sun. Mayadanava had made such a weapon that would work its poison into a person as soon as the sun set and it would completely destroy a person at sunrise. So, essentially Rama's army had only the time between sunset and sun rise to revive Lakshmana by bringing an antidote to the poison. While everyone in the army was crying, Jambavan was busy looking for Hanuman who was engaged in a brutal fight on the other end of the battlefield. He knew that as usual the only person who could save the day was Hanuman. Giving him a proper brief of the whole matter, Jambavan instructed Hanuman to immediately depart to fetch the herbs that were required as an antidote to the poison.

By the time Hanuman left it was close to midnight. As he began his ascent, he saw something else rising parallel to him almost simultaneously. He was shocked to see that it was the sun, rising at midnight! Only a few hours back the sun had set, so how could it rise so early? The moon was as confused as Hanuman. It was his stipulated time to rule the skies. How did the sun come back, out of turn? In the middle of that crazy confusion,

Hanuman heard a shrill laughter. He turned around in mid-air and discovered the source of that laughter to be Ravana. As soon as he saw that naughty look on his face, he deciphered that Lankeshwar Ravana was the cause behind the unnatural phenomenon. Of course he had the power, ability, and insensitivity to change the course of nature according to his whims. Hanuman realized that there was no point in trying to do anything with Ravana since time was of essence now. There was no time to waste in arguments or fights since Lakshmana's life was at stake.

Rather than rushing towards the mountains to bring back the life-saving herbs, Hanuman soared towards the sun in an attempt to prevent it from rising so early. He had treaded this path many times before. Once as a baby hungry for food, once as a young child hungry for knowledge, and now as a dynamic youth hungry for service. Though his prime service at this point was to get the herbs back, the secondary condition was to get it on time before sunrise. He decided to first take care of the secondary condition and thus ensure his primary service got completed on time.

Reaching the sun god Surya who was seated on his sun chariot, Hanuman landed with a thud. He needed to have a private chat with the Sun god who had also been his teacher. Obviously with the charioteer Aruna being around there was no question of privacy. Thus Hanuman kicked out Aruna from the chariot and took charge of it, bringing it to a screeching halt. Surya was now completely dumbfounded. What did this monkey want from him now? He was never sure what mood Hanuman approached him in. Sometimes he was aggressive and sometimes so humble. In that state of confusion, he asked Hanuman why was he behaving so violently. Hanuman glared at him. Surya immediately understood what that meant. He confessed to Hanuman that he was dead scared of Ravana's wrath. But Hanuman's question was how could that make him do something that would cause harm to Rama? Fear shouldn't make us change our loyalty. Hanuman reminded Surya that Rama was his ultimate master and that he derived all his strength from the Supreme Lord. While Surya seemed to agree to Hanuman's points, his eyes kept darting towards Ravana's palace where Ravana was stationed on the balcony monitoring the sun's rise.

Hanuman realized that there was no point in discussing with someone who was overcome with fear. Fear makes one do foolish things. He said something that immediately seemed to draw Surya's attention. He told Surya that he had a brilliant idea that could help both of them simultaneously. He could win Ravana's trust as well as Rama's favour with this brilliant idea.

To get Surya to trust him even more, Hanuman used a brilliant emotional connect. He told Surya that since he was called Bhanu and he, Hanuman, was called Hanu, therefore, since their names were similar, they could do something nice together. Now that Surya was open to listening to his idea, Hanuman called him closer to whisper the idea into his ears, lest someone heard it and conveyed to Ravana. The innocent Surya bent closer and offered his ears to Hanuman. Hanuman informally put his arm across Surya's neck as if bringing him closer and suddenly grasped the neck firmly with his arm, locking the sun god in the grip of his armpit.

Shocked by the sudden turn of events, Surya tried to pry himself out of Hanuman's grip but in vain. The more he struggled, the more Hanuman tightened his grip. Now Surya realized that his fate was sealed. He stopped struggling and Hanuman took a leap from the chariot with the sun god in his armpit. No more was sunrise a concern because the sun god himself was under his control. When Hanuman began to fly with the sun under his armpit, everyone below in Lanka was amazed. Ravana was totally taken aback. How could a monkey control the sun like that?

As Hanuman flew, his armpits glowed effulgently with the sun god trapped in there. Without any further obstacles, he reached the mountains, home to the particular herbs and plucked them in a large quantity and brought them back to Lanka. While Jambavan and Shushena busied themselves reviving Lakshmana, Hanuman flew back to the stationary sun chariot to release the captive sun god. As soon as he released the sun god, he begged forgiveness from him for his audacity. Though it was extremely embarrassing for the sun god, he did not take offense knowing that Hanuman's intention was right though his action may have been wrong. Not that he had been happy serving Ravana. But he had no option other than obeying, sponsored by his fear. Thus, in one way Hanuman prevented him from serving Ravana and saved him from making a ghastly mistake. Surya concluded that the embarrassment of being under Hanuman's armpit was better than the embarrassment of rising at the wrong time on the orders of Ravana.

This was the third time Hanuman did *juga sahasra jojana para bhānū*

prabhu mudrikā meli mukha māhī।
jaladhi lāghi gaye acharaja nāhī॥ 19 ॥

With the Lord's ring in your mouth,
You jumped across the Ocean—no wonder in that. (19)

When the monkey army was being allotted different directions to search for Mother Sita, Sugriva addressed Hanuman, who was in the group going south, headed by Angad and assisted by Jambavan and others: "If Jambavan is the wisdom and Angad the youthful dynamism behind this group, then you are the strength that carries everyone along. The success of the entire mission of searching for Mother Sita rests on you. There can never be any impediment big enough to stop you in your transit on land, sea, or sky. You are like your father, Vayu, the wind god. I don't think anyone can match your prowess, astuteness, adventurous spirit, or intellect in the three worlds. However, more than any of these things, your greatest asset is your spotless character. I have a lot of hope pinned on you. Somehow, please find Sita."

Rama was intrigued and inspired as He watched Sugriva single out Hanuman for such attention and praise. Hanuman had definitely impressed Him right from the moment He saw him disguised as that beggar. In fact, every act and speech of Hanuman's had touched Rama very deeply. His sensitivity, intelligence, strength, resourcefulness, kindness, skills, and servitude together made him stand out in the crowd of the vanara sena. Now that Sugriva was so effusive in his praise for Hanuman, Rama's appreciation for Hanuman went up several notches. By this time Rama had developed good faith in Sugriva's abilities to judge people. Sugriva would only give such importance to someone whose record had been outstanding. In fact, Rama was now convinced that Hanuman was one of the most special beings in his world.

"O' Hanuman, I totally depend on you now!" Hanuman's heart melted with Rama's first words of dependence. Rama continued, "I am convinced you will succeed in the current expedition. With this conviction, what I am going to offer you right now is the most valuable thing in the universe!"

Rama held out something glittering in His right hand. Hanuman bent down on one knee, cupped his palms and extended them to Rama. Rama dropped that glittering object into his palms. As soon as it touched Hanuman's hands, a shiver ran through his body. It was a golden ring studded with a large precious stone on top and two small stones below. Hanuman noticed, inscribed on the larger top stone, the syllable Sri and on the lower stones, the syllables Ra and Ma. Originally, this ring must have been Sita's. It couldn't have been Rama's. A humble person like Rama wouldn't arrogantly wear a ring with His name inscribed on it. Sita wore this ring on Her finger to remind Her always of the protection of Rama's name in Her life. When the boatman Kevat ferried them across Ganga, Sita had given this ring to Rama to offer it as a token of gratitude to Kevat. He hadn't of course accepted it. From then on, Rama had retained the ring on His finger. Sita had wanted to ask Rama back then about why He had kept the ring, but She let it go, concluding that Her husband always backed His action with some good reason. Rama had probably known that this ring would unite them someday.

Hanuman rose to his feet, held the ring between the index finger and the thumb of his right hand and touched it reverentially to his head. He then safely tucked it away in his waistcloth. Hanuman then bent low and held Lord Rama's feet. With the blessings of Rama in his heart and the ring in his hand he left for the search mission. He began to wonder where to keep that special, invaluable, and extremely potent ring, in the course of his arduous journey. He wanted to keep it in a place that was respectful and yet secure. He definitely could not wear the ring on his finger since it belonged to Lord Rama. That would be arrogance. He couldn't find any place in his clothes that would be safe enough. The long journey and tough encounters on the way would make it impossible to retain it within the folds of his clothes. He couldn't tie it on to his sacred thread, as it would be too visible and also too susceptible to the risk of falling off or accidentally snapping off the thread during the journey.

He possibly couldn't keep it in his hands as it could fall off during a careless moment or even when he would have to use his hands to climb or fight. Hanuman finally got his answer. There was only one place where the holy name of Lord Rama really belonged. And that was the tongue. The tongue should ideally reverberate the holy names of Rama constantly. Presence of the ring in his mouth was symbolic of the holy name of Lord Rama being constantly on his tongue. Moreover, it would act as a constant reminder to him to absorb his mind in the holy names. *prabhu mudrikā meli mukha māhī*

The ring has a special place in Ramayana. It served to unite Rama and Sita more than once. It so happened in Ayodhya that Rama and Sita had an argument one day and stopped talking to each other. Few days passed and neither took the initiative to break the deadlock. Neither wanted to admit His or Her mistake. Although Sita was very anxious to end the impasse, Rama seemed determined to continue. Unknown to Sita, Rama too longed to talk to Sita and forget the argument.

One day as they were sitting in the royal garden, together but not talking, Sita had an idea. She purposely dropped her ring in the nearby bushes and called out aloud, "Is there anyone here who can help me find my ring?" Rama immediately sprang up from his seat to search for the ring. Having found it victoriously, He slipped it back on Sita's hand. Sita smiled happily and this loving gesture broke the ice. They embraced each other and promised to never argue again.

When the whole vanara army was contemplating who would cross the 800-mile ocean, Jambavan reminded Hanuman of his powers. Of course Hanuman wasn't aware of his own powers but very well knew of a greater power that was with him. The ring of Lord Rama with His holy name inscribed. Other monkeys did not have that ring. Angad was confident of jumping to Lanka but he doubted he could come back. Angad, a visionary, knew none of them had the means to cross the ocean. Though Lord Rama sent all of them but he gave the ring only to Hanuman. So if anyone could cross the ocean, it was Hanuman.

In that jump of Hanuman's, the five elements were involved intricately. He himself being the son of the wind god, so the air element was involved. Because the jump was over the ocean, the water element was involved. He used the skyway and thus the ether element was involved. Since the whole search mission was to find Sita who is Bhumi suta or the daughter of the earth, the earth element was also involved. And while he was in Lanka, he set the whole city on fire, thus involving the fire element. Hanuman strongly believed that everything in one's disposal should be involved in the service of Lord Rama and this Hanuman proved in his mystical jump to Lanka by involving all the elements in Rama's service.

Not only was the jump long but it was dangerous. Hanuman came across four obstacles during his jump across the ocean, each of which tested his commitment to the mission. Along with his character, intelligence, and strength. The first obstacle was a golden mountain named Mynaka that arose from deep within the sea. The presiding deity of that mountain invited Hanuman for a break and to enjoy the pleasures of life before proceeding ahead on that arduous journey. A break was completely justified, considering that Hanuman had already been on a two-month intense search operation that took him across thousands of miles. Not just that, the journey that was waiting for him ahead was going to be more intense and dangerous. But instead of choosing to accept it, Hanuman outrightly rejected it. For Hanuman, everything including personal comforts and conveniences came after his service to Lord Rama. There was absolutely no scope for personal space. His love for the Lord and His mission superseded his need for comforts and relaxation.

If Mynaka pushed him to focus on his comforts, the next obstacle distracted him from the goal, pushing him to focus on proving his greatness. The obstacle was named Surasa. She was sent by the demigods to test Hanuman's preparedness for Lanka. The gods weren't sure if Hanuman was equipped enough to handle the diplomacy and power of Ravana. She rose from the ocean and blocked Hanuman's path stating that she had Brahma's boon that anyone who passed over the ocean would have to enter into her mouth. Very humbly Hanuman requested her to step away from his path and allow him to execute his mission. Surasa reacted by increasing the size of her mouth to block his forward movements. That angered Hanuman who increased his size assuming a size bigger than her. Surasa beat him in size and then Hanuman became even bigger. She outdid Hanuman once again. As this went on, Hanuman realized that in trying to prove that he was better than her, he was forgetting his goal and his mission. His destination was Sita that could only be attained by humility. Sita represents bhakti devi and bhakti is the path of reducing oneself to nothingness. It is a path that teaches you that god is everything and you are nothing. Surasa represented the desire for greatness and self-promotion. Hanuman realized that the only way to deal with the Surasa mentality was by admitting defeat and showing yourself to be insignificant and humble. The only way you can deal with desire is to become zero. Hanuman not just became small but *atilaghu* which means very small. When you make yourself zero, which means when you take shelter of the Lord, then desire can't eat you. Hanuman became very small and entered her mouth and came out, thus fulfilling Brahma's boon. Surasa was impressed with his intelligence and in turn blessed him to be victorious. The demigods certified Hanuman to be the right candidate to thwart Ravana's fortitude.

After covering a considerable distance, Hanuman found himself locked in mid-air. He couldn't move an inch in any direction. Suddenly he was sucked in towards the ocean with great force. He fell into the open mouth of a demoness named Simhika who could capture anyone by their shadow. She swallowed Hanuman completely in one gulp without realizing what a huge mistake that was. Even before she realized it, Hanuman tore open her belly from the inside and swam out of the bloody waters and once again rose into the sky heading towards Lanka. Simhika represents an envious mind-set who is drowning in an ocean of envy. The nature of envy is to drag down high-flying people using one single fault of theirs as a hook. Hanuman realized that the only way to deal with envy is by destroying it. Envy pulls you down and does not allow one to reach bhakti devi and thus shouldn't have any place in our lives.

Finally when he reached Lanka on the other side of the ocean, he came across his fourth obstacle in the form of Lankini, the security chief of Lanka. When Hanuman tried to enter, she pushed him out forcefully. The angered Hanuman punched her. With that punch, she came to her senses and realized who her real master was. She was serving a master that was feeding her but had forgotten that master who had brought her to existence. With that realization, Lankini gave up the service of her false master Ravana and began to serve her true master Rama.

Though the journey was arduous for anyone, but for Hanuman who held the holy name of the Lord in his mouth, the blessings of the Lord in his heart, and the remembrance of the Lord's constant presence and protection in his mind, nothing was difficult and impossible. Crossing over the ocean of difficulties wasn't at all a tough task for Hanuman. *jaladhi lāghi gaye acharaja nāhī*

durgama kāja jagata ke jete।
sugama anugraha tumhare tete॥ 20 ॥

All impossible tasks in this world,
Become easily doable with your mercy. (20)

Some acharyas analyse that Sita represents the Jivatma and Rama, Parmatma. Whereas Ravana represents pride or false ego. Hanuman achieves the difficult task of uniting the soul with the Parmatma by defeating ego.

Hanuman had found Sita in Ashok Vatika and passed Rama's message on to her. With Sita's blessings and permission, Hanuman proceeded to observe the city of Lanka. As he was scrutinizing the strategic points in the city, he noticed a shining golden altar. Situated on the golden altar under the canopy of a giant Ashok tree was a beautiful temple. Hanuman crept inside the temple and saw an effulgent dark complexioned goddess. The goddess was beauty personified with her three eyes resembling Cupid's bow. Wearing a garland of skulls, she was dancing to the auspicious sounds of drums and bells that she played with her four hands. Surrounding her were her followers dressed as yoginis. All of them were eulogizing Ravana. Shouts of 'Hail Ravana', 'Victory to Ravana' filled the room. Hanuman was disgusted at this sight. Letting out an angry roar, he jumped into their midst terrifying the yoginis. The goddess herself was startled at the sudden intrusion. Pacifying her frightened followers, she asked Hanuman, "Who are you, O' Vanara? And how did you get in here?"

Hanuman introduced himself, "My name is Hanuman. I am the son of the Wind God. I have accepted the servitude of Lord Rama by whose mercy I can destroy the entire earth with its oceans and forests. I came here searching for Mother Sita who has been held captive by wicked Ravana. Who are you and why are you wishing for the victory of a sinner like Ravana?" The goddess replied, "I am the daughter of Himalayas residing in Chandasvarupa. Hence, I am known as Chandika. I am also known as Parvati and Kali. Ravana has conquered me with his devotional worship due to which I shield him from his enemies. O' monkey, kindly show me your colossal form about which you were boasting some time ago."

Hanuman obliged by expanding himself. Eyes popped out as the goddess and her followers observed his gargantuan size. The goddess could see different rakshasas smashed and shred into pieces dangling from Hanuman's sharp nails and teeth. From his pores emerged innumerable colossal vanaras who were annihilating the rakshasa army. On Hanuman's head shone the beautiful emerald complexioned Lord Rama killing Ravana with his arrows. He held the severed head of the giant Kumbhakaran in his hand that wielded the bow. On Hanuman's forehead stood Lakshmana whose complexion was like gorochan. Fixing his gaze upon the lotus feet of Rama and Sita, Lakshmana destroyed Meghanada, Ravana's unconquerable son. A blazing and burnt Lanka lay between Hanuman's eyebrows and the pious Vibhishan ruling Lanka as the king could be seen in Hanuman's heart. The goddess was astounded looking at Hanuman's wondrous form.

Humbly, she prayed, "O' divine monkey, it is certain that you are none other than Lord Shiva himself who has appeared as a vanara for the annihilation of Ravana and his clan. It is for this very purpose that you have accepted the service of Lord Rama. Please let go of your anger and command me as to what can I do for you." Hanuman assumed his original form and said, "O' divine goddess, I request you to leave Lanka at this very instant. Why do you wish victory for a sinner like Ravana? The entire universe will be in chaos if he doesn't die. If you continue to protect Ravana, the expansion of my energy in you will also be contaminated for siding with this sinner."

The goddess replied, "The one who insulted Sita

has also insulted me. I will leave Lanka as you have instructed."

Hanuman said, "O' Parvatnandini Maheshwari, you are worshipped by the great trinity, Brahma, Vishnu, and Mahesha. You are the great illusory energy that maintains this material world. You are the Adishakti and maintainer of all the demigods and Brahma, Vishnu, and Mahesha. Please bless Rama with victory and assist him in eliminating Ravana."

Goddess Chandika blessed Rama, saying, "Sri Rama will surely gain victory over Ravana and shine as the sun of the glorious Ikshvaku dynasty. He has all my blessings to annihilate Ravana. O' Hanuman, the demigods are obliged to anyone who appeases them by performing rituals as prescribed in the Vedas. In the Pousha Magha month, the period for worshipping demigods is 13 days, which has passed. Thus, Ravana cannot restrict me now. Had this been the stipulated worship period, it would have been difficult for me to leave Lanka. Since I am not compelled now, I bless Rama with victory."

Chandika then departed from Lanka. Hanuman returned to Ashoka Vatika. He killed the rakshasas that tried to resist him and offered them to Goddess Chandika with their blood. Uprooting the trees, he offered them as flowers unto her. Ravana's son Akshay Kumar was her sacrificial offering. When Hanuman was finally captured by Indrajeet and his tail set on fire, he lit up the entire Lanka and set it ablaze as offering of incense and lamps unto the goddess. After having completed his mission, Hanuman went to Mother Sita to seek her blessings. After bidding her farewell, he leapt over the ocean and returned to his eagerly awaiting retinue to convey Sita's message to Rama. *durgama kāja jagata ke jete | sugama anugraha tumhare tete*

Every time Rama would sever his limb, it would rejoin once again. It was magnetism of the highest order. It appeared as if Ravana was practically immortal. Even when all his heads were chopped off, they would roll back into place. Even when Rama threw his severed arms far into the ocean, they would fly back and rejoin the body instantly. It had been more than an hour since Rama had been trying his best. By now he had come to the conclusion that it was impossible to eliminate Ravana by normal methods. There had to be a secret to this whole thing, and obviously a well-guarded secret at that. Vibhishan walked towards him and reconfirmed his premonition. The secret was in a boon that Lord Brahma had offered Ravana. It was definitely a boon, but there was a condition to it that could prove to be useful to Rama.

Vibhishan explained that Lord Brahma had offered the boon to Ravana that his limbs even if severed, would rejoin instantly. Thus his body could never be destroyed. Technically he had ensured Ravana's immortality. But while giving this boon, Brahma also offered him an arrow within which he had locked Ravana's destiny. He warned Ravana that his life was literally within that arrow. If this arrow was shot at his navel, it would instantly sap away all his strength, eliminating him that very moment. As long as that arrow remained protected, Ravana's life remained protected.

The monkeys became really excited that some hope was still there, though they also wondered if they would ever find that wonder arrow. Of course, as usual Vibhishan had an answer to that too. He announced that the only person other than Ravana who knew the whereabouts of that arrow was Mandodari.

The question now was who would do the impossible. Hanuman immediately stepped in and said that he could try. *durgama kāja jagata ke jete*, all the arduous tasks of this world Hanuman would be always eager to try. Taking the blessings of Rama and with a loud cry of Jai Sri Rama, Hanuman leaped towards the inner sanctorum of Lanka. When he landed, he wasn't Hanuman the vanara hero anymore but an old frail and wise astrologer who had to walk with the help of a stick since he was stooped with wisdom. Every demon in Lanka flocked to him to hear predictions about their life and that of their family members. The mothers were especially worried about their sons who had gone to war. The old astrologer was so accurate with anything he told that people were astounded. Soon word spread across the length of Lanka till it did rounds of the royal palace and reached the ears of Mandodari. She immediately wanted a private audience with him. Soon the astrologer was wobbling into the palace with a naughty grin on his wrinkled old face.

The moment they were alone, Mandodari broke down. She was really worried about the safety of her husband. She had almost lost everyone she considered a relative and now her world only revolved around one person, Ravana. She wanted to know from the astrologer whether her husband would win. She wanted to know if there was any processes that would ensure his victory. Looking very grim, the astrologer began to study his astrological charts intensely. Finally he declared that today was doomsday. Either Ravana would rule forever or he would be dead. The word death sent a shiver down Mandodari's spine. When she asked for a plan that could seal his victory, the astrologer looked at her very seriously.

He told her that her husband's life was safe as long as she held the secret a secret. She was confused what that meant. At the same time, she felt that he was referring to the secret arrow that she had hidden away carefully. But when he told her to not to give it to anyone who comes to her asking for it including Lord Brahma himself, she knew that he knew about that secret arrow. Reassured that he was her well-wisher, Mandodari promised him that she would not give to anyone, no matter who. The astrologer smiled at her and got up to leave. Just as he was stepping out of the room, he turned around partially and asked her if she was sure that the secret hideout was really a secret after all this time especially since Vibhishan had now joined the enemies. He knew every small and big secret of the palace. What was the guarantee that he didn't know about the secret arrow?

That question made Mandodari think a bit. But after a moment she snapped out of her thoughts and reassured the astrologer that there was no way Vibhishan or anyone else could know about the secret place. But not wanting to take any risk since it was the question of her husband's life, she asked the astrologer if he had a better place to house the arrow than the glass pillar within which she had embedded it. The moment she pointed out to the pillar, the next moment itself the pillar shattered to pieces with a thunderous sound followed by an intense chant of Jai Sri Rama. The shocked Mandodari saw Hanuman jump out of her window with the secret arrow in his hand. That was the end of Ravana! *sugama anugraha tumhare tete*

rāma duāre tuma rakhavāre।
hota na āgnyā binu paisāre॥ 21 ॥

You stand guarding Rama's gate,
No one can enter without your consent. (21)

When the bridge construction was almost complete and the monkeys were set to march to Lanka, Vibhishan felt restless and uncomfortable. He wasn't satisfied with the information from Lanka that his spies had brought him. His intuition said something else. That something sinister was cooking on the other side of the ocean. Taking the form of a pigeon, Vibhishan flew across the ocean and landed on the dome of the Lankan royal courtroom. Before he could hear a single word, what he saw was enough to increase his heartbeat. Two robust rakshasas stood before Ravana with a smirk on their faces. From the size of the two, Vibhishan realized the size of trouble.

Soon leaders of the monkey army along with Rama and Lakshmana were gathered around Vibhishan. He shared with them the problem ahead. It wasn't a single but a double-edged problem. The name of the problem was Ahiravana-Mahiravana. These were two cruel magician friends of Ravana who derived great pleasure in tricking innocent people into their sinister web and offering them as human sacrifice. Vibhishan had reliable information that they had been contracted for killing Rama and Lakshmana. Vibhishan warned the monkey leaders that dealing with these two meant dealing with a lot of treachery. The two brothers could change their form at will and pull off any trick, possible or impossible, in the blink of an eye. The primary goal now was to ensure that Rama and Lakshmana remain in a highly protected environment.

In order to safeguard them, the entire monkey army assembled together to form circular layers. They were fully armed and fully alert. Around the concentric wall of monkeys, Hanuman made another robust wall with his tail. Only a small entry gate remained through which a single person could walk in or out. Hanuman personally stood guarding that. When Vibhishan studied the entire protective structure, he was delighted with their efforts. Vibhishan requested Rama to invoke the Sudarshan chakra to guard the sky ways which was the only loophole left in the whole structure. Placing Sugriva and Angad inside to guard Rama and Lakshmana personally, Vibhishan chose to station himself outside the wall to be in continuous interaction with Hanuman.

To be doubly sure that there was no loophole in their security system, Vibhishan walked around the wall in circles and Hanuman stayed put at the gate. *rāma duāre tuma rakhavāre hota na āgnyā binu paisāre.*

Hanuman guarded the gate of Lord Rama and no one could enter without his consent.

As soon as Vibhishan turned around the corner out of sight, an elderly royal king approached Hanuman. Introducing himself as Dasharatha, the father of Rama and Lakshmana, he begged to be allowed in to spend some time with his sons whom he hadn't seen for more than a decade now. Immediately Vibhishan's warning struck in Hanuman's mind. Mahiravana and Ahiravana were masters of illusion. Not wanting to take a risk and yet at the same time not wanting to be disrespectful to Dasharatha, he requested the king to wait a little till Vibhishan arrived. But Dasharatha left in a hurry saying that he would return soon. When the confused Hanuman explained the incident to Vibhishan, he warned Hanuman that even if his father Kesari comes, he should not let him in without Vibhishan's approval. The instruction was clear now. From then on Hanuman had no hesitation denying entry to Bharata, Rama's brother, then to Kaushalya, Rama's mother, and even Janak Maharaj, Sita's father. Vibhishan was extremely pleased with Hanuman's alertness. The system was working very well and so far there was nothing to worry as long as they maintained this vigil.

With a pat on Hanuman's back, Vibhishan continued his stroll around the wall. In a matter of a few minutes he was suddenly back. Hanuman was surprised but concluded that there must have been some emergency he perceived due to which he had returned hastily. Speaking with a sense of urgency, Vibhishan asked Hanuman to step aside and allow him to enter the gate to inspect the situation inside. Hanuman complied and Vibhishan entered swiftly. Sealing the gate once again Hanuman stood on high alert. In a few minutes, Vibhishan came to the gate once again. How was this possible? When he had already entered, how could he come back again outside? Hanuman initially thought that this was the imposter Ahiravana or Mahiravana. But when Vibhishan gave him some solid proof, Hanuman panicked understanding that he had sent the imposter inside. Dismantling the tail, Hanuman and Vibhishan entered only to find that every single monkey inside was lying unconscious and both Rama and Lakshmana were missing. The question was where were they now? The answer stood right in front of them in the form of a pit. Not wanting to waste any time, Hanuman leaped into the pit, promising to bring back the divine brothers.

The pit was actually a portal that led him all the way

to the netherworld or the Patalaloka. When Hanuman
fell into the beautiful city of Patala, he transformed
himself into a regular monkey. Suddenly an old lady
saw him and began to scream. When a few onlookers
gathered, she pointed out to the monkey and said that the
king had a curse that the day monkeys and humans enter
his city, it will mark the end of it. She warned everyone
to leave the city soon. Hanuman jumped away from the
crowd, happy to hear good news on arrival. While he
was in another corner of the city, he heard another lady
conversing with someone that there was going to be a
huge festival inside the palace today where the king
would be performing a human sacrifice for the pleasure
of Goddess Mahamaya. He learnt from that conversation
that the brothers Ahiravana and Mahiravana had brought
two handsome humans for that purpose. Armed with this
information, Hanuman assumed a very tiny form and
found entry into the palace in spite of heavy security
and inspection.

Once inside, Hanuman began his search. He came
across a heavily guarded door, which he deduced to be
the sacrificial arena. When he tried to sneak through
the door in his really tiny form, he was stopped by a
very powerful looking personality. His face resembled
a vanara's and his body resembled a crocodile's. He
pounced on Hanuman and a tremendous fight ensued,

with Hanuman finally tying up that half-vanara half-crocodile with ropes and hurling him onto the ground. Thus humbled, the guard introduced himself as Makharadhwaja, the son of Hanuman. This unexpected introduction bewildered Hanuman who had never been married. How could he have a son that he didn't know of? When questioned, Makharadhwaja explained that when Hanuman had burnt Lanka and then dipped his tail into the ocean to quench the fire, a drop of sweat had fallen into the ocean, which had been swallowed by a female crocodile. From that crocodile, Makharadhwaja was born. Hanuman was happy to meet his son and Makharadhwaja promised to help his father in finding Rama and eliminating all the Ravanas.

Makharadhwaja suggested Hanuman to meet Chitrasena who was a Nagakanya held captive by Ahiravana and Mahiravana. She held many secrets of the demonic brothers and could definitely help Hanuman find a solution. From what Vibhishan had told him, Hanuman knew that killing the brothers wouldn't be easy and straightforward, as they would have magical ways to remain immortal. Thus it was imperative that Hanuman met Chitrasena and gain her confidence so that she would reveal the inner secrets of the demons. Taking the form of a small bumblebee, Hanuman entered the room of Chitrasena and hovered over her. When he had managed to capture her attention, Hanuman revealed his original form to her and began a conversation. Initially she wasn't ready to believe him because he could be one of the evil brothers who had taken a vanara form just to test her loyalty. But when she saw the genuineness and the love he had for Lord Rama, she was convinced that this could not be them, as there was not even a shade of evil in his persona. She agreed to help Hanuman on one condition. Her condition was that Rama would have to marry her in return for the favour she was going to do to help them save their lives. Seeing no way out, Hanuman agreed to her condition but not before posing a condition of his own. As a condition to her condition. His condition was that Rama would marry her only if her bed could handle the weight of Rama. Not seeing any harm in it, she agreed to his condition. She was a great devotee of Lord Vishnu and the moment she had seen Rama, she had completely surrendered her heart to him.

Chitrasena then revealed few of the well-guarded secrets of the evil brothers. She explained that Mahiravana had once saved the lives of a group of honeybees who became so grateful that they always resided in the palace, assisting the demons. Whenever one of the brothers got killed in a battle, the bees would fly out and sprinkle celestial nectar, that could revive the dead, into his mouth. Thus, as long as these bees were alive, the brothers would live. She further disclosed that the lives of the two brothers existed only partly in their bodies; the rest of their lives were stored elsewhere. The life of Ahiravana was stored in a large diamond and the life of Mahiravana was stored in five lamps that were constantly lit in five adjacent caves in a nearby mountain. Along with actually killing the brothers, the two life sources had to be destroyed simultaneously, only then would the demons die.

Having learnt their secrets, Hanuman took the form of a bumblebee once again and ventured out to find the hideout of the bees. What followed was a tremendous battle with the bees. He slaughtered all the bees in that hive one by one until there was just one bee left who helplessly took shelter of Hanuman promising to assist him in every possible way. Hanuman smiled. He had just the right idea for using this bee's services. He instructed the bee to proceed to Chitrasena's room and make her bed hollow and weak internally. While the bee left to do its service, Hanuman made his way into the temple of the goddess Mahamaya also known as Kamakshi devi. There he spent some time with the goddess, explaining to her the entire situation and asking her permission to do something drastic in her presence. The goddess blessed Hanuman to save the lives of Rama and Lakshmana. He next proceeded to the prison where Rama and Lakshmana were held captive and explained to them the whole plan.

By the time Hanuman finished explaining, guards had arrived to take them to the sacrificial arena. Hanuman immediately proceeded to the five caves where a herculean task awaited him. Meanwhile, Mahiravana and Ahiravana asked Rama and Lakshmana to bend themselves and place their necks on the pedestal. Feigning ignorance, Rama asked for a demonstration. The brothers bent down to show what is the right way to place the neck in the pedestal for an easy chop. That very moment both Rama and Lakshmana broke open their shackles and picked up the swords that were placed close by and lopped their heads off. Immediately, Lakshmana jumped up with a hammer to the place where the diamond was kept. Rama began his onslaught to massacre all the remaining demons in that arena.

Hanuman had reached the cave and began to blow off the lamps one by one in the five caves. To his consternation, by the time he blew off one lamp, the previous lamp would light up again. It was obvious to him that all five needed to be blown off simultaneously. Since the caves were in five different directions, he took up a five-headed form known as Panchamukhi Hanuman. Facing north was the Varaha or boar face, facing south was Narsimha or lion face, facing west was the Garuda or eagle face, facing east was Hanuman's original face, and facing up was the Hayagriva or horse face. With one blow, he extinguished all the five lamps at one go. Exactly at the same time, Lakshmana smashed the diamond. Thus permanently eliminating the two demonic brothers.

Returning to Rama and Lakshmana, Hanuman touched their feet and they happily embraced him. Of course there was still a small problem left to deal with. Hanuman explained the promise to Chitrasena in order to get her to divulge her secrets. Without asking Rama, he had agreed for the marriage proposal from her. Rama smiled and went to her room. Chitrasena was so happy that she was going to be finally united with her worshippable Lord and master. But as soon as Rama sat on the bed, it broke. Chitrasena immediately realized that this must be a trick of Hanuman's. But even before she could express her anger on him, Lord Rama, with a sweet smile on his face, explained to her that in this life he had taken eka-patni vrata and thus he could marry no one other than Sita. But he assured her that in his next incarnation as Krishna, he would surely marry her and she would be one of his chief queens named Satyabhama. Satisfied with that assurance, Chitrasena decided to wait for the right time to come back and stepped aside.

Rama then coroneted Makharadhwaja as the king of Patalaloka. Once everything was in order, Makharadhwaja handed over the responsibilities of the kingdom to the ministers and decided to travel with his father for assisting him in his mission. Hanuman lifted Rama and Makharadhwaja lifted Lakshmana on their shoulders and zoomed out of the Patalaloka to return to the eagerly awaiting monkey army. Cheers broke out when the monkeys saw Hanuman safely back with Rama and Lakshmana.

With Hanuman present at Rama's door, who can dare to defy and enter forcefully?

saba sukha lahai tumhārī saranā।
tuma rakshaka kāhū ko daranā॥ 22 ॥

There's all happiness under your shelter
When you give protection, there's nothing to fear. (22)

"These villages were given to us by Lord Rama and Hanuman was a witness," the brahmanas cried out in unison.

The brahmanas of Kanyakubja had been in possession of about 4,400 villages, which they claimed that their ancestors were gifted by Lord Rama, with Hanuman as the witness. But King Kumaarpala would not believe them. Where was the proof? He wanted tangible proof of ownership. If they couldn't prove it, the villages belonged to him. It was as simple as that.

Having lost their home and all their possessions overnight, the brahmanas wondered how they could gather proof. Their only hope was finding Lord Rama or Hanuman. They decided to search for them and three thousand brahmanas left on foot on a journey to south to validate their claim.

It was a difficult journey. They crossed dense jungles, dangerous rivers, and difficult terrains. They survived on fruits and roots. Day by day, they became weaker and weaker in mind and body. Till one day they could not go any further. Helplessly, they prayed to Lord Rama to come to their rescue. Instead of Rama, an old yogi came. He asked what they were doing in the middle of nowhere and when the brahmanas informed him about their mission to find Rama, he discouraged them totally. However, the brahmanas did not have any other proof, so they continued their journey to Rameshwaram.

Next day, they met another travelling yogi. He too thought they were wasting time searching for Rama. Who has ever met Him, he asked. It's all a fairy tale, with no substance of truth. But the brahmanas, instead of believing him, were suspicious of who this yogi really was.

"Are you the same yogi who met us yesterday?" they asked suspiciously, "or are you Hanuman himself?"

The yogi smiled broadly and assumed his original form. The brahmanas gasped in astonishment as they saw Hanuman standing in front of them. Tears flowed as they bowed down to him and paid obeisance. Hanuman held out his palm and offered them fruits. These were divine fruits that would satiate hunger and bring them joy. Next, what he did made no sense. He plucked a hair from his right armpit and placed it in a pouch. He plucked another hair from his left armpit and placed it in a separate pouch. He wrapped both the pouches with tree bark and handed it over to the brahmanas.

"Go back to Kanyakubja and tell the king I have instructed him to return the land to you. If he refuses, then remove the hair from the left pouch. Once the king begs forgiveness and promises to return your land, use the right pouch. Follow these instructions carefully and you will get your land back."

The brahmanas were delighted with Hanuman's assurance and danced joyfully. Hanuman then flattened a rock and asked them to spend their night peacefully on it. Whilst they slept, Hanuman lifted the rock and carried them back to their homeland in a matter of hours which otherwise would have taken them months to cross. When the brahmanas woke up, they were shocked to find themselves back home. They thanked Hanuman from the bottom of their hearts.

They proceeded to the palace to convey Hanuman's instruction to the king. But as expected, the king only laughed at them. "You expect me to believe you met Hanuman?" he scoffed at them. "Get lost now!"

The brahmanas removed the hair from the left armpit pouch and dropped it. The king sneered even more. As soon as the brahmanas left the palace, they turned behind to see a cloud of smoke rising up from it. Within minutes the palace was on fire. People ran out from there trying to save their lives. Miraculously, only the palace was on fire. The fire did not spread anywhere else. They were not surprised to see the king also trying to save his life. He hurried towards them, bewildered and humbled. There was no need for any words. His eyes begged them to stop the fire and take the land. The brahmanas dropped the hair from the other pouch and lo and behold, the fire disappeared, restoring the palace to its original condition.

He immediately issued a decree to return the land to the brahmanas, stating that it belonged to them forever. He had enough proof to believe that now. The brahmanas could only thank Hanuman for giving them shelter and returning their life, their homes, and happiness. Hanuman never disappointed his devotees. *saba sukha lahai tumhārī saranā*

This was calamity no one knew how to heal with. The vanaras could handle weapons used by Ravana's army but what they saw right now was just one man! He was walking all over the battlefield, burning everything. He was a resident of Patalaloka. It could only be Ravana who invited this terrible demon named Bhasmalochana. With the departure of his brother Kumbhakarna, Ravana had lost his mental balance. He had even started attacking his own people in madness and fear. All of a sudden, he remembered Bhasmalochana. Who could be better than Bhasmalochana to lead his dwindling army and lend confidence to his attack?

Bhasmalochana did what was expected of him. He strode out with an air of confidence to take on the monkey army. Such was his confidence that he was not only alone, he was also blindfolded! At first, it seemed funny and audacious on his part, but as he came closer, he became more and more visible and menacing. They could see the glow surrounding his eyes, underneath the band. They wondered if his eyes could be glowing. Realization dawned on the monkeys, then. Bhasmalochana! He was none other than the man who could burn with his sight! From humour, the monkeys turned to panic. They ran helter-skelter, not wanting to turn into ashes. They wanted to be nowhere around when he opened his blindfold. The entire monkey army was in chaos all of a sudden.

The generals and leaders of the army were equally stunned. They were all overwhelmed with fear, thinking of what step to take to protect themselves. Attack was no longer a priority. Saving themselves was. In the midst of all this, Bhasmalochana uncovered his eyes. His eyes dazzled like the sun in all its glory. When he looked at someone, there was a flash of light, followed by a scream. Then came the smell of flesh and finally a heap of ashes. It all happened so quickly that the ashes were not even hot. Because the burning process that normally took hours was reduced to nano seconds.

As this mass destruction was taking place, Hanuman came into action. But instead of running towards them, he began to run in the opposite direction. The monkeys were horrified to see him running away from the site of disaster. Why was he abandoning them and fleeing? The monkeys had no hope left now. There was no way they could survive if Hanuman himself was running away. While they were drowning in sorrow, they caught a glimpse of Lakshmana smiling. He had in fact seen Rama whisper into Hanuman's ears so he knew Hanuman was up to something brave.

Now the monkeys could also see a masterplan behind Hanuman's actions. They saw Hanuman climbing high up. "Look! Where Hanuman has reached! He is so amazing." All the monkeys huddled together to watch their hero Hanuman. It was fascinating to watch him and guess what he was up to. Despite the impending danger, there was sudden excitement in the air. Hope had returned. They could now see Hanuman's tiny figure at a distance, scaling up the fortress of Ravana. He had reached the city. Naturally he would not run into the enemy camp if he was trying to save himself. There was a deeper motive behind this. What could it be? They didn't have to wait too long to find out because they saw Hanuman flying out of the fort with a huge plank of iron on his back.

Holding the plank with one hand and his tail, he balanced himself in air. He used his other hand to navigate the flight. But it was still a mystery as to what Hanuman was planning to do. Lord Rama and Lakshmana showed no such anxiety. The monkeys even saw them exchange a knowing glance. Hanuman had now landed right behind Bhasmalochana. Whereas the monkeys were behind rocks, trees, inside water bodies—anywhere at all, to hide themselves from the demon's fiery glance. Peeping out of their hiding places, they were less concerned about their own safety and more curious about Hanuman's next step. Hanuman's agile tail shot up to carry the iron plank high in the air over Bhasmalochana's head. He then expertly twisted the tail and flipped the iron plank.

Wow! What brilliance! The tail was the centre of attraction as it began to lower the vertical iron plank such that it came right in front of Bhasmalochana in the path of his vision. As soon as he brought it in front, there was a deafening sound. Boooom! It was an explosion. Bhasmalochana had turned into a pile of ashes. A huge cheer went out from the monkey army as they ran to hug their saviour. There were a few who had not yet grasped what exactly Hanuman had done to blast their enemy. They looked at the iron plank. What a surprise, it was a mirror! Hanuman showed Bhasmalochana a mirror to see himself! With this heroic act, Hanuman easily overcame something that could have potentially won the war for Ravana, wiping out the monkey army. The vanaras had nothing to fear as long as Hanuman was there. His devotees have nothing to fear as long as they sought protection from Hanuman. *tuma rakshaka kāhū ko daranā*

Draupadi worshipped Hanuman for the protection of Pandavas. A deity of Hanuman is present in every household altar. Because he overcomes difficulties for gods also. He rescued all gods from Ravana's prison. Whether it is Suryadeva or Varuna or Agnideva, or even Sita, everyone takes Hanuman's shelter.

āpana teja samhāro āpaiı
tinau loka hāka te kāpaiıı 23 ıı

You alone can face your radiant strength,
The three worlds tremble in fear when you roar. (23)

Even before Hanuman was born, his parents Kesari and
Anjana had received a boon for him. Sages had blessed
their marriage with a child who would rock the three
worlds!

Anjana was meditating in a cave on top of a secluded
mountain. Her eyes were shut in deep meditation, but
she felt like she was being watched—intensely. When
she opened her eyes, in front of her was a sight so
grotesque that she backed off with a startle and hit the
wall of the cave inside which she was seated. Standing
a few metres away from her, blocking the entrance of
the cave was this intensely ugly, extremely frightening,
gigantic rakshasa. There was no escape from the
demon's cruel intent to ravish her then and there. She
stood up, pushed him and rushed out of the cave. Her
shove was so intense that the rakshasa tripped. The few
moments he took to recover from the shove were enough

for her to make her escape toward the closest village. An intense chase began. She used every ounce of her energy to save her life. She had heard of a wise sage who lived somewhere in this village. His fame rested on the fact that he had answers to the most complex problems that existed. Right now, what could be more complex than this demon? She barged in, crashing down at the feet of the saint who was seated inside with his eyes closed in deep absorption. The sage looked at the distraught girl and said, "This is a powerful asura, Sambasadhana. No one can do anything to stop him from achieving what he seeks to achieve. He is indestructible. It appears as if Lord Shiva himself has empowered him to destroy everything in this universe. As far as I know, barring the monkey-hero Kesari, no one has the power to destroy him. I have no idea where he could be at this time and how to even convince him to come to your aid."

Suddenly Sambasadhana broke open the hermitage and the two were exposed to his gruesome stare. As he took the next step toward her in an attempt to grab her, he was hit by something so hard that his ears began to ring loudly and he felt torturously deafened by a relentless buzzing. Unable to bear the pain any longer, he collapsed on his knees. He turned around to see a strong vanara standing with his hands on his hips and a grin on his face. "Kesari!" the sage exclaimed. The girl opened her eyes with a smile. Miraculously Kesari had appeared there just in the nick of time.

Sambasadhana, unable to bear the insult, lunged at the standing monkey. Although he was massive, Kesari's power was formidable and matched his. The two of them pounded each other's bodies ferociously. When fists were not enough, they uprooted trees to attack each other. The entire village including all the sages assembled to see this close-quarter fight. Just then something unimaginable happened. Sambasadhana transformed into a giant elephant. He was now ten times his original size and appeared to be ten times stronger. He began demolishing everything within his reach, razing the entire village to the ground. Not one house was left standing. To the horror of the villagers and sages, even Kesari seemed clueless.

But the next moment Kesari did something that surprised all of the onlookers. He shrank himself down to a tiny size, jumped onto the elephant and began pounding him on the forehead with his tightly clenched fist. Although he was tiny, Kesari's blows were powerful enough to hurt Sambasadhana the elephant. Kesari was relentless with his punches, knowing well that the forehead was an elephant's weakest spot. Soon Sambasadhana was bleeding profusely, his blood dripping all over the village as he ran amok shaking his head violently, trying to throw Kesari off. No matter how much he bled, Sambasadhana wasn't dying. Anjana knew that the answer to all problems lies in prayers. She began to pray intensely to Lord Shiva for direction and in her inner voice she heard "Blood!"

She got up and started running toward where Kesari had initially appeared. There she found what she was looking for, his quiver of arrows and his bow. She quickly picked up the bow and an arrow and rushed to the combat area. She stopped at a particular spot and crouched onto her knees. She carefully dipped the tip of the arrow in the puddle of blood that had dripped from the demon's body. Despite being at each other's throats, both Kesari and Sambasadhana noticed the girl's action. But Kesari also caught the fleeting moment of panic in Sambasadhana's eyes.

Pulling himself away from the demon, Kesari ran toward the girl who stood arms outstretched with the bow and arrow. In one swift move, he grabbed the bow from her hand, nocked the arrow, and in an instant released it straight into Sambasadhana's chest. As soon as the arrow hit the demon, he fell dead!

The sages and the villagers jumped up in joy hailing their saviour Kesari. They lifted him on their shoulders and began to dance around. The girl's eyes brimmed with tears—tears of joy and gratitude. The sages sat

Kesari down in front of her. Kesari was just as grateful to her as she was to him. The sages proposed that it was apt that Kesari accept Anjana as his wife. The two stole glances at each other and smiled in agreement. The sages thus blessed the happy couple, saying, "Through this marriage will be born a historic figure that will create a revolution in the world of devotion! His splendour will be so intense that the three worlds will tremble seeing his prowess."

Thus Hanuman was born, blessed with such power even before his birth. *āpana teja samhāro āpai / tinau loka hāka te kāpai*

Hanuman's 'teja' continued even as he was at a ripe old age. A much older Hanuman was once meditating on the shore of the ocean. It was the same ocean that had been the site of many adventures that he had had with Lord Rama. This was not just an ordinary ocean for Hanuman but rather a very important place of worship. Every time he visited this place, he would go on a mental journey back into the past and relive all his adventures. Soon he was totally immersed in his internal ecstasies. He was so immersed that he didn't even feel the touch on his arms. Only when that touch became a nudge did he even feel it. But when that nudge became a shove, he opened his eyes and saw a threatening figure looming over him. Hanuman chose not to react in his meditative mood.

But the dark figure began to provoke Hanuman, demanding a fight. Least bothered, Hanuman waved him off. He had dealt with enough arrogant people in his younger days and couldn't care less for one more. Introducing himself as Shani, the dark figure began to challenge Hanuman for a fight for establishing supremacy. Hanuman straightaway refused, declaring that he had better things to focus on. Shani then went on to tease him harshly. Calling him a foolish monkey, Shani announced that his time was up and his days were up. Kali yuga was his era where Hanuman had no say and no control. Though Hanuman had rescued him from Ravana's clutches in Treta yuga and he was grateful for that, that was old history that had no relevance today. Shani began to push Hanuman with great force.

The next moment something unexpected happened. Shani was suddenly flying in the air, held tightly in the grip of Hanuman's tail. Hanuman took him straight into the ocean and began to bang him hard on all the rocks and stones of the ocean. Badly bruised and swollen all over, Shani was totally dazed. It happened so fast he didn't even have time to react. After the bang, Hanuman asked him if he still wanted to have a fight. Shani was, of course, hurt physically and experiencing great amount of pain but his ego, that was seething for revenge and self-establishment, was in a greater pain.

Shani arrogantly proclaimed that Hanuman maybe stronger physically but he was much stronger mentally. There was no way Hanuman could defeat him in a mental game. If only he entered Hanuman's mind, then he could wreak havoc there till Hanuman submitted. He had been given the authority to influence every human being on earth for seven and half years every twenty-two and half years. Not wanting to continue this discussion, Hanuman told Shani that he wasn't a normal human being and was considered amongst the celestials. But Shani was not ready to agree. He argued that anyone who had lived on the earthly realms was under his jurisdiction. Just to irritate Hanuman a bit more, he added that his favourite targets were old people who were closer to death. That statement really broke the straw. Hanuman was extremely put off by his snobbish interaction.

He asked Shani to demonstrate how he influenced people's minds. Jumping at the chance, Shani immediately leaped into Hanuman's head, giving him an intense headache. Hanuman walked towards a nearby mountain and picked it up placing it on his head. Though the mountain was so huge, Hanuman didn't even feel its weight on his head. But deep inside Hanuman's head Shani could experience the whole weight of the mountain on his back. He suddenly realized that he was in big trouble. The headache hadn't decreased. So Hanuman picked up another mountain and placed it on top of the first one. The pressure on Shani's back grew exponentially and he began to scream aloud. But Hanuman wasn't satisfied with even two mountains stationed on his head. He placed a third one and then a fourth one. When he was about to stack a fifth mountain over his head, Shani broke out, wailing loudly. He begged Hanuman to let him go. Hanuman feigned surprise. Shani began to plead helplessly. He was ready for a compromise now. He promised that he wouldn't stay that long in the body of Hanuman but rather only stay for two and half days instead of seven and half years. Hanuman didn't care for his promises and proceeded to pick up the fifth mountain. Shani became hysterical and declared that he would never ever even think of entering into Hanuman's mind and not only that he would not even trouble anybody who chanted Hanuman's name. He begged for relief from his suffering.

Hanuman dropped the mountains one by one. Finally Shani flew out of Hanuman's head and fell on the ground writhing in great pain. He literally begged Hanuman for some oil to massage every sore limb of his body. Hanuman being a recluse, had no access to oils and other luxuries. He advised him to beg for oil from those people whom he troubles. From that day onwards, everyone who visits the temple of Shani offers a little oil to soothe his pains. Of course, Shani's temples are almost always near Hanuman temples just to commemorate this story and connection. Also to remind Shani of the splendour and valour of Hanuman which is famous all over the world. *āpana teja samhāro āpai / tinau loka hāka te kāpai*

bhūta pishācha nikata nahi āvai।
mahābīra jaba nāma sunāvai॥ 24 ॥

Ghosts and demons dare not come near,
When one chants your name Mahavir. (24)

When offering oblations to the sun one evening, Hanuman heard an intense chanting of mantras from a distance. He completed his worship and followed the sound. What he saw surprised him. Four divine-looking people were worshipping the earth with special mantras. He realized that these were the gods in charge of dharma, artha, kama, and moksha. And that they were invoking mother earth to accept them within her. Why would they do such a thing? Then Hanuman saw that the earth had actually split open and they were about to enter into the earth's womb. Immediately Hanuman knew that this would be a disaster if these four went missing from earth. Without the boundary of these four to regulate human life, only animalistic civilisation could remain. These four were in fact the very source of strength for the demigods. He stopped them just in the nick of time, before they could jump off into the crater. When asked for an explanation, they expressed that there was no point in them staying on the earth planet. They didn't want to be misused by a new demon named Trayambakasura, who had recently acquired great strengths and was systematically taking over all affairs of the universe. They explained to Hanuman that this demon had such a herculean body that he was overshadowing even the demigods in the heaven. When the demigods cannot protect themselves against his atrocities, then who could they rely on?

Trayambakasura was the great-great- grandson of Mahisasura. He was the only person in the universe who had managed to please the holy trinity of Brahma, Vishnu, and Mahesh and received a boon from all three simultaneously. As every demon tries, he also initially tried asking for eternality. But when they flatly refused, he resorted to asking them a boon each. First he asked Lord Brahma for creative abilities like Brahma's. Lord Brahma approved the request. Then he asked Lord Shiva to grant him the boon that he would never be killed by any weapon or carrier of weapons. Lord Shiva granted it. Then he turned to Lord Vishnu, the maintainer of the whole universe. Since Lord Vishnu is the Paramatma within everyone's heart, Trayambakasura asked him for vision to see both the visible and invisible things. Vishnu gave him the ability to see anyone hidden anywhere. Soon Trayambakasura declared war against the gods in the heavens, and these four Purusharthas personified fled. Trayambakasura ordered his minister to capture them and get them back. Unfortunately for him, Hanuman came in between. Using his mace, Hanuman hit the minister and flung him far away. Then Hanuman hid the four Purusharthas in four trees. He hid dharma inside a banyan tree. Artha inside a golden leaf tree. Kama inside a kadamba tree and Moksha inside a peepal tree. Hanuman then called Jambavan to protect these four Purusharthas camping inside the trees, and then left to deal with the Trayambakasura demon.

In the heavens, an interesting type of combat was happening. This was perhaps the most unique war scenario ever in the history of civilization. Trayambakasura, with his creative abilities, had created duplicates of each demigod. Since Lord Brahma had blessed him with his own creative abilities, he was able to replicate an exact clone of each god with the same strength and abilities. The only hitch was that although the duplicates possessed the exact strength as the originals, their intelligence did not quite match up to theirs. Indra's clone was fighting with Indra. Agni's clone was fighting with Agni. There was complete mayhem all around. The original demigods ran to seek shelter of Vishnu, Shiva, and Brahma. But when they reached them, they were shocked to see clones of the three as well.

The beaten-up minister of Trayambakasura returned with a bruised face. He told his master of his inability to capture the four Purusharthas personified due to the presence of a vanara child who had beaten him black and blue and then hidden the Purusharthas. Trayambakasura needed to annihilate the four of them urgently since they were the source of strength of the demigods. Once they were done with, it would be easier to finish off the gods too. Using his Vishnu-given power, Trayambakasura discovered that the four had been stowed away in Aranyavan by Hanuman. When he reached there, Hanuman came and stood between them. Without batting an eyelid, Trayambakasura created a duplicate of Hanuman to fight with him. The only difference was that the duplicate was of a blackish complexion (shyam varna). But he had the same strength.

A fantastic fight began between the two Hanumans creating wild tremors. Trying to bring the matter under control, the three principle deities appeared and explained to the shyam varna Hanuman that although he had been created by an asuric force, he should still behave like the real Hanuman. Though he did not have the intelligence of the real Hanuman, the duplicate one comprehended and readily cooperated. The real Hanuman explained to his clone that since the asuric forces had created him, he had to cease to exist. But at the same time, because he was so cooperative, they would ensure that he is respected by everyone. The real Hanuman then created another clone of himself, which was exactly like the shyam varna Hanuman created by Trayambakasura. Then the two shyam varna Hanumans merged into one and immediately took on a deity form. The three principle gods blessed the shyam varna Hanuman with the boon that he would be worshipped in this form. When souls troubled by ghosts, pisaach, and evil forces worship shyam varna Hanuman, they will immediately be relieved of all such troubles. Thus shyam varna Hanuman continues to reside on earth in a deity form. *bhūta pishācha nikata nahi āvai / mahābīra jaba nāma sunāvai*

Once that was taken care of, Hanuman returned to the demigods who were still in fear of the demon. He requested Surabhi cow to allow the demigods to reside in her body as the demon Trayambakasura was determined to kill them all and would find them from anywhere else they hide. She gracefully agreed and all the demigods took different positions in her body. Finally Hanuman requested Jambavan to get the four Purusharthas there too. Precisely at that time, Trayambakasura reached there and challenged Jambavan. A long fight ensued and ended with Jambavan using the Brahmapasha to tie up the demon. While the demon was struggling to free himself from bondage, Jambavan took the four Purusharthas to the place where Hanuman and Surabhi were waiting. The four of them gratefully entered into the four legs of the cow. Next, Hanuman hid Surabhi in Matanga Rishi's ashram. Yet again, Trayambakasura understood the trick and kidnapped the cow, taking her to Patalaloka. His plan was to perform a Gomedha yagya, which would culminate in the cow being sacrificed and thus killed. But Hanuman made an appearance just before the sacrifice was completed and created a whirlwind effect, blowing away everything and destroying the whole sacrificial arena. Trayambakasura was livid at Hanuman and rushed to kill him. But before he could fight with Hanuman, Surabhi came in between them. Suddenly it dawned on Hanuman that the only way this demon would die was through Surabhi, without any weapons. No matter how much anyone else tried, it would not work. Surabhi being innocent and weapon-less was the ideal candidate to kill him. Using her horns, which were not weapons technically, the cow continuously attacked the demon till his life ebbed away.

The demigods then appeared out of Surabhi and declared that since she protected them like a mother, she would eternally be worshipped as a mother all over the world. They also blessed Hanuman profusely for not giving up till the end and thus saving the world. Neither evil spirits nor demons could harm any devotee of Hanuman.

nāsai roga harai saba pīrā।
japata nirantara hanumata bīrā॥ 25 ॥

Diseases are destroyed and pains disappear,
By constantly chanting the name
of brave Hanuman. (25)

Bodily functions are controlled by the five winds or vayu.
These are prana, apana, vyana, samana, and udana. They
take care of the different automatic functions of the body
like breathing, digestion, excretion and so on, which we
are not aware of. There is a figure of Hanuman with
five heads, Panchmukhi Hanuman, which corresponds
to these five winds. Thus it is said that Hanuman is in
charge of our involuntary functions and devotion to him
will give us health.

This time, Ravana had come up with a foolproof plan.
He had not sent the usual kind of demon who depended
on physical strength alone. Neither was it a demon who
looked like a demon. Ravana's evil mind had come up

with a unique scheme. He had deployed Panchphan, a five-hooded snake, to manipulate the waters of the rivers in Sumeru. He was not to poison the rivers but to tamper with them in such a way that those who drank the water, their minds become weak and they get hypnotized by Ravana. Once hypnotized, Ravana would have full control over everyone. Becoming puppets in his hand. Rubbing his hands in glee, Ravana began to gloat over how he would exact revenge on the powerful vanara clan.

However, King Kesari realized that their water was being contaminated and they started digging wells to find an alternative source of water. Hanuman quickened the process by using his tail as a drilling machine and soon hundreds of wells sprouted all over their kingdom, nullifying Ravana's well-laid plan.

But Hanuman was not satisfied by simply digging wells. He ran after Panchphan to punish him for his wrongdoing. But Panchphan escaped to live another day. He sneaked in again the following night and bit Kesari. He was too frightened of Hanuman so he targeted his father. This was too much for Hanuman to bear. He caught hold of the wicked snake in anger and pulled out the precious gems from the top of his hood. The gems on a snake's hood are considered his crowning glory, his pride. Breaking them is breaking that pride. Hanuman proceeded to do exactly that.

Controlling the snake with his power, Hanuman ripped off the gems. His hand was on the fifth one when someone stopped him. He turned to see who it was, with his grip firmly on Panchphan. Who else but a mother would protect a son, however wicked he may be. Panchphan would have died if his fifth gem were dislodged. But his mother appeared on time. "O' Hanuman, I beg of you to release my son. I give you my word that if you let him go, he will never trouble any living being ever. He will turn over a new leaf. I have heard your mighty power comes from your large heart, please show compassion to my son."

Hanuman, although he looked dangerous in anger, could be as gentle as a lamb too. Nor would he disobey a mother. He loosened his grip and the fearful snake slithered out to save his life. He had heard his mother's promise and resolved to fulfil her words. He fell at Hanuman's feet asking for forgiveness. Hanuman forgave easily and Panchphan became a devotee of Hanuman.

Now Panchphan was afraid that what he had done would yield disastrous consequences. He revealed, "I have done an abominable act by biting your father and your kith and kin. If we don't get the cure for them within two days, they will die." And he hung his head in shame. Feeling remorseful, he shared what could revive the dying. "We can ask Shukracharaya, the guru of all demons, to give his Sanjivani mantra which has curative powers to bring everyone back to life."

Since Panchphan had been a demon himself and knew Shukracharaya intimately, he volunteered to go to him and make a request. But he was in for a disappointment. Demons did not believe in going out of the way to help others. But he did suggest another option. Panchphan returned and told Hanuman, "To save your clan, we need to procure a herb called Vaishali karna pushpa which only grows on an island called Prabal Dvip. Not only the path to this island is dangerous, it is also accessible only to a select few. One who satisfies three criteria—of being an innocent child, a brahmachari, and a Trideva, only he can enter Prabal Dvip, a hundred yojans away in the south." He also warned that the red coloured flowers there were guarded by a ferocious brahmarakshasa. No ordinary mortal was a match for this monster. Even before Panchphan could complete the warnings, Hanuman had leapt into the air. He did not care for the obstacles on the way when he was on a mission.

Not knowing the exact location of the island, he stopped on the way for directions. Unfortunately for him, it was Mayasura who came and guided him under a disguise. Not wanting him to succeed, Mayasura sent him on a wild goose chase. After going round and round for many hours, Hanuman finally reached his destination. As expected, the island was guarded by a brahmarakshasa. The brahmarakshasa was famous for swallowing everything he saw. In fact, he was on a mission of finding a cure by swallowing everything. He had been a rishi in another birth and been cursed to become a brahmarakshasa. The curse would only nullify when a divine energy entered his mouth. Not knowing what that divine energy was, he swallowed, whatever came his way, hungrily. And that is why, Hanuman too entered his mouth. Hanuman, being that divine energy, killed the demon and released him from the curse. The rishi was so thankful to be liberated from the curse that he offered the rare flowers to Hanuman, which Hanuman accepted gratefully and flew back to his own territory. He administered the flower remedy in the mouth of his father and every sickly monkey and soon, all of them stirred and sat up as if getting up from sleep. The other monkeys cheered for Hanuman because Hanuman had all the solutions for every ailment and could revive even the dying. *nāsai roga harai saba pīrā*

Suryadeva was not sure if he should speak his mind. It was time for Hanuman to give guru dakshina to his guru and Suryadeva was choking with emotions. He was exhilarated that his brilliant student had mastered the entire gamut of knowledge in a record-breaking time. Simultaneously, he felt pained at the thought of his loving student leaving his school. To top that, Hanuman wanted to give guru dakshina. Suryadeva had two pressing problems and Hanuman could solve both of them. Should he open his heart? Or should he suffer in silence? Finally he decided to speak.

"My dear Hanuman. I want you to do things for me. One is to take care of my son Sugriva and save him from Vali's wrath. And second, which is more difficult, is to bring back my son Shani to me. Shani is an angry young man full of pride. But please convince him to come back," said an emotionally distressed Suryadeva.

Hanuman, of course, was eager to fulfil his duty to his guru. He immediately departed to bring back Shani. Sugriva, he could take care of when back on earth.

On the way to Shani's abode, Hanuman bumped into planet Mangal, who tried to obstruct his path. Mangal is the God of combat, more specifically, wrestling. Yet, Hanuman overpowered Mangal easily and tucked him under his arm to continue his search for Shani. When he neared the domain of Shani, he was stopped by Tamra

Mai, the guard. She tried to bribe him into not entering by offering him unlimited wealth. Hanuman naturally refused her offer and removed her from his path. He meted out the same treatment to the next obstacle Ratna Mai. Then he encountered Swarna Mai, popularly known as Saadhe saati. He subdued her also and finally reached the innermost region of Shani. Shani, by now, was fuming and fretting because all his expertise had failed in stopping Hanuman. He threatened to burn down Hanuman with his glance. Hanuman kept his cool and requested Shani to return with him, but when Shani attacked him on his head, Hanuman had no option but to fight back. Very soon, Shani was overpowered by Hanuman. Now that he was helpless, Shani asked for forgiveness and agreed to return and even ask for forgiveness from his father. He declared that on worshipping Hanuman every Saturday, his devotees would not feel the negative effect of Shani. Mangal too bestowed a similar benediction. Those who worshipped Hanuman on Tuesdays would escape the destructive impact of Mangal.

Suryadeva was overjoyed to have his son back and actually begging forgiveness from him. Shani, feeling emotional, showered more blessings on Hanuman for being instrumental in the reunion. He promised that he would stay clear from the path of all those who take the path of devotion and truthfulness by chanting the name of Hanuman. Never would he trouble those who believed in the power of Hanuman's name. *japata nirantara hanumata bīrā*

Lanka was burning, with the fire spreading wildly and the winds blowing strongly but did Ravana understand? Rama had sent His best doctor with the best medicine to cure him but if the patient refused to take medicine then how would he get cured? Here was a patient with a serious disease called lust, but he couldn't get cured with any ordinary medicine, he needed a special treatment . . . comprising of gold, silver, pearl, and other kinds of ashes. Lanka was full of precious metals and stones; Rama sent a clue to Hanuman to burn all that and use the ash. Hanuman did exactly that. But Ravana did not consider himself sick. He did not think he needed treatment, so he did not take the medicine, did not listen to the doctor; instead he laughed at the doctor. Thus Ravana was incurable.

sankata te hanumāna chhudāvai।
mana krama bachana dhyāna jo lāvai॥ 26 ॥

Hanuman removes all hardships
For those who meditate on him in thoughts,
words or deeds. (26)

Hanuman is supposed to be pratyaksha devata, or the most efficient living deity of the present age of Kali, since he is ever ready and ever eager to help his devotees out of trouble. He alone is said to be capable of bestowing all the four aims of life (dharma, artha, kama, and moksha) and for those who desire, he also gives the fifth fruit, i.e. bhakti.

Sambhasadan, the demon, had been killed by Kesari. His fellow demons were still mourning his death. Without him, they were a defeated lot. Their energies had seeped out and so had their motivation—like orphans with no one to care for them.

Meanwhile, Anjana was angry with little Hanuman

for all the mischief that he always did. All the sages had been complaining to her about how he disrupted their meditation. How he interrupted their rituals. How he played pranks on them. Unable to control the little prankster, Anjana decided to tie up Hanuman physically so he wouldn't go anywhere. There was no other way this bundle of energy could be restrained. Thus, Anjana tied him up using iron shackles. Satisfied that Hanuman was now restrained, she relaxed and went back to her chores.

At the other end of the jungle, demonic followers of Sambhasadan were in for a shock of their lives when they saw him alive, walking towards them. They rubbed their eyes, unable to believe what they were seeing. Some demons fled, thinking it was a ghost. However, the figure turned out to be not Sambhasadan but Kumbhasadan, his brother.

"Where is Sambhasadan?" he thundered at the assembled demons.

"Oh! Have you not heard?" they wailed. "Your brother Sambhasadan is dead. Killed mercilessly by the vanara king Kesari."

Kumbhasadan staggered and nearly fainted, roaring with pain on hearing the news. How could his brother be dead? "I will avenge my brother's death!" he avowed.

Now all the demons came back to life. They were fully inspired to do what they did best. Fight! Flushed with excitement, they began to make a plan to eliminate Kesari.

Hanuman, who was all tied up, could perceive that evil forces were plotting against his innocent father. He had to do something to stop it. He broke open his shackles and in one leap crossed the vast jungle to land on Kumbhasadan. Although he was a baby monkey, small in size, he could be really heavy in weight. Hanuman's landing imbalanced Kumbhasadan and he fell flat on the ground. Hanuman simply did not allow him to get up. The other demons came to lift him but he flung them far away with one flick of his finger. Soon the entire area was clear of all demons and Kumbhasadan was left alone. Then Hanuman lifted him with one hand and punched him hard with the other. That was the end of Kumbhasadan. He dropped dead like a lifeless doll. There was no danger for Kesari now. *sankata te hanumāna chhudāvai*

Guhasura was sleeping peacefully in the cave. No one dared to disturb him because if he woke up, they were dead. This was one cave everyone was scared of entering, including the vanara friends of Hanuman. They never ventured to play out there. One day when

Hanuman was playing with them, he asked them why they stayed away from the big cave that seemed like an inviting place to play to their heart's content.

"We can't go there," they all shouted in panic, "because Guhasura is sleeping there!"

Hanuman looked at them blankly, unsure of who Guhasura was.

"Guhasura is a demon who sleeps for six months. And when he wakes up he breathes so hard that all the surrounding insects get pulled towards him and he gobbles them all. So if he wakes up and we also get pulled by his breathing then we're dead!" his friends explained. "From last time's experience, we know he ate up many of our friends."

But nothing could stop the fearless Hanuman from playing in that cave. "Come with me and I will see what Guhasura can do."

All his friends followed him inside. It was pitch dark. Slowly their eyes adjusted to the darkness. Guhasura lay like a big truck there, snoring away joyfully. Hanuman devised a new game of jumping over Guhasura to see who could jump the farthest. One by one the playful vanaras jumped over him, giggling and laughing. Playing with Hanuman was so exciting. Some vanaras even fell on Guhasura. His huge abdomen made for a soft landing and then they would roll down on the ground and stand. It was good fun. Guhasura seemed unconscious, undisturbed by their play. The vanaras got bolder with every minute and some started jumping on him. Soon not one or two but the entire gang was playing on top of him.

Suddenly Guhasura stirred. He was coming back to consciousness. Oh, what now? The monkeys panicked. It was too late to escape. They looked helplessly at Hanuman who was keenly observing Guhasura. As soon as Guhasura woke up, his breath would be fatal for all. Should he allow him to wake up? Hanuman wondered. Or should he kill him in sleep, before he took a single breath? Deciding on the latter, Hanuman jumped on Guhasura. Before Guhasura could react, he jumped again. And again. Guhasura had no chance of escaping. Traumatised by Hanuman's weight, his body started bleeding internally and slowly, he bled to death. All the monkeys were now dancing ecstatically, without any fear of the dangerous enemy. They could play in the cave without any cares. Hanuman had come to their rescue once again. *sankata te hanumāna chhudāvai*

"Call the saint to court immediately," ordered the Mughal king. He was eager to meet the saint Tulsidas whose name and fame had reached his ears. Every person in his kingdom was queuing up to meet him and take his blessings. The king wanted to see what was so extraordinary about him.

When Tulsidas entered the court, the king was shocked. He was shocked to see how every person in his court stood up on seeing the saint. How could a mere mortal command so much respect? More than a king? Envy stirred the king's heart and he felt his chest burning. Meanwhile, the saint was indifferent to all that was going on. Turning beads on his fingers, he was immersed in chanting the holy name. "Rama . . . Rama . . . Rama . . ."

Without showing any respect, the king ordered the saint, "I have heard that you have mystical powers. Show me what you can do. Let me see what the truth behind your fame is."

The king crossed his arms and sat back on his throne, expecting to see some entertainment program. But he was in for some disappointment. Tulsidas replied, "I have no magical powers. I only know how to chant Rama's name which has the power of purifying hearts. That's the only magic I know and believe in. The holy name is not chanted to show off or to acquire name and fame. Neither am I looking for any instant publicity."

The king was taken aback by the saint's answer. He

felt humiliated in front of the entire court. "Throw him into the dungeon!" he barked at his guards, swallowing the insult.

The guards jumped into action and caught the saint. Without any fear, the saint folded his hands and started chanting Hanuman's names. Then he sang out a prayer to Lord Hanuman; the intensity and purity of his prayers was both stunning and soothing. Everyone present there had a supremely spiritual experience hearing his divine voice.

Suddenly the atmosphere was disturbed by shattering of glass. Not just glass, but everything in the court seemed to be shattering. Within moments, an army of monkeys had entered the guarded premises, breaking everything they could lay their hands on. Total chaos prevailed. They plundered the chairs, tore down the curtains and even pulled away the weapons and beards of soldiers. The king sat dumbstruck. He had no idea what had happened and how to handle the catastrophe. He trembled at the scene unfolding in front of his eyes. Then he noticed the saint. He was calm and composed, still standing there with his eyes closed. Unbelievably, the monkeys had not touched him. In fact, a few monkeys had formed a protective circle around him, sitting at his feet.

Now the king realized how he could save himself.

He climbed down his throne and ran to him, falling at his feet.

"Save me, O' saint," he begged with tears flowing down his cheeks, "save me from these dangerous monkeys."

When the king pleaded again and again, Tulsidas opened his eyes. As soon as he stopped chanting, the monkeys quietened down and walked away. Soon the courtroom was empty. The monkeys had gone and so had the king's pride and arrogance. What remained was the saint, untouched by any harm.

When one remembers Hanuman sincerely, chants his names, meditates on him, Hanuman does everything to protect his devotee. *sankata te hanumāna chhudāvai / mana krama bachana dhyāna jo lāvai*

saba para rāma tapasvī rājā।
tina ke kāja sakala tuma sājā॥ 27 ॥

Rama, a renunciant king reigning over all,
And it's you who carries out His every task. (27)

Everyone in Ayodhya loved Rama infinitely and waited
eagerly to serve Him. *saba para rāma tapasvī rājā*. But
Hanuman was much more eager than all of the others put
together to serve Rama. So much so that he practically
usurped everyone's seva and did it all himself.
tina ke kāja sakala tuma sājā. Thoroughly disgruntled
with Hanuman, everyone decided to block him from
doing any seva. Even Sita and Bharata had agreed to
this proposal of keeping Hanuman out of the palace.
They were not envious of Hanuman but rather hungry
for rendering some service. Out of desperation, first they
sent him on a mission out of Ayodhya for a week. In his
absence, they drew up a list of all the services required
for Rama. They painstakingly wrote each and every
small service that was needed, making sure nothing,
absolutely nothing, was left out. Next, they assigned
all the sevas amongst themselves, leaving nothing for

Hanuman. Now all they needed was Rama's approval to implement it. Would he give his approval? Considering that Hanuman was very dear to him. They could only wait and watch.

Next day Sita presented the list to Rama to complete the formality. Everyone waited with bated breath, anxious about the outcome. Would Rama cooperate? Would Rama ever deny Sita's request? And to their joy and relief, Rama looked at the list, smiled and gave his nod. It was as simple as that. There was euphoria all around which extended into celebration. Finally, they would get to serve Rama without being overshadowed by Hanuman.

When Hanuman returned, he saw the celebratory mood and big smiles everywhere. He was happy to see the mood of joy. But his greatest joy was in serving Rama. Immediately he got into action and ran to do some service. But every place he went to render some service, he was stopped and shown the list of duties. Finally irritated with the list in everyone's hand, he decided to inspect it carefully. He scrolled down the list, dismayed at his name missing from each and every seva. He was further distressed to see Rama's royal seal on the list, indicating it had Rama's approval. He barged into the courtroom for more answers. Rama calmly advised him to see if there was any seva that was left out, then he could surely take that up. Hanuman thought and thought, scratching his head, if he could do something that was not already taken up. Meanwhile, everyone was enjoying the scene of successfully keeping Hanuman out of every seva.

Not surprisingly, Hanuman's clever mind came up with a unique seva. He claimed that there was one seva not included in the list. The conspirers were shocked. What had they missed out? He revealed they had missed the seva of snapping. He would snap his fingers every time the Lord yawned. There was no one assigned to this very important seva. When Rama nodded in acceptance of his proposal, everyone was disappointed.

Happy to be back near Rama, Hanuman performed his task sincerely all day. Night came and he followed Rama to his private chambers, anticipating being with him all night, just in case he yawned.

Now Sita was not at all happy with this intrusion in her private space. She asked Hanuman to leave the room. But Hanuman asked what if Rama yawned at night? He had Rama's permission to carry out the seva and no one could stop him. Sita was speechless. Their plan had backfired. Now Hanuman was stuck to Rama not only all day but also all night. She kept silent, not knowing how to react. After a few hours, when Hanuman was still on active duty, Sita asked him to leave, using a very rude tone of voice. Hanuman did not want to create trouble so he left against his wishes. But how could Hanuman give up his seva to his master? He went on the roof above and continued to snap his fingers, unwilling to stop serving. Just in case Rama yawned below, at least he would be doing his service, and if not from close then at least from afar. He went into a trance, chanting names and snapping his fingers to counteract all the possible yawns.

Meanwhile, in the room below Hanuman, a lot of drama was going on. Rama's jaws had gone into a spasm because of continuously yawning. He just could not stop yawning. How could He, when His devotee had not stopped snapping his fingers? When a true devotee serves Him, He has to respond. One after the other the yawns kept coming. His eyes began to water. His face became distorted. Sita was horrified as to what had happened to Rama. Scared to death, she called her mother-in-law. Soon the entire family had gathered around Rama, trying to stop his spasms. But there was little they could do. Someone then called sage Vashishtha as the situation was getting out of hand.

Sage Vashishtha arrived and assessed the scene. "Where is Ramadoot?" he enquired at once. Sita humbly admitted that she had asked him to vacate the room. Maybe she had offended him, questioning his right to serve Rama.

Everyone now began searching for Hanuman. The royal staff scanned the entire palace but Hanuman was untraceable. Finally sage Vashishtha heard some strange sounds coming from above. They all scrambled up on the roof and found Hanuman in a trance, chanting and snapping his fingers. Vashishtha shook him to break his meditation and Hanuman came out of his snapping spree. He looked at all of them, embarrassed to be surrounded by so many people. As soon as he stopped snapping, Rama miraculously stopped yawning. Relieved that the agony had ended, Rama jokingly asked them to assign some other seva to Hanuman. There was no need for Hanuman to worry now. His bond with Rama was unshakeable. His zeal for seva was unmatched. He was unanimously assigned all the sevas he wanted to do without any restrictions! Though everyone loved to serve Rama and Rama ruled over everyone *saba para rāma tapasvī rājā* but in comparison to Hanuman, who would carry out every service to Lord Rama, *tina ke kāja sakala tuma sājā,* no one could match his eagerness and zeal to serve.

Nal and Neel had spanned the ocean with a bridge that was a hundred leagues long and ten leagues wide. As the monkey army eagerly tried to reach Lanka using the bridge, Ravana hurled two missiles and destroyed the two ends of it, leaving them stranded in the middle of the ocean. They could neither reach Lanka nor return. Hanuman came up with an excellent idea. Increasing his size he stretched himself flat holding the edge of Lanka with his hands and the end of the bridge with his legs. The entire army scrambled over his back to reach the golden Lanka. In this way, he never allowed any task of Rama's to be left incomplete or unsuccessful. *tina ke kāja sakala tuma sājā*

aura manoratha jo koī lāvai।
sohi amita jīvana phala pāvai॥ 28 ॥

And when approached with heartfelt desires
You fulfil them with unlimited nectar like fruits. (28)

When a devotee asked Hanuman, "Should we have desires or should we be desire-less?" Hanuman gave a pleasant answer. He said, "I don't like anyone asking anything from my Lord Rama. So I wish that no one should ask anything from Lord Rama." So the devotee asked again, "Does that mean we should not have any desires?"

Hanuman replied, "No, no! Please have desires. Because I take the responsibility to fulfil every desire. It is my vow to fulfil a devotee's desire so that my master Rama need not be hassled about it."

Hanuman was himself detachment personified. A renunciant in all aspects. But he helped others like Sugriva and Vibhishan in fulfilling their wishes. ***aura manoratha jo koī lāvai / sohi amita jīvana phala pāvai***

Hanuman's search for Sita had reached its culmination. Sitting under the Ashoka tree was Mother Sita herself. Draped scarcely in a single cloth, she looked emaciated. Probably due to months of fasting. Her eyes revealed a trail of continuous tears. She appeared an epitome of divinity.

He shuddered when he glanced upon those guarding her. They were one-eyed, vicious looking demonesses. Their very appearance was enough to plunge the sturdiest of hearts into a state of horror and depression. And they were no less than 700 of them. Hanuman understood Ravana's trick. By surrounding Sita with such monsters who abused her constantly, he was playing a psychological game of weakening her determination. Although Sita had resisted a nervous breakdown till now, she could not hold off anymore. After Ravana's last visit, which Hanuman had been a witness to, Sita decided it was not worth living. If Rama had not come till now, He may not be coming at all. She had been chanting Rama's holy name since many months now but there was no sign of Rama rescuing her from the evil Ravana.

Hanuman wondered how best to approach Sita so that she did not doubt his words and intentions. The presence of security demonesses also hampered him in contacting Mother Sita. But what he saw next took his breath away. Her long hair was tied to a branch and looped around her neck. It did not need a genius to figure out what she was about to do. Before Sita could take another step, Hanuman began what he knew best. Narrating Rama katha in a dialect from Ayodhya. That was the only language which would not create panic in Sita. Beginning from birth, he described Lord Rama's efforts in searching for Sita and how he was sent there with a message from her dear Rama.

His words had the desired effect on her and she relaxed. She unlooped her hair and sat under the tree, looking up to find the speaker. Hanuman took a miniature form and landed in front of her. Now she was completely at ease with a complete stranger knowing that he was an intimate associate of Rama. They chatted with each other for a long time, exchanging all the facts that had brought them together. Sita was further overwhelmed and tears gushed from her eyes when Hanuman produced the ring given to him by Rama for Sita. Hanuman too was so moved that he immediately offered to take her out of Lanka on his back.

Sita said to him, "Son, you have managed to fly across the ocean to reach me which is by no means an easy task. So surely you are powerful and intelligent. But I have a doubt. I am confused. What is your real size?"

Hanuman was quick to realize that because he had appeared in a very small form in front of her, Sita could not imagine how he could take her back. It was a valid question from her. At the same time, he was thrilled being addressed as 'son'. It made him very joyful.

He said, "I am very small, mother. But by Lord Rama's grace, I can become very big when the need arises. God's power is so great that I can also grow big by taking his shelter. But my real size is small, mother," with all the innocence of a child.

Sita was touched by Hanuman's profound answer. He had appeared like a rainbow in the skies of her gloomy mind, adding colour to all her forlorn desires of escaping Lanka and uniting with Rama. As long as Hanuman was there, he would see to it that her wellbeing was taken care of. *aura manoratha jo koī lāvai*

It was the last day of Rama's exile. It was the day Bharat expected Rama to reach Ayodhya. If Rama failed to keep his word, it would not just be the last day of his exile but the last day of Bharat's life as well. He could not wait a minute longer than the fourteen years. And Rama very well knew the consequence of any delay. Just a few more minutes were left for the day to end and there was no sight of Rama. Bharat was prepared to die. It was inevitable. There was no stopping him now.

His brother Shatrughana, his ministers, citizens of Ayodhya were all present around him. A heavy cloud of darkness hung in the air and no one knew how to convince Bharat to change his decision. He had made up his mind to jump into the pyre of fire at the end of the day. Unknown to all, help was nearby. Hanuman. He sat on a tree above, wondering what the right step would be to stop Bharat. He had been sent by Rama to inform Bharat of his arrival. But before he could do that, Bharat was already planning to jump in to the pyre.

Hanuman recollected that just a few weeks back he was in the middle of a similar situation. He was on a tree and Mother Sita had been contemplating suicide. This time it was Bharat. Whenever he found himself staring at a dead-end, Hanuman resorted to only one solution. It had always worked. It had worked when all the monkeys were dejected on the shore of the ocean. It had worked in Lanka for Sita. And he would use the same strategy again today. Rama katha. When he narrated Rama katha to the monkeys, Sampatti had come to their rescue. When he narrated Rama katha to Sita, she had been inspired to live. It would not let him down today either.

He began his narration in his sweetest voice, a voice that could melt even stones. He began from the beginning of Rama lila to the point where Rama reached Bhardwaj muni's ashram that was on the way to Ayodhya. When Bharat heard the message that Rama was on the way, he quickly dropped the idea of ending his life. He was eager to unite with his venerable brother again.

Once again Hanuman had saved the day by fulfilling Bharat's wish with his message. From Rama. He had fulfilled Sita's wish by giving her hope of Rama's arrival to rescue her. Whenever any wish needed to be fulfilled, Hanuman was always there on the horizon, not only to fulfil the wish but to fulfil it as quickly as possible. *sohi amita jīvana phala pāvai*

chāro juga para tāpa tumhārā।
hai parasiddha jagata ujiyyārā॥ 29 ॥

Your glory spreads in all four yugas,
Your fame radiates across the universe. (29)

There are seven chiranjivis, granted the boon to live forever: Ashwathhama, Vyas, Kripacharya, Markandeya, Bali, Vibhishan, and Hanuman. Their divine attainments have made them immortal unlike others who are destined to die. Hanuman is one of the greatest personalities in all the four yugas and anyone taking his refuge, is freed from all troubles. Immortality has two forms—of body and of name. Hanuman has immortality of body as well as of name, active to carry out the job allotted by his Lord.

At one point in his life, Jambavan began to experience a weird type of dream that kept repeating every single night. The dream was about a group of four people shooting arrows at him and eventually stabbing him to death. At this point in his life, Jambavan was really old. He had been alive for more than a yuga now. He was born at the beginning of Satya yuga and it was already a long way into the Treta yuga now. Being the son of Brahma and having lived through such a long life span, Jambavan was the most experienced person on the earth. In fact, he had been a witness to so many events, like the incarnations of the Supreme Lord as Vamana avatar, Parashuram avatar and now was about to be a part of Rama avatar. While awaiting the beginning of Rama lila, he was already a part of Hanuman lila. Living in Kishkinda, Jambavan considered Kesari and Anjana to be like his own children, and Hanuman to be like his grandchild.

When Jambavan began getting the weird disturbing dreams, he lost himself in thoughts. Hanuman guessed that something serious was troubling Jambavan. Jambavan had been seriously praying to his father Brahma, seeking direction and clarity from the creator of the world. His father's gentle voice revealed to him that it was time to wind up his life on earthly realms in this body and move on to another destination where yet another adventure awaited him. Brahma explained that his end would come while desperately trying to save an innocent girl who was a great devotee of Lord Vishnu. Now that Jambavan knew all the details, he felt less anxious. It was a noble way to die!

Believing his father's words, Jambavan mentally prepared himself for the inevitable. Leaving behind a message for Anjana, Kesari, and Hanuman, he quietly departed in the middle of the night. When Hanuman received the message of Jambavan's departure, he was terribly shaken up. He refused to accept that Jambavan was going to die soon. He decided to defy even death itself to bring Jambavan back to Kishkinda. Taking permission from his parents, Hanuman departed to look out for Jambavan.

Meanwhile, Jambavan had ventured far into the forest where Kaal purush appeared to him in the form of a sage. Kaal purush is the time factor that decides everyone's destiny. He is only visible in the beginning and at the end of one's life. When he appears he either gives life or takes life. Disguised as a sage, Kaal purush invited Jambavan to his ashram where he claimed that a young girl needed his help. Jambavan immediately understood that it was a call of destiny, directing him towards his death. He followed him silently, deeper into the forest.

After an intense search, Hanuman reached the place where Jambavan had met the sage. When Hanuman studied the footprints, he was in for a shock. The footprints of Jambavan went in one direction and right next to him he saw another print embedded on the ground! Print of a snake slithering right next to him. Hanuman clearly knew what that meant. Print of a serpent slithering parallelly implied imminent death. This scary thought impelled Hanuman to speed up and catch up with Jambavan. Though Kaal purush tried his best to prevent Hanuman from meeting Jambavan, he wasn't successful in his attempts. Hanuman began to explain to Jambavan that it was important for him to stay back in this world as Rama was about to make his way to Kishkinda and he had a very important role in Rama lila. Especially with the experience that he had, surely his assistance would be crucial for the new incarnation of the Lord. On Hanuman's insistence, Jambavan actually contemplated returning but Kaal purush, disguised as a sage requested him to at least visit his ashram. Jambavan agreed and together the three of them reached the ashram.

Kaal purush suggested that Jambavan take a bath in the lake close by so that he felt fresh. In spite of Hanuman warning him, Jambavan left to go to the lakeside. As soon as he reached there, he heard a girl crying out for help. He ran towards the direction of the voice and saw three men, armed with weapons, chasing a traumatized young girl. The girl was dressed like an ascetic. When she saw Jambavan, she ran towards him and begged him to save her. She informed him that she had deeply desired to only have Lord Vishnu as her husband, but these men were forcing her to marry a mortal. Jambavan assured her of his protection and turned around to face the armed men. When he tried to reason with the men, they were hardly interested in a discussion. Instead, they began shooting arrows at him and injured him severely. Jambavan was startled to realize that this was the exact scene he had seen in his dreams repeatedly. He immediately called Hanuman for help. Jambavan mentally prepared himself for the inevitable and focused his mind on the Supreme Lord.

When Hanuman reached the scene, he thrashed the men and drove them away; and fell on his knees holding the bleeding Jambavan. Precisely at that time, Yamaraj arrived on his buffalo to take away the soul of Jambavan to his next destination. Recognizing the expansion of Lord Shiva, Yamaraj offered his respects to Hanuman. When Hanuman refused to let go of Jambavan, Yamaraj was disturbed. How could anyone change the will of destiny? Not wanting to upset Hanuman and yet wanting to follow his call of duty, Yamaraj put a condition. He briefed Hanuman that he had to cross the eight gross layers and three subtle layers of the material world in order to reach Yamaloka. Within that time frame, if Hanuman could manage to convince Lord Brahma to let Jambavan live, then he would abide by that. If he failed, then Hanuman would have to just give up and accept the will of providence. Hanuman agreed to that condition and immediately prepared to leave for Brahmaloka. He requested the girl whose life Jambavan had saved, to take care of his body while he completed his mission. The girl, feeling guilty, promised to not move an inch from there till Jambavan was revived. She felt so responsible for all that had happened that she wanted to do something at least to set things right for him.

Hanuman travelled at the speed of wind and reached Brahmaloka, begging Lord Brahma to allow Jambavan to live. Lord Brahma flatly denied since he had no rights to change the laws of nature. Hanuman pleaded with every god for help but none could. After all his efforts, with no one responding, Hanuman got furious. His Rudra form took over and he began to dance in great anger. The tandava dance that is done by Lord Shiva during the time of annihilation could be seen at that time. Everyone including the gods trembled in fear. Lord Vishnu personally intervened, pacified Hanuman and explained to Lord Brahma that sometimes the laws of nature have to be tweaked to accommodate some important exceptions that are beneficial for the betterment of society and that ensure greater good. With that grant by Lord Vishnu, Lord Brahma ordered Yamaraj to return Jambavan.

Yamaraj released Jambavan's soul and he got his life back. Hanuman embraced Jambavan in great joy. Lord Vishnu explained to Jambavan how Hanuman was so eager for his revival that they had to change the laws of the world to fulfil his desire. Of course, Lord Vishnu had a special relationship with Jambavan from the previous yuga. Lord Vishnu blessed that Jambavan would be alive for all four yugas and would participate in the pastimes of the Lord in each of the yugas. He would wind up his time on earth after helping Kalki annihilate the universe. Jambavan expressed his gratitude in being allowed to serve in the Supreme Lord's eternal pastimes. Lord Vishnu also blessed the young girl desirous of marrying him, that she would get fulfilment of that desire in Dwapar yuga; when she would be born as Jambavati, the daughter of Jambavan. She was very happy to know that she would be reborn as the daughter of Jambavan who had protected her like a father. Once all the gods vanished, Jambavan expressed his gratitude to Hanuman for saving his life and allowing him few more yugas of service to the Lord. Jambavan glorified Hanuman's greatness to influence the world across yugas. The happy duo returned to Kishkinda and waited in great anticipation for Rama lila to begin. *chāro juga para tāpa tumhārā / hai parasiddha jagata ujiyyārā*

sādhu santa ke tuma rakhavāre।
asura nikandana rāma dulāre॥ 30 ॥

You protect the ascetics and saintly people
You destroy demons and are dear to Rama. (30)

From the time Hanuman was a small baby, he had a special affinity and fascination for saints and rishis. He loved their compassionate faces and their busy activities. That's why he always hung around them and in all his innocence, even troubled them by pulling their beards and jumping on their laps in the middle of yagyas. Even when the sadhus complained to mother Anjana about his disruptive behaviour, she never stopped Hanuman from going there because she wanted him to have as much saintly association as possible. Later on, when he realized his powers, he never lost any opportunity to protect them.

When it came to demons, Hanuman was as good as their death call. In fact after Hanuman freed Yamaraj from the bondage of Ravana in Lanka, he gave him a boon. He said to Hanuman, "During the battle, whenever you look at any demon, I will straightaway take away his life."

Sage Angirasa belonged to a group of sages called Saptarishis, the most exalted rishis in the world. So when he experienced his body burning like fire, he had no idea why. He had never experienced anything this before. His eyes were blazing. His head was boiling like hot water. His limbs were trembling with intense heat. His full body was burning like hot charcoal. Normally, ordinary illnesses and sufferings had no effect on him. His powerful mind could safeguard his body from any physical attack. But this was a totally different experience.

Unable to solve the mystery, he approached Mother Lakshmi for advice. Here's what she said, "Sage Angirasa, the reason your body is burning is because of the sin you have committed. And that is why you are suffering."

"The sage was aghast to hear this from the goddess. He was a Brahmarishi. Committing a sin was impossible, he thought. What sin have I committed?" he asked her.

"Your sin is," the goddess said, revealing the mystery to him, "that you have done injustice to Shukracharya and been partial to your own son Brihaspati."

Angirasa had recently appointed his son Brihaspati as the guru of the demigods. Although Shukra was coveting that post for himself, Sage Angirasa thought otherwise. When Brihaspati was declared the guru, Shukracharya vowed to take revenge. He appointed himself as the guru of the demons. The demons and the demigods were always engaged in battle and Shukra was determined to extract revenge by helping the demons win over the gods.

"Because you favoured your son, it went against you," explained Goddess Lakshmi.

Sage Angirasa was devastated. He asked the goddess for a solution to stop the burning. The goddess said, "Take shelter of Hanuman. Hear from him stories of ashta siddhis. Hearing it will gradually reduce your sin and soon you will become free of it."

Sage Angirasa rushed to meet Hanuman and asked him to narrate the katha to him. Hanuman was only too glad to oblige. But he was on another mission so he asked the sage to travel with him and hear it at the same time. He also asked the sage to hear the tale with a peaceful and attentive mind. With this instruction, Hanuman started the narration while on the move.

Shukracharya, was in fact, more qualified than Brihaspati to be the guru of the devatas. However, he had the mind-set of demons. His attitude was more demonic than godly. He was proud and also full of anger. When denied the post he so badly wanted, he did not accept it easily. He was carried away by his desire to take revenge. The feeling of revenge was so powerful that he became the demon's guru just to harass the demigods. And just like he was burning with the desire for revenge, he wanted Angirasa to burn in the fire of sin.

So it was alarming for him when Sage Angirasa began to hear the katha from Hanuman to atone for his sin. He did his best to stop him from hearing it. Every day, he created new demons and sent them to hamper the process, to prevent the sage from hearing the tale so he could suffer the reactions of his sin eternally.

The latest demon he created from his yagya kunda was the menacing Bhadrasura. He ordered him to kill the sage. Bhadrasura knew that the sage was immortal and killing him was next to impossible. Easier than killing would be to swallow him into his stomach where the fire of his digestion would slowly but surely burn him down. The huge fire in his stomach could not fail. One day soon he succeeded in swallowing the sage, when the sage had retired for the day and was all alone. And as the demon had rightly anticipated, the sage started feeling his life force ebbing in the presence of the huge fire in his belly. Keeping calm, he prayed to Hanuman to rescue him; he had no other shelter other than Hanuman's and he offered his heartfelt prayers to him.

Hanuman heard the prayers but he didn't know from

where it was coming. He searched for him but before
he could do anything, Shukracharya sent a yakshini
to bewilder him. The yakshini created an illusory
garden from where Hanuman plucked some fruits. As
soon as he plucked them, the garden changed. From a
flourishing green vegetation, it became dry and yellow.
The yakshini then told him to fetch water from a desert
for the garden to flourish again. The innocent Hanuman
used his mystical powers to dig out water from a desert
also. As he was going back, he met an old woman who
was thirsty and asked him for water. Now Hanuman
realized that something was fishy and he poured water
from his pot but again he used his mystic energies so
that the water kept flowing and did not get over. Then
he poured that water over the entire forest and the forest
became a lively green hub again. But before he could
leave, the yakshini told him join the fruits that he had
plucked back to the branches he had plucked them from.
Hanuman already knew by this time that the yakshini
was preventing him from finding the sage. So he told
her to pick up the fruits and give them to him. As soon
as she picked one, he made the fruit so heavy that it
was unbearable. She found herself caving in with the
huge weight. Realizing he was stronger than her, she
asked for forgiveness and told him where he could find
Sage Angirasa. "He has been swallowed by the demon

Bhadrasura," she said, leaking out this life saving information. Hanuman immediately located Bhadrasura and killed him with his mace. He then pulled out the sage from his stomach. Angirasa was in a bad shape and Hanuman nurtured him back to health. Once the sage was strong enough, they resumed the katha so as to nullify the effects of the sin. At the end of the katha, the sage offered sanctified food to five brahmanas. This was the last stage of the purification and Shukracharya knew he had to stop this from happening. Using his illusory power, he converted the sattvic food into tamsic food. When the brahmanas saw they had been served with animal flesh and stale foods, they lost their temper at the sage's audacity. They cursed him to be afflicted by leprosy. Once again, sage Angirasa turned towards Hanuman to rescue him from this calamity. Hanuman felt sorry for the sage because it was not his doing. Rather, Hanuman's fury for Shukracharya grew manifold because of his endless atrocities. Hanuman informed the brahamanas the truth behind the food turning tamsic. The brahmanas then repented cursing the exalted sage and told him to worship Suryadeva for undoing the curse. In this way, thanks to Hanuman's interventions and timely actions, Sage Angirasa became robust and healthy once again.

All the saints and sages wisely turn to Hanuman

when in difficulty because he is the only one who can rescue them. *sādhu santa ke tuma rakhavāre / asura nikandana*

One day Hanuman had a guest and it was none other than his music teacher and the great devotee Narada. When the two met, they had so many beautiful things to discuss. Hours passed as if they were just seconds. On this occasion, Narada had a very peculiar question to ask Hanuman. Of the millions of great devotees of the Supreme Lord in the universe, he was really inquisitive to know who the greatest devotee was. To Hanuman that question was irrelevant as he always felt that there was no need to compare the greatness of devotees. Everyone was special in his or her own way. Plus each one had their unique relationship with God that would be so different from all others'. Thus there was no common ground also to compare. But when Narada insisted that he really wanted to know the answer to his burning question, Hanuman said something that totally surprised Narada.

Hanuman told him that instead of speculating and arguing about who the topmost devotee of the Lord was, it would be best to verify directly by going through Lord Rama's diary. Hanuman explained that the diary contained the names of all the greatest devotees of the Lord from all over the universe. Narada's excitement knew no bounds when he heard about this fascinating diary. Though he knew the Lord so well, he didn't know this facet of the Lord that he actually maintained a database of his great devotees in a diary. He ran at great speed in order to reach Lord Rama at the earliest. Though tired after running such a distance, Narada, without catching his breath, asked the Lord if he had a diary with the database of his greatest devotees.

Rama pointed in a particular direction without even looking. He seemed too preoccupied in something more important. Following the direction of Lord Rama's hand, Narada saw a huge diary that was placed on an ornately carved table. He rushed towards it with great eagerness to immerse himself in that holy list of the greatest devotees in the universe. With a small prayer on his lips, Narada opened the diary with the hope that he find his name there somehow. He got the greatest surprise of his life when he saw his name on the top of the list. He was thrilled. He carefully went through the whole list, immersing himself in the names of all the great devotees of the Lord, many of whom he had personal connect with. But though he scrutinized every page in that diary, he was surprised to find Hanuman's name missing. How was that even possible?

With mixed feelings he ran back to Hanuman. He first thanked him for sharing with him the information of the existence of a diary with the names of the greatest devotees of the Lord. If it hadn't been for Hanuman, he wouldn't have ever known that he was listed as the topmost devotee in that list of devotees across the universe. Though he was happy that the Lord had recognized his devotion, he was at the same time sad that Hanuman's name hadn't featured in the entire list though he was such a wonderful devotee. Narada expressed the same to Hanuman. As soon as he said this, Hanuman asked him a question that literally slipped the ground beneath Narada's feet. With a sweet smile Hanuman asked him whether he had seen Lord Rama's small diary. Now what was that? Was there another diary?

Without waiting for any more clarity, Narada ran back to Lord Rama's palace. Barging in he asked Rama if he had another small diary. This time there was a distinct change in Lord Rama's mood. He dropped everything he was doing and looked at Narada with great love. His eyes seemed to moisten at the very remembrance of that small diary. Gracefully he removed that small diary from a pocket close to his heart and handed it over to Narada. Rama seemed to be lost in some special memories as he kept staring at the precious diary that was in Narada's trembling hands now. Narada opened it, as if he was opening a great treasure. If Rama kept this diary so close to his heart always, it simply meant that the contents of this diary were really special. As soon as he opened the diary, he got the biggest shock of his life to see the name of Hanuman as the first name in that list of names. The one whose name wasn't even there in the big diary was the first name in the small diary. Suddenly a thought hit him and he began to frantically study all the other names in the small diary only to discover, to his dismay, that his name didn't feature in the small diary at all. What did all this mean? Some names are in the big diary and some names are in the small diary. Names that were in the big one were not in the small one and the names in the small one were not there in the big diary. With a disturbed mind, Narada inquired about the secret behind the two diaries.

Lord Rama explained to the great devotee Narada that the big diary contained the names of all those devotees who constantly remembered him and the small diary contained the names of all those devotees whom the Lord constantly remembered. Tears flowed incessantly from Narada's eyes as he ran from Lord Rama's abode to that of Hanuman's and fell at his feet. Hanuman gently picked him and embraced him. What was the need to know the name of the greatest devotee?

Narada learnt from his student Hanuman that the need was to act in such an exemplary way that the Lord strives to remember you. Now Narada very well understood how dear Hanuman was to Lord Rama (*rāma dulāre*) and how much he had to work on himself to get into that small diary of Lord Rama's.

Hanuman is addressed as Shankar suvan, Kesari nandan, and also Pavan tanay. But after Hanuman returned from Lanka, he got one more identity—Rama called him his son. Rama said, "Every son on the earth owes his parents a debt but you are the only son whose father owes you a debt. We attained you without any difficulties of raising you up. But you have gone through a lot of difficulties for us. You have reversed the norm of parent-child relationship. A father carries his son but you are a son who carried his father. You are my precious son." That's how much Hanuman meant to Rama. *rāma dulāre*

ashta siddhi nau nidhi ke dātā।
asa bara dīnha jānakī mātā॥ 31 ॥

You bestow eight mystical powers
and nine divine treasures
As given to you by Mother Sita. (31)

As a small baby, Hanuman received 14 boons from
Brahma, Indra, and other demigods. And he received 21
boons during his service and association with Rama and
Sita. With these boons, he became the most blessed and
prosperous being, which elevated him to the status of
God in his vanara body form.

Sita had also blessed him with 8 siddhis and 9 nidhis.
Siddhis refer to supernatural and mystical powers
attained through yoga and meditation. There are many
siddhis described in Vedic literature out of which eight
are most famous and termed as ashta siddhi.

These are the 8 siddhis that Hanuman had:

1. Anima - The ability to shrink his body to the size
   of a molecule.
2. Mahima - Ability to expand the body to any size.

3. Garima - The ability to make the body extremely heavy.
4. Laghima - Ability to lighten the body.
5. Prapti - Ability to go to any place without interruption.
6. Prakāmya - The ability to fulfil any desire.
7. Isitva - Ability to have absolute authority over anything and everything.
8. Vasitva - The ability to manipulate every living being.

Nidhis refer to divine treasures belonging to Kuvera, the god of wealth. Each nidhi is personified as a goddess.

The nine nidhis Hanuman had are:

Mahapadma:	Great lotus flower
Padma:	Lotus/ a Himalayan lake with treasures
Shankha:	Conch shell
Makara:	Crocodile
Kachchhapa:	Tortoise or turtle shell
Mukunda:	Cinnabar
Kunda:	Jasmine
Nila:	Sapphire
Kharva:	Dwarf

"Help, help!" Hanuman heard a faint voice of someone calling for help. From the sound of it, it could only be a small child. Hanuman was so sensitive he could not ignore any pleas for help. He instantly zeroed in on the source of the sound and landed over there. He found a little girl, Mamta, crying out from a deep ditch in a forest on a mountain. Extending his hand to her, he pulled her out easily. Expecting the little girl to be in shock and take some time to recover, he was surprised to see her run around collecting twigs and sticks.

"What are you doing?" he asked with surprise. "Won't you rest a while?"

"Oh no! My stepmother had sent me to gather sticks to cook for them. If I reach later and their food gets delayed, she and my stepsisters will beat me a lot. I have to go. Thank you for saving me." And little Mamta sped away like a frightened squirrel to complete her chores.

Hanuman was intrigued. There was fear and sincerity in the child. He followed her to see what the cause of her anxiety was. What he saw next shook him. The stepmother and stepsisters beat her harshly for coming late. And the little girl was so tiny that she could not even protect herself. Instead she continuously begged for forgiveness. And reassuring them that she would complete all the work including cooking for them. More than feeling sympathy for Mamta, Hanuman admired her patience and tolerance. Wanting to help her, Hanuman planned to teach the wicked family a lesson or two.

He went to meet them, disguised as a herbal doctor for beauty treatment. The stepsisters wanted to become the most beautiful girls so they could marry a prince. Hanuman gave them a herbal face pack to apply on her face. But the treatment was attached to a condition. He warned them, "After applying these herbs on your face, do not think ill of anyone. If you do, your face will turn black. For a pure heart, this will enhance beauty. But an impure heart will become uglier with this."

In their over enthusiasm to become beautiful, they disregarded his warning. Not only the stepsisters but the stepmother too applied the Ayurvedic pack to turn fair and lovely. But alas, their hearts were impure. They harboured only negative and vile thoughts for the innocent Mamta. No sooner had they applied the pack with much eagerness, that their faces turned as black as a moonless night. This time they started cursing Hanuman along with Mamta for turning them into blackened monsters. Hearing their evil words, Mamta began to cry helplessly. She had no other shelter and no one to turn to.

Hanuman pacified Mamta and gave advice to the wicked family. He said, "It is not Mamta's fault that you have turned black. It is you yourself who have brought this upon yourself. By mistreating her and always thinking the worst for her. Beauty of the heart is more important than external beauty. A heart full of love and compassion is the most beautiful. When you develop this beauty, your face will automatically glow."

Turning to Mamta, he assured her that he would always protect her as a brother. Giving her a leaf (apta patta) he sealed his relationship with her. The apta patta was symbolic of happy relationships, health, and wealth. With his blessings, Mamta happily tied the knot with a prince.

The Goddess of Laghima siddhi, who represented love and happiness, was extremely pleased with Hanuman. She promised him that she would always be with him because Hanuman had gone out of his way to fight with fate and bring love and joy in the little girl's life. *ashta siddhi nau nidhi ke dātā*

Kashyap nidhi, the rarest of nidhis, was a symbol of wealth and prosperity. It was possessed only by Indra, given to him by Goddess Laxmi.

When Indra heard that Hanuman was out on a search for Kashyap nidhi, he became upset. No way did he want

Hanuman to have it and become greater than him. He decided to implant obstacles on his path to waylay him.

Kashyap nidhi was in Kashyap loka, an ocean full of tortoises. The king tortoise was Kashyap. When Hanuman reached there, the guards arrested him and presented him before King Kashyap. The king told Hanuman that to obtain the Kashyap nidhi, he would have to go through very tough tasks and maybe he should drop the idea. But Hanuman replied that he was there on order of his guru Suryadeva and he could not even think of giving up. This pleased the king very much. He said, "Tell me, what are the three qualities required to protect wealth?"

Hanuman replied, "To protect wealth one needs to be powerful. One also should know how to make good use of the wealth else he will lose it soon. And religious consciousness is very important to know who is worthy of sharing the wealth with."

King Kashyap agreed with Hanuman and said, "I will take your test on these three parameters. If you pass all three, I will give you Kashyap nidhi."

The first test was about power. Hanuman had to fight a gigantic tortoise to prove his strength. The tortoise was so formidable that he could break a mountain on his back. Even Indra had refused to fight with him. But Hanuman engaged himself in a terrible battle with the super huge tortoise, fighting with great passion and fairness. Midway, the tortoise stopped the fight and told King Kashyap, "I accept defeat because Hanuman has fought with great love and compassion. He is worthy of the Kashyap nidhi."

The next test involved knowing whether Hanuman was a good judge of how to use wealth. He was given some wealth to spend on earth and the king would watch how he spent it. On earth, Hanuman met a lady who was in a bad shape. But Hanuman refused to help her. He explained that there were many people around her eyeing to snatch her wealth away. She was too weak to keep it safely and use it for herself.

A little ahead, Hanuman saw a man beating his children for wanting to eat food. However, he ignored him too because, as he explained later, one does not value what comes easily, without any effort.

Then he saw a businessman who was on the verge of bankruptcy. He was eating in a hotel but when a few poor children came to him for food, he happily gave his plate to them. Hanuman reflected that this was a good candidate to give wealth to because he could help more people by being a fair employer and he would also not hesitate in giving to charity. So Hanuman gave a little of his wealth to the businessman who in turn helped many others.

Now Indra decided that it was high time he stepped

into the picture. He created a scene where he, disguised as a moneylender, severely harassed a few people for not returning a loan. Hanuman decided to give some wealth to those people to repay their loans but they instead spent it on their pleasures. Immediately King Kashyap appeared and informed Hanuman that he had failed the test. But Hanuman justified that had he not given them money, the moneylender would have killed them. In this case, he gave life more importance than wealth. Satisfied with his answer, King Kashyap passed him and took him for the next test on consciousness.

He told Hanuman to enter a kingdom from the northern gate. It was a kingdom created by King Kashyap especially for this test. The law there was that whoever entered the kingdom from the northern gate after the king died, would be crowned as the new king. And since Hanuman was told to enter from there, he was offered garlands and announced as their king. Hanuman was aghast at this senseless method of finding a new king. He was not attracted to the throne or the wealth of the kingdom, rather he was interested in making sensible rules for the future. So he travelled around the kingdom to find someone who was fit to be king. After a long and arduous search, just as he was about to give up, he happened to see a farmer tilling his land without the help of bulls. Hanuman talked to the farmer and learnt that since he did not want to trouble his bulls, he was ploughing himself. Hanuman became happy to learn that the farmer was concerned about the welfare of animals. Then Hanuman asked for water. The farmer took him home and offered food as well along with the water. Hanuman looked at the simple fare on the plate and asked if he ate this simple food daily. The farmer replied that he believed in simple living and high thinking. Rather than the satisfaction of delicious food, he preferred the satisfaction of helping people. Hanuman further asked him about his family to which the farmer replied that the entire kingdom was his family and he provided them with food by farming. Hanuman was delighted that he had found the right person to be crowned as the king. But he also wanted to judge how powerful he was because a king should have physical strength.

Just then a few people came with sticks to attack the farmer. They had to settle an old score with him. The farmer, fearlessly, fought single-handedly. He picked up a stout stick and wielded with such agility that all the thugs scrambled for their lives. Finding an opportunity, Indra also came in disguise to fight with the farmer. The poor farmer was no match for him. Observing the expertise of the new entrant, Hanuman looked closely and realized he was Indra, trying to foil his plans. He immediately transferred some of his power to the farmer and soon the farmer overcame the last challenge as well. Hanuman announced to the royal order that the farmer was suitable in every way to be the king of the land.

Had it been anyone else, he would have fallen for the attraction of the throne and power. But not Hanuman. He had no attachment for all of this. Moreover, he made sure that the right person sat on the throne. Thus, King Kashap was happy to see Hanuman emerge victorious in all his tests and handed over the Kashyap nidhi to him. Kashyap nidhi herself was more than happy to be with Hanuman, fully convinced that Hanuman would use the divine wealth only for the welfare and wellbeing of all living beings. *ashta siddhi nau nidhi ke dātā*

After the war, Rama sent Hanuman to inform Mother Sita of Rama's victory over Ravana. Hearing the fantastic news, blessings flowed out of Sita's heart for Hanuman. "May all worthy virtues abide in your heart. May the Lord of Kaushal be ever gracious to you. Because this day is so auspicious, it will be known as Mangalvar and you will be worshipped on this day. May you be blessed with the ashta siddhis and the nava nidhis." *asa bara dīnha jānakī mātā*

rāma rasāyana tumhare pāsā।
sadā raho raghupati ke dāsā॥ 32 ॥

You have the treasure of the holy name of Rama,
And may you remain in service of Rama eternally. (32)

The King of Kashi was very confused after meeting
Narada Muni. Why would he give him such a strange
instruction? Usually saints teach you to be very
respectful to one and all, but this saint was teaching
exactly the opposite. "I guess that is why they say that
one can never decipher the minds of pure devotees!"
With this argument he pacified his reeling mind. He
didn't have the audacity to argue in front of the saint.
He decided to act immediately, lest his mind presented
more arguments that challenged the saint's instruction.

The journey from Kashi to Ayodhya was long but
the king sweetened the journey with remembrance of
Lord Rama's adventures. The more he recalled the great
adventures of Lord Rama in Lanka, the more excited
he became about the meeting. The arduous journey
passed in a jiffy, absorbed in divine remembrance. Soon
he was inside the royal palace of Ayodhya, right in the

exalted presence of Lord Rama. As soon as he saw his worshippable Supreme Lord, he immediately fell flat on the ground, offering his respectful obeisance. He was so absorbed in looking at his divine master that everything else and everyone else in the vicinity ceased to exist. Without even realizing it, he was following Narada's instructions to the last letter. He stood with his hands folded in supplication looking at the divine form of Lord Rama. Tears flowed from his eyes and his lips quivered in great joy.

Suddenly he was shaken out of his meditation by a shrill voice. Someone was furious. He broke his line of vision to see a sage furiously walking towards the Lord from a distance, shouting while pointing fingers at the king of Kashi. What had he done to attract this kind of wrath from the sage? He had walked in only a few minutes back. Then he realized what the anger was about. It was about his following Narada's instructions. Of course, no one knew that he was only following Narada's instructions. Everyone including the angry sage Vishwamitra had concluded that he was simply arrogant and disrespectful. Though he had offered respects to Lord Rama, he had completely ignored and been disrespectful to all the exalted sages present in that assembly. Though many others would have been also offended, they all chose to remain quiet. But

Vishwamitra wasn't the one to stay quiet when a gross error was committed in his presence. He demanded justice from Lord Rama for the impudence of the king of Kashi. Rama was in a fix. Though he understood the mood of the king, he had to also appease his guru.

He extracted three arrows from his quiver and held it out for all to see. He then declared that with these three arrows, he would behead the king of Kashi by sunset that day. Those words immediately pacified Vishwamitra who stopped speaking and smirked with satisfaction at the devastated king. While Vishwamitra returned to his asana peacefully, the king of Kashi fled like a madman. A minute back, he was staring at Lord Rama with so much love and now all he wanted was to run as far away as possible from Him before sunset. Though in panic, he wondered why Rama had given him time till sunset when He could have finished him off immediately. And why did He choose three arrows when every single arrow of His never failed the mark? Of course now wasn't the time to think about confusing actions of great personalities. He had to first go and seek help from the same person whose very instructions had got him in this trouble to begin with.

Instead of empathizing with him, Narada Muni laughed aloud. In fact, he told him that this was exactly what he had expected. The king of Kashi wondered why

Narada was being so sadistic in spite of being aware of his sorry plight. Narada said that the only person who could help him in this situation was Anjana, Hanuman's mother. If he convinced her that his life was in danger, without mentioning who was trying to kill him, she would ask her son to help. That seemed like a good suggestion. The desperate king immediately ran to Anjana and fell at her feet, begging her to save his life. The compassionate mother immediately called her supremely powerful son Hanuman and instructed him to save the king's life from whoever was attempting to kill him. Hanuman promised his mother all help and spoke to the king.

Hanuman wanted to know the details of the whole story that led him to the death threat. When the king of Kashi explained everything and concluded that the person who had vowed to kill him by sunset was none other than Lord Rama, Hanuman was in a fix. On one hand, he had vowed to his mother to save the king and on the other hand was his loyalty to Lord Rama. For the first time in his life, he was in a situation where he had to stand up against Rama. He repented committing to his mother before understanding the complete problem. If only his mother had known that it was Rama that Hanuman had to stand against, she wouldn't have even recommended this mission. Anyway, it was too late now. Hanuman had to find a solution somehow. The only solution that he had was the holy name of Lord Rama and that, he was convinced, was the solution to all problems of life. *rāma rasāyana tumhare pāsā*

Touching the king of Kashi on his shoulder, Hanuman suggested that he stand neck-deep in the waters of the Sarayu river and incessantly chant the name of Lord Rama. As directed by Hanuman, the king of Kashi desperately began to chant the name of Lord Rama while Hanuman sat on the riverbank doing the same. With the ticking of time, the desperation of the king grew and so did the loudness of his chanting. By sunset, he was crying out the name of Lord Rama intensely. Exactly at sunset, a loud thunderous sound was heard followed by a whooshing sound that increased by the second. The first arrow of Lord Rama had been released. Rama had directed the arrow to sever the head of the king of Kashi wherever he may be at that moment. The arrow flawlessly made its way towards the Sarayu river. The king of Kashi increasingly became aware of his approaching death. His intensity of chanting Rama's name also increased. Just when the arrow was about to hit the neck of the king, it stopped. Less than an inch away from the neck! The king opened his eyes and swallowed a lump of bile that had gathered in his throat. He realized that the arrow had been held by the powerful hand of Hanuman, just an inch before it penetrated into his throat. Hanuman took the arrow away and broke it into two and threw it into the river. As the two pieces of the arrow floated away with the current of the river, the king of Kashi took a deep breath.

Before long, a second thunderous sound was heard with the release of the second arrow by Lord Rama. Immediately, the king of Kashi began chanting Rama's name intensely. This time he was well aware of Hanuman's presence right next to him. Though his mind was more peaceful with that awareness, his heart refused to stop beating intensely. Which heart wouldn't beat so furiously when well aware that Rama's arrow was speeding towards his throat? As soon as the second arrow reached its marked destination, Hanuman's ever alert hands managed to catch it just in the nick of time yet again, saving the king's life. The broken arrow was soon floating away. In a few minutes, the third arrow also met the same fate. The king was thrilled that all three arrows were gone and he was still very much alive. He began to dance inside the water in great joy, thanking Hanuman profusely. Just as the private celebration of the king was on, a huge crowd gathered on the banks of the river. Soon Lord Rama himself was standing there with his hands on his hips, severely angry at Hanuman for thwarting his attempts thrice.

Rama demanded to know from Hanuman how he

dared to stop the arrows of his master. Had his loyalty changed? With great humility, Hanuman explained to the Lord and to everyone assembled there that it was his duty to save Lord Rama's devotee and especially one who chanted his name. Since the king of Kashi was so intensely chanting the names of Rama, he was duty bound to save his life from any sort of danger. Even if that danger came from Lord Rama himself. Rama couldn't refute the argument. Now he was in a fix! How could he fulfil his vow to Vishwamitra without disagreeing with Hanuman?

Narada Muni was watching the scene with great interest. This was exactly what he wanted the world to understand. The holy name of Rama was even more powerful than Rama himself and that Hanuman would always protect those chanting the holy names of Lord Rama. Now since that was established, he silently signalled the king to run and offer obeisance to Sage Vishwamitra. The king promptly fell at the feet of the great sage and begged forgiveness for his disrespectfulness. The sage forgave him instantly and instructed Rama to let the king live, thus solving the dilemma of the Lord for good. The king was immensely grateful to Hanuman for giving him the right direction and saving his life so dramatically. Finally Rama smiled at Hanuman. This servant of his was so special that he somehow knew how to win over his master's heart by hook or by crook. *rāma rasāyana tumhare pāsā / sadā raho raghupati ke dāsā*

Hanuman leaps across the ocean, constantly remembering his master Lord Rama. He remembers that he is the Lord's arrow. The arrow travels swiftly in air not because of its own power but because of the bow and the power of the arms that holds the bow. Similarly, Hanuman believed that it was not his capability that took him across the ocean but the power of the arms that shot him. He was simply the arrow that reached the target because of the skills of the shooter. He gave all credit of success to his master Rama's shelter. *sadā raho raghupati ke dāsā*

tumhare bhajana rāma ko pāvai।
janama janama ke dukha bisarāvai॥ 33 ॥

By singing your praises, one obtains Rama,
And sorrows of many-many past
lives are forgotten. (33)

The freedom that Hanuman enjoyed in Ayodhya was probably unlike that experienced by anyone else. He had won the heart of not just Lord Rama, but also of every citizen of Ayodhya. If anyone was loved the most after Rama, it was definitely Hanuman. His innocence and purity was the reason for such openness in accepting him as a part of every family in Ayodhya, especially the royal household. No one ever stopped him from entering the royal household. That's why when he followed Sita everywhere one day, no one questioned him, nor did Sita mind it. He was like an innocent son, oversized but a little child at heart. A day before, Hanuman had seen the way Rama expressed his love for Sita; and of course he had been a part of the whole war Rama had waged to get her back. He understood that Rama loved her too much but he what he could not fathom was why. There must be some secret Sita held, due to which Rama loved her so madly. If only he could wrangle out Sita's secret then he too could be loved by Rama as much. That was his single-point agenda for the day. He decided he would keep Mother Sita under constant vigilance for a whole day and surely then, he would stumble upon the secret.

Sita noticed Hanuman's strange behaviour the whole day. She realized that he was up to something. But she didn't want to confront or embarrass him. Everything he did was somehow always about trying to please Rama. How he did things was not always conventional or even the most acceptable, but she just tolerated his obvious snooping around, observing her constantly. Finally evening came and she sat in front of a huge mirror and began decorating herself. Hanuman stood at a distance with his finger on his lips, thoughtfully observing her getting ornamented. Though he didn't find much meaning in all those ornaments she wore, he kept his keen observation centred on her. Finally, he observed her do something he didn't quite comprehend. Sita took a pinch of red vermillion and placed it on her forehead slightly rubbing it into the parting of her hair. That seemed strange to Hanuman. He immediately stepped forward and inquired from Sita what she had just done. Sita wondered how to explain a monkey the deep meaning behind the ritual of wearing a red vermillion paste on the parting of hair for a married woman. That too, to Hanuman, who being a brahmachari, or a lifelong celibate, had no experience of the nuances of a married life. She wanted to make it simple for him in a language that he best understood. So she said that this little red dot on her head pleased Lord Rama a lot and also ensured a long life span for Him.

That was it! Hanuman had found what he was looking for. He could now end his long day of research and observation. He had stumbled upon Sita's secret. Her secret of how she managed to please Lord Rama had finally leaked out. He ran out of the bedroom with great joy. Sita couldn't understand what had come over him so suddenly that he ran away right in the middle of a discussion. Anyway, it was futile trying to understand his ways. While she continued decorating herself, Hanuman ran through the streets of Ayodhya in a frenzy. He ran and ran until he came across a shop that he was looking for. Running into that shop, he asked the shopkeeper for some red vermillion that Sita applied on her forehead. The shopkeeper handed over a little box containing red vermillion. Hanuman was surprised at the tiny quantity the shopkeeper offered him. He asked for more and the shopkeeper gave him four small boxes containing red vermillion. He told Hanuman that it would last Sita for at least six months even if she applied thrice a day. Hanuman didn't want to argue with him. He simply asked him where he stocked the red vermillion powder. The clueless shopkeeper pointed to a storeroom that was at the back of his shop.

Hanuman walked into that storeroom and after a few minutes walked out with a huge sack over his shoulder. Walking right into the middle of the street, Hanuman emptied the contents of that sack on the ground and spread the red vermillion powder. By then, many onlookers had gathered to watch the humorous actions of Hanuman. Throwing away the empty sack, Hanuman began to roll on the ground, all over the red vermillion powder. Soon every inch of Hanuman's body was covered with the red powder. The red monkey stood up. Peals of laughter vibrated from every corner of the street. No one had ever seen a red monkey. Hanuman then began to walk with a proud gait towards the royal courtroom. When he entered the courtroom, a serious discussion was going on. As soon as he stepped in, giggles could be heard from different corners. Soon Rama noticed that everyone was laughing hysterically. He turned towards the door of the courtroom and found a red monkey standing there with folded hands. The whole scene was so hilarious that Rama couldn't control his laughter. Soon Rama was laughing his heart out too. Seeing their king in so much mirth, the entire courtroom drowned in laugher.

Rama's expansive laughter gave much satisfaction

to Hanuman's heart. He had always wanted to please the Lord. Rama not just seemed pleased but supremely pleased with him. After everyone had laughed to their hearts' content, Rama asked Hanuman what had he done to himself. Why was he red all over? With an innocent childlike smile, Hanuman explained how he had discovered Sita's secret of pleasing him. He told Rama how Sita had revealed that putting a little red dot on her head pleased him and also increased his life span. "If a little red dot on her head can please you so much and increase your life span considerably, then I thought how much you would be pleased if I completely covered myself from top to bottom in red vermillion. Not just that, how much would your lifespan increase if I applied so much red powder all over myself!"

Lord Rama's heart simply melted at Hanuman's innocence and intense desire to please him. He blessed Hanuman with a benediction that anyone who worshipped Hanuman with red vermillion will never have difficulties and suffering in their lives. *tumhare bhajana rāma ko pāvai / janama janama ke dukha bisarāvai.* If one worships Hanuman, one finds Rama and also finds the end of innumerable miseries. Hanuman always responds to the call of his devotees and grants them their cherished prayers, irrespective of time and place.

anta kāla raghubara pura jāī।
jahā janma hari bhakta kahāī॥ 34 ॥

*At death, your devotee goes to Rama's abode
Or takes birth as a devotee of Hari.* (34)

Jambumali, a demon who lived in the golden city of Lanka, a city of sense gratification, was a demon who loved liquor over anything else. So much so that he did not just drink it but was constantly floating in a lake of liquor. He never wanted to come out of the intoxicated state. He did not want to wait for the liquor to be served to him. So Ravana had gifted him a lake of liquor that had become his home.

However, with the arrival of Hanuman in Lanka and the destruction of Ashoka Vatika, Ravana had to ring the alarm bell and get Jambumali out of his stupor. Jambu was one of his best attacks. And he needed him now to stop the monkey's rampage.

Jambumali was very agitated when the soldiers literally pulled him out of the lake. But when Ravana mentioned that a good fight was waiting for him, he cheered up. He loved fights. "Who is my opponent, is it Indra or Agni?" he asked in excitement.

"Neither. It's a monkey!" informed Ravana with disgust.

Jambumali smashed the glass of liquor in his hand on the floor in anger.

"Is this a joke?" he demanded, ready to return to his stupor. "I don't fight with petty monkeys."

Ravana then told him what this monkey was capable of. He had destroyed the entire Ashoka Vatika and many of their soldiers. He was not an ordinary monkey. Reluctantly, Jambumali prepared for the fight, which he thought would be over in a few minutes. How much time would he need to finish a monkey anyway?

When he reached Ashoka Vatika, he found the gigantic monkey sitting on a dome, feasting on fruits. Hanuman saw Jambumali and threw him a challenge. "Who wants to meet death today?"

Jambumali was so furious he yelled a few curse words at Hanuman and shot arrows at him. Hanuman caught the arrows and sent them back to him. None of their missiles or weapons had any impact on him. When he had played enough, he stepped down, uprooted a tree and hurled it at the army. That was followed by a volley of rocks and stones. It only took this much for Jambumali to stop physical combat and turn to magical tactics. He expanded his size to an extent that he towered over Hanuman. But Hanuman grew four times in size and Jambumali found himself staring at Hanuman's knees. This wasn't working either so Jambu came back to his normal size.

Hanuman did not want to kill him without giving him a fair chance. He said, "Listen, Jambu. If you like, I can teach you a small mantra that can save your life. It will undo all your sins that you have accumulated over many lifetimes. And if you insist on dying, chant this mantra to take you to a higher destination. The result of devotion is always God's own abode. *anta kāla raghubara pura jāī*

"What nonsense," Jambu yelled in hysteria, "a monkey will teach me a mantra?"

Seeing his reluctance, Hanuman picked him up and balancing him on one finger, he spun him around, all the while chanting Ra-ma, Ra-ma . . . and he flung him away causing instant death. He had wanted Jambu to chant so that he could attain the status of a bhakta but Jambu was unwilling. Hanuman shrugged, anyway he would continue to spread the mantra that elevated the soul. *jahā janma hari bhakta kahāī*

When Rama left the world to return to his divine abode, he instructed Hanuman to stay behind and preach Rama katha to one and all so that everyone got the opportunity for bhakti in this lifetime itself.

aura devatā chitta na dharaī।
hanumata sei sarba sukha karaī॥ 35 ॥

Even if one does not meditate on any other god,
Only serving Hanuman makes one blissful. (35)

After the war ended with Rama's victory, Rama asked
Hanuman to inform Sita about it. Hearing the supremely
good news, Sita blessed Hanuman for bringing the
message to her. She declared that auspicious day as
'Mangalvar' (Tuesday) when Hanuman would be
worshipped. However, Hanuman never accepts worship
for himself but dedicates it to Lord Rama. Lord Rama,
being the supreme Lord, blesses devotees of Hanuman,
granting all their desires and therefore worshipping
Hanuman surpasses worshipping of any other demigod.

Shukracharya, guru of the demons, instigated a demon
king named Viprachit to organize a tamasic yagya. A
tamasic yagya is a negative fire sacrifice that creates a
high amount of inauspiciousness with exactly opposite

results as compared to regular fire sacrifices. He instructed him to harass the sages who were expert in performing yagyas and force them to do a tamasic yagya using abominable ingredients such as flesh and blood. Shukhracharya knew the science of yagyas and was well aware of the fact that the offerings of any yagya had to be personally accepted by demigods. When tamasic yagyas were commenced under the dictate of Viprachit, all the demigods began to get sick one after another. The sun god himself was so sick that the speed of the sun cycle reduced drastically, resulting in widespread climatic changes all over the world. The rising and setting of the sun became irregular too. Since the sun cycle was disturbed, every living being on the earth naturally got disturbed and began to get sick. Different varieties of infections and diseases spread across the globe.

When this came to Hanuman's notice, he immediately reached out to Suryadeva, his teacher and guide. But he did not respond to his calls. That was strange because his teacher had never ignored him before. Hanuman personally went all the way to meet Surya and find out the cause of all the abnormal events. As soon as he saw his teacher in that miserable sickly condition, he got his answer. Surya urged Hanuman to somehow stop the tamasic yagya instigated by Shukracharya and thereby save the universe from such an unprecedented calamity.

Since nothing was ever hidden from Surya's vision, he shared with Hanuman the location of the tamasic yagya being conducted under the protection of the demon king Viprachit. Surya even showed him the place where the demon king had imprisoned all the sages involved in that yagya. Following the direction, Hanuman reached the prison where the sages were held captive. He learnt from them that they were conducting the yagya under compulsion and not choice. The demon king had imprisoned all their relatives and had threatened to kill them one by one if they didn't obey him in performance of the tamasic yagya. Not only the sages but even their relatives were imprisoned in a prison created by powerful spells that could not be penetrated by ordinary means. Hanuman first decided to tackle the root of the fear of the sages.

The next morning when the demon king and Shukracharya were busy with the tamasic yagya, Hanuman went to the mountaintop where the relatives of the sages were imprisoned. He sat facing the prison and began to chant the holy names of Lord Rama. As soon as the holy names of the Supreme Lord began to reverberate, the spell simply collapsed and the prison disintegrated, releasing all the prisoners. Shukracharya came to know by his mystical powers that the spell had been broken and he sent the rakshasa army to handle the situation. Hanuman, who was waiting to receive the upcoming army, slaughtered each and every rakshasa using his powerful mace. He then instructed the sages to stop performing the tamasic yagya. Shukracharya and the demon king were furious at his impudence. When the demon king attacked him, Hanuman assumed a form so big that Viprachit retreated fearfully. Hanuman was about to kill Viprachit when Shukracharya stepped in to protect his disciple. Leaving Viprachit with a warning, Hanuman freed all the sages and requested them to begin conducting regular yagyas to restore the balance that had tilted towards gross negativity. Shukracharya helplessly watched the tamasic yagya being dissolved by Hanuman and the whole arena being demolished right in front of his eyes.

Only when he returned with the sages, Hanuman realized the extent of the impact of the tamasic yagya across the world. Even after the tamasic yagya had stopped, the demigods had not cured. Most of them were still reeling under its effect. Under Hanuman's direction, all the demigods were taken to Dhanvantari for cure. Dhanvantari examined them and concluded that only a particular quality of pearl exclusively found in Mansarovar could cure them. In addition to the pearl, he also required a twig from the navaratna tree, which was a combination of nine different trees growing as one. A yagya should then be conducted using the twigs with the special pearls tied on them. The ashes obtained from that yagya, when mixed with waters from the Ganges, was the magical cure for the illnesses of the gods. Immediately, Hanuman left for Mansarovar to obtain the necessary ingredients for the magic potion to cure the sick demigods.

However, Shukracharya had not stopped fighting the war. By his yogic powers, he had created duplicate pearls that looked exactly like the original but without the same curative potency as the original. But Hanuman outsmarted him and found the real pearls with the help of the divine swans of Mansarovar. Bringing back the pearls along with the sticks of the navaratna tree, Hanuman ensured completion of the yagya as per the instructions of Dhanvantari. And to the delight of all demigods, all of them bounced back to health again.

After this experience, Hanuman realized that health was of paramount importance. He asked Dhanvantari for a permanent cure for all health problems. Dhanvantari told him about the treasure of health, or swastha nidhi, which can bestow permanent good health. However, the catch was that this treasure was not in existence and could only be created by Lord Brahma. So Hanuman, together with the demigods, reached Brahmaloka. Brahma told them the formula for swastha nidhi. It required 16 different types of rudraksha formed from the tears of Lord Shiva. Hanuman was aware that rudrakshas ranged from one-mukhi to sixteen-mukhi with each one having the power of curing different diseases. Brahma told Hanuman to perform a mahayagya with 16 rudrakshas, as from that yagya would appear the swastha nidhi. Hanuman was excited at the thought of performing the mahayagya and left to collect the 16 ingredients from holy dhams.

As usual, Shukracharya came to know what the demigods were up to. He instructed Viprachit to foil their plan. Viprachit met the king of owls and told them to destroy all the rudrakshas. Because of the owls, Hanuman was unable to find a single rudraksha. He sought Garuda to ask who was behind this mischief. Garuda informed Hanuman that owls were the culprit but no one could take anything from the King of owl without his permission. That's a boon that they had.

So Hanuman reached the land of owls. The king refused to part with the rudrakshas. On asking why, the king revealed that the entire owl family was saddened by the public perception that they were inauspicious. They wanted a better status in society. Feeling sympathy for the owls Hanuman took the king to Mother Laxmi. On Hanuman's request, Laxmi blessed the owls that they would no longer be considered inauspicious. In fact, she accepted them as her vehicle so they would be associated with wealth and hence be considered auspicious.

Feeling on top of the world, the owls returned the rudrakshas gratefully to Hanuman. Hanuman gave them to Brahma, who, along with the demigods, began the yagya. But to their surprise, Agni dev refused to light up. The reason was that Viprachit was still on the throne of heaven and controlling the power of the demigods. In a fit of anger, Hanuman rushed to Indraloka and gave him one tight kick. Viprachit directly landed in Patal-loka and lost all his powers.

With the departure of Viprachit, the demigods regained their powers. The yagya was performed and swastha nidhi personified assured the demigods of continued good health. Hanuman asked for the same assurance for Mrityu loka and swastha nidhi agreed to be present in Mrityu loka as well as Swarga loka. She also thanked Hanuman for invoking her presence and gave him a blessing that whoever prayed to Hanuman will have her special mercy. All the demigods thanked Hanuman profusely. *aura devatā chitta na dharaī ॥ hanumata sei sarba sukha karaī*

sankata katai mitai saba pīrā।
jo sumirai hanumata balabīrā॥ 36 ॥

All difficulties are wiped away and all pain vanish,
By remembering the mighty Hanuman. (36)

During one of his travels, Hanuman saw a very weird
scene. A group of people were lighting a funeral
pyre, but surprisingly, they were not burning a human
body but rather a wooden statue! And though it was
a lifeless wooden statue, an old lady nearby was
bawling her heart out. She lamented continuously
about her dead son. Next to her stood a small boy
trying to console his wailing grandmother by assuring
her that his father was not dead. He was astonished
why she was conducting the last rites of someone who
was alive.

Hanuman was bewildered to see this awkward
scene. Inquisitiveness made him approach the old lady
to question her. He wanted to understand the entire
situation to make sense of it. Why was she burning a
wooden statue of her son while her son was still alive
according to her grandson?

The old lady shared her complicated story with Hanuman. She said that though her son was alive, he was as good as dead. Whoever was called by King Baladhari never came back. Hanuman could sense something sinister in her words. There seemed to be some connection between the disappearance of her son (and many others) and the evil king. He wanted to know more about the king and his whereabouts. Hanuman promised her that he would get to the root of the whole problem and retrieve her son. When she saw a ray of hope knocking at her door, the old lady revealed everything she knew about the atrocious king. Hanuman set about on a mission to find her lost son, Gajashakti, and to find out everything about the activities of the mysterious king.

While Hanuman was almost at the kingdom of King Baladhari, he came across two very weak and emaciated men who were about to jump off a cliff to commit suicide. Immediately Hanuman intervened and prevented them from doing so. They got furious with Hanuman for stopping them from ending their lives. Hanuman explained compassionately that suicide was not a solution to any problem. He encouraged them to face their problems with courage and not give up without trying their best. When Hanuman assured them all help, they confided in him.

At one time, they were the most powerful wrestlers in the entire village. But one day, King Baladhari invited them for a wrestling competition. Eager to exhibit their strength and talent, they accepted the invitation. But to their horror, King Baladhari sucked away all their energies and strengths. All that was left of them was simply a bag of bones while all their strengths had been transferred into the king. Hanuman was surprised hearing this tale. How did he get this kind of incomprehensible power? The two former wrestlers said that all this was the grace of Lord Brahma on him. Lord Brahma had been pleased with his tapasya and offered him a boon by which he could extract the entire physical strength of anyone standing in front of him. And that's how he got his name Baladhari, due to this boon. But there was a flipside to this. As soon as that person died, his strength would leave from Baladhari's body. Thus in order to retain their strength in his body, he would not allow those people to die. He would imprison them and keep them well fed so that they live. The two unfortunate men had somehow managed to escape from that cave. They were hoping that by ending their life, the king's strength would decrease and there would be a greater probability of him being defeated.

Hanuman then confirmed that Gajashakti was also in the king's captivity. They narrated that Gajashakti too was a powerful wrestler with the strength of an elephant and was always in the forefront to protect the village from any kind of calamity. Obviously, he came into the king's radar and was thus invited by the king to a wrestling match where all his strength was siphoned off. They sadly explained that now Gajashakti was reduced to a mere shadow of himself, in a sad emaciated state in the prison. The king additionally gave Gajashakti a warning that if he tried to escape, he would kill his family members and slaughter everyone in his village.

Equipped with all this information, Hanuman headed for a meeting with King Baladhari. Considering him to be an ordinary vanara soldier, the king heaped insults on Hanuman. Then he sent his soldiers to kill him. In a matter of a few seconds, Hanuman destroyed all the soldiers. Baladhari then took Hanuman seriously and stepped forward to fight. Hanuman defeated Baladhari easily. Baladhari tried to suck away Hanuman's energy by holding his hand. What he didn't realize was the vast difference between their two bodies! His body was limited in its capacity but Hanuman being Rudransh, an expansion of Lord Shiva, was unlimited in his capacity. When Hanuman's energy began entering Baladhari, he, very soon, reached the upper limit of his capacity to handle more energy. He wanted to let go of Hanuman's hand but Hanuman wasn't ready to. Thus Hanuman's energy flowed into his body with a tremendous rush and when Baladhari's body crossed the tipping point, it blasted into millions of pieces which scattered all over the place.

Liberating all the weak wrestlers, Hanuman inspired them to not give up on themselves. He taught them the importance of exercise to regain their lost physical strength. He created akhadas or wrestling arenas where they could practice intense exercises and recover their strength. Once Gajashakti found his strength, Hanuman took him back to his mother. The old mother became really happy and blessed Hanuman profusely. At that point, Narada made his appearance and requested Hanuman that he should see to it that never again can another Baladhari exploit people's strengths. Thus for the future, Hanuman created a beautiful reddish deity of himself known as Balanidhi. And he said, "This form will always reside in all akhadas and wrestling arenas. Anyone who worships this form of mine and performs physical activities and exercises will be able to acquire great strength. Physical activity will keep one strong and lack of it will make one weak. From now on no one will be able to steal the strength of another, like Baladhari did."

Narada was very happy and satisfied to know that there would be no more exploitation and pain. *sankata katai mitai saba pīrā । jo sumirai hanumata balabīrā*

Tulsidas recommended installation of Hanuman deity in every akhada to gain Hanuman's blessings for strength for wrestling.

In Ashoka Vatika, when Hanuman assured Mother Sita that Lord Rama would free her from the bondage of the evil Ravana, Sita was so pleased that she plucked a betel leaf from a tree, put it on Hanuman's forehead and blessed him with immortality. All those who seek success in life and wish to be free from fear, pray to Hanuman and appease him with a betel leaf garland.

jaya jaya jaya hanumāna gosāī।
kripā karahu gurudeva kī nāī॥ 37 ॥

Victory, victory, victory to Lord Hanuman
Please shower your mercy as
would a divine master. (37)

Hanuman was once on a mission of obtaining the ashta siddhis or the eight mystical powers. On the way, he suddenly felt hunger pangs. He looked around to find something to satiate his hunger with but what he found was an opposite effect. It made him forget his hunger. What a strange sight it was! An austere woman crying while performing a fire sacrifice. From her radiance he could guess that she had spent a lifetime in austerities. But why was she crying? It made no sense at all. Who would cry during a yagya? When he approached her he also saw that her ears were bleeding profusely. The mystery was getting complicated. He asked her, "Mother, are you in any pain? Please tell me what is troubling you."

"I am doing a yagya and evoking my death because I have no purpose left in life," she replied, sobbing and wiping her tears with her shoulders as her hands were engaged in giving offerings in the yagya. On further encouragement by Hanuman, she narrated her woes.

"After a long and tough period of austerities, I was blessed with a pair of divine earrings. Such was their blessing that wearing them gave me the power to obtain anything I wanted, go anywhere I desired, and take any boon from any demigod at any time."

Hanuman gasped at the powers she had. He anticipated what happened next and said sympathetically, "And now are they stolen?"

She nodded her head sadly. "They were snatched from me by dacoits. But I'm not concerned about the fact that they got stolen. What worries me is that they will fall in the wrong hands and be misused and exploited. It could be used to harass innocent people. All because of me."

Hanuman, who always did his best to help everyone, could not leave without helping her. After learning that the dacoits had headed towards the jungle, Hanuman too took off to find them. He followed the footprints left by the horses, which easily led him to them. But another surprise awaited him there. The dacoits were dead. All but one. He was on the verge of dying too. Answering Hanuman's queries, he revealed before dying, "We were bitten by Nagaraj so that he could take the earrings away from us."

Hanuman followed the trail of Nagaraj and reached the ocean. Since the Nagaloka was located inside the ocean, Hanuman dived deep down. On reaching the gates of Nagaloka, he punched the guards and entered. There he met Nagaraj Kartak and asked him to return the precious earrings. Of course, the Nagaraj refused and laughed at Hanuman's suggestion. Instead he bit him because that's what he did best. But naturally, Hanuman, being a Rudra avatar did not get affected by these trivial bites. He gave him a good thrashing and defeated all the nagas and took away the earrings. But to his horror, the minute he picked up the earrings in his hand, all the nagas fell lifeless. Was there a connection between the two? To confirm, he put the earrings back again and to his amazement, the snakes sprang back to life! The earring belonged to an ascetic woman; how could it have a life and death impact on the naga clan underwater? This was truly bewildering for Hanuman.

Nagaraj Kartak explained, "These divine earrings are a source of our power. This is actually unnatural but unfortunately some days back, our nagamani was stolen. When I went to retrieve it, I found some dacoits who possessed this pair of earring. And this pair of earring gave us the same strength as we had from the nagamani. So I abandoned my search for the mani and carried these earrings back to Nagaloka. Now if you take them away, we will die."

Hanuman was in a catch-22 situation. If he took the earrings back, the innocent nagas would die. If he didn't, the ascetic woman would give up her life. The naga king folded his hands humbly and said, "We will abide by your decision."

Hanuman did not want to choose one over the other. He had to save everyone without any discrimination. He had to find a third way out. He asked Nagaraj, "What if I bring back the nagamani for you? Will you return the earrings then?"

Nagaraj had no objection to this. In fact he appreciated Hanuman's thoughtfulness, his sensitivity and his compassion for them. No one had ever shown any sympathy to their lot. They were always looked down upon with hatred and vengeance by the entire world. With tears in his eyes, he thanked Hanuman for his concern for them.

Hanuman now had to think like a detective. "Where did you lose the mani?" he enquired.

"On Shivaratri, we had gone to Lord Shiva's abode to participate in the celebration. That's where it was stolen. And since then we have been lifeless."

"Do you suspect anyone? Is there any clue to find it?"

"Whoever has stolen the mani will naturally hide it. But he will have no option but to take it out on every full moon day or Purnima because the moon is the source of nourishment for it."

This was sufficient information for Hanuman. He waited for the arrival of Purnima. On that full moon night, he began his hunt for the mani. His keen observation made him realize that all the moonlight was being pulled to one spot on earth. He quickly reached that spot, an obscure village not far from Nagaloka. But the thief was intelligent and knowing it was risky to expose the nagamani for too long, had tucked the mani away much before daylight. When Hanuman reached, he could no longer find the trail of the mani. Since he was sure the mani was in that village itself, he roamed around looking for clues. He came across a huge crowd where a rich man was donating wealth to the villagers. He overheard a few comments about how this man had become wealthy overnight. Hanuman was now certain he had found the thief. He kept an eye on the man and followed him home. The man appeared very nervous and restless. Something was surely bothering him. He told his servants he was going hunting to find some peace of mind. Hanuman followed him to the forest. The forest was a breeding ground for tigers and the foolish man had gone all alone. He was soon attacked by a hungry tiger.

Had it not been for Hanuman, he would have lost his life. Hanuman had stopped the tiger and carried the man in his arms to a safer part of the forest. The man was so grateful that he agreed to handover the mani to him. He confided in Hanuman that stealing the mani had been the worst mistake of his life. It had brought him nothing but misery and misfortune.

A relieved Hanuman took the naga mani and returned it to Nagaraj. An elated Nagaraj returned the divine earrings to Hanuman who in turn handed them back to its rightful owner. The ascetic mother was so pleased with Hanuman that she wanted to give him a blessing of his choice.

"Please bless me that I reach Siddhiloka at the earliest, without any obstacles. That is my destination." The woman not only blessed him but also gave him the earrings. Hanuman was quite stunned with the gift and he did not know what to do with it.

"Because you are always ready to help others in distress, and because your heart is full of compassion, you rightly deserve the divine earrings." She instructed the earrings to accept Hanuman as their master. "Use them in your welfare work. Your merciful nature will win many hearts. You will be hailed as a guru and a hero worldwide for all your good work." *jaya jaya jaya hanumāna gosāī । kripā karahu gurudeva kī nāī*

When things are going smoothly in life, we can easily experience the mercy of God. If we are happy, satisfied, and get what we desired, then we tell others that Lord is very merciful. But if things are not going as per plan, we experience bouts of doubts during sadhana. This is the time we need to have faith.

Lord's mercy can come in many different ways, and to see mercy in difficult situations, we need eyes like Hanuman's. Rama sent Hanuman to find Sita (bhakti) only because he could see God's mercy in favourable and unfavourable conditions.

So while in search of bhakti, if you can feel faith and mercy in dark situations, only then you can successfully find her even in a place like Lanka.

jo shata bāra pātha kara koīı
chhūtahi bandi mahā sukha hoīıı 38 ıı

By reciting this a hundred times
Gives freedom from bondage and pure bliss. (38)

King Rama's sacrificial horse for Ashwamedha yagya
had been captured. Who could show such audacity? It
was Champak, the son of the king of Surat. His act meant
there would be war between the two armies. Before that,
Angad was sent to negotiate. Angad had always proven
himself to be a skilled negotiator. Perhaps, he could
avert the war even this time.

However, he failed to convince the king to release
the horse. For unknown reasons, the king of Surat was
adamant on fighting a war. He refused to hear a word
on that matter. Unhappy with the turn of events, Angad
returned. On his way back, he overheard two soldiers
talking. The few words he could make sense of were
that their king was immortal, thanks to a boon granted
to him by the god of death. Confused at how a mere
mortal could be immortal, Angad hurried back with a
heavy heart.

War was declared. A small chunk of the army was led by Pushkala, the son of Bharat, to fight the army of Champaka. Champaka was a war veteran and easily defeated Pushkala. Instead of continuing the war, Hanuman decided to meet the king. He had heard that the king was a pious man and he thought that it should not be too difficult to convince him. After all, no sane person would want to go through the trauma of war if it was avoidable. But how much ever Hanuman tried to persuade, the king would not move from his stand. His obstinacy made Hanuman suspicious. He went back but returned to the court in a small form so that no one could see him.

What he heard cleared the entire mystery. The king was telling his son, "Yamaraj had told me that I could leave this body only if Lord Rama himself comes to my abode to release me from the cycle of birth and death. My intention is not to fight the war. My intention is not to trouble his devotees. But how else will Lord Rama come here? I have to do all this for my selfish reasons." Hanuman heard all of this and saw the crying king being consoled by his son. Hanuman felt a stab of pain in his heart. How he wished he could help this pious king.

Next day, Hanuman came into the war zone. To match his power, the king of Surat ventured out too. They fought tooth and nail, causing a large number of casualties on both sides. But the scene changed suddenly when the king, showing tremendous valour, tied up Hanuman and made him a prisoner of war. With Hanuman out of action, the entire army gave up hope.

Hanuman closed his eyes and did what he thought was best under the circumstances. He chanted Lord Rama's names. Rama . . . Rama . . . Rama. The holy name echoed in the sky filling the entire space with potent vibrations. Suddenly there was a blinding flash and blowing of conches. Lord Rama appeared with a smile on his lotus face. Hanuman's ropes fell off and the king of Surat fell too—on the ground to offer his obeisance. His body trembled in delight. His hair stood on edge. His eyes crying profusely. Showing all symptoms of ecstasy, the King of Surat attained his desired goal of liberation. Hanuman had willingly tied himself to allow freedom to someone deserving. When Hanuman gives blessings, freedom from material bondage is possible. *chhūtahi bandi mahā sukha hoī*

jo yaha padhai hanumāna chālīsā।
hoya siddha sākhī gaurīsā॥ 39 ॥

Reading this Hanuman Chalisa
Gives mystical powers. Shiva,
the lord of Gauri bears witness to it. (39)

Satyavati, the queen of Kankhal, would be dead had it not been for Hanuman who saved her from committing suicide. Hanuman found her trying to drown in a river and stopped her from doing the abominable act. When he escorted her back home, he realized she was none other than the queen herself. Shocked, he asked her, "What is it that is lacking in your life that you took the extreme step of jumping into the river?" Hanuman was even a little bit angry at the bad example the queen was setting for the common people.

"No one can give me what I lack," was her strange and sorrowful reply. "I want a child. I am not able to have a child. I have failed in giving the king a successor to continue his legacy. How can I face anyone?" And she burst into tears, despondent at still being alive.

Hanuman's face softened. He felt sorry for her. King of Kankhal, King Narottam, and the Rajmata visited him and expressed their gratitude to Hanuman for saving the royal family from a tragedy. They also confided how unhappy they were at not having a child. None of them had any purpose in life anymore. Hanuman could not bear to see their deep grief and promised to help them. Although he had never encountered a problem like this before, he knew he had to do something to help them. He could not simply walk away. He had never done that and he was not going to start now.

Hanuman decided to meditate on Matang rishi, who he believed had answers to all his questions. After an intense period of meditation, Matang rishi appeared. Hanuman paid his obeisance to him and came to the point. "I am sorry for calling out to you but the matter is urgent. King Narottam of Kankhal kingdom is unable to have a child. Because of which the kingdom is in a crisis. Can you please suggest what can be done in this situation?"

"They cannot have a child," announced the muni to Hanuman, "because of their past sinful karmas. Nothing can be done about it."

"Is there not a single deed in their past karma that could save them now? Is there nothing they can do now?" Hanuman persisted. He would not let go so easily.

"Yes, there's always something that can be done," Matang muni smiled at Hanuman's sincerity in spreading joy for others. "They must attempt to please their pitras or forefathers."

Hanuman's face brightened as the muni continued to give instructions, "If the pitras are pleased, they will be happy to take birth in the king's dynasty." The simple solution delighted Hanuman and he thanked the sage profusely before taking his leave. He hurried to convey the message to King Narottam.

Meanwhile, unknown to all, Shukracharya was planning another attack on the demigods. He had interrupted a powerful demon named Davanal from his penance, to help him in his plan. Shukracharya excitedly told him his modus operandi for this attack. "Davanal, this is a fool proof plan. I want you to go to Pitraloka and capture all the pitras along with Aryaman, their king. Once they are in our power, we will force them to take birth in demon families. In this way the quantitative strength of demons with multiply and our might will increase manifold. In this way we can overpower demigods."

Davanal was amazed at the brilliant plan. There was only one doubt in his mind which Shukracharya immediately dispelled. "I will give you the power to enter Pitraloka." Davanal beamed and prepared his army for the attack.

While Shukracharya and Davanal were orchestrating the attack on Pitraloka, Hanuman was helping King Narottam in Pitra puja. At the time of Pinda daan (charity to the body of the deceased), Hanuman evoked Goddess Swaddha, who is designated to accept the pinda on behalf of the pitras and bless them in return. She came to accept the charity but she informed Hanuman that the pitras had attained moksha and were on their way to a higher planet. None of them would want to come back and take birth on earth again.

Hanuman was once again in a lurch and again he sought Matang rishi for further guidance. Matang rishi advised Hanuman to go to Pitraloka to meet Aryaman and convince the king's pitras to take birth from the womb of Satyavati.

Hanuman abided by the instruction and reached Pitraloka. There Aryaman revealed that he was helpless because the process worked on auto mode. "It is never my decision or the pitras' decision where they will take birth. It is dependent on their past karmas and desires. Why don't you ask the pitras where their future birth is?"

The pitras informed Hanuman that they have been liberated and couldn't accede to his wish of taking birth again. But there's one pitra who understood Hanuman's keen and urgent desire to save King Narottam and agreed to change his path for him.

While Hanuman was conversing with the pitras, Davanal was leading the demons in a battle against the demigods led by Indra. The demigods killed the demons but they couldn't match Davanal's powers. Davanal alone conquered all the demigods and entered Pitraloka. When the pitras realized they had been attacked, they hid themselves inside a golden peepal tree. Davanal searched for them all over, even walked past the golden tree but could not find them. Just then, he heard a telepathic message from Shukracharya to uproot the golden tree and bring it back to him as all the pitras were inside that.

However, the pitra who had volunteered to go with Hanuman had already left with Hanuman and entered Satyavati's womb making her pregnant. The remaining pitras were transported to the abode of demons where they were spell bound by Shukracharya to become motionless. He then performed a yagya so that the pitras could die and be ready to be born again as demons. He forced Aryaman to instruct the pitras to take birth in demon wombs. For the second time Aryaman repeated the same words that he had said to Hanuman. "It is never my decision or the pitras' decision where they will take birth. It is dependent on their past karmas and desires and not on brute force."

But Shukracharya was adamant. "I will force them to take birth as per my wishes," he boasted.

Because of Shukracharya's yagya, all pitras had died. And a consequence of this was that Satyavati too delivered a dead child. For the third time, Hanuman set out to find the cause behind this unexpected occurrence. His search led him to Shukracharya where he fought Davanal, killed him and warned Shukracharya to stay out of matters of Pitraloka.

After freeing the pitras, he consulted the demigods and with their approval they established a rule that nobody could bind spirits to take birth forcefully in any loka or species. The only criterion to take birth was past life activities and desires. The goddess of progeny was very thankful to Hanuman. In the presence of all demigods, she blessed him that those who glorify Hanuman will be blessed by siddhis. *jo yaha padhai hanumāna chālīsā hoya siddha sākhī gaurīsā*

tulasīdāsa sadā hari cherāı
kījai nātha hridaya maha derāıı 40 ıı

Tulsidas, servant of Lord Hari,
Says, 'Lord, please reside in my heart.' (40)

Tulsidas became a poet after Lord Rama bestowed his causeless mercy on his ardent devotee. He eventually came to be known as a maha-kavya, with a little help from Hanuman.

Tulsidas's compassionate heart won the favour of a spirit residing on a babool tree in Kashi. Every morning, after his morning ablutions, Tulsidas would throw the remaining water near the tree, which the thirsty spirit would gulp down. That water had sustained the thirsty spirit all along. He felt eternally grateful to Tulsidas for his kind service. One day when Tulsidas poured out the water, he was startled to see a shadow emerging from the tree and then he heard a voice, "You have pleased me immensely. I will grant you a boon. Please ask for your heart's desire."

"Who are you?" asked Tulsidas, "And why do you want to give me a boon?"

"I am a spirit ghost," replied the friendly voice, "and I am happy with you. I have not had anything to eat or drink since many, many years. But after I made this tree my home, I got nourishment from the water a pure soul like you gave the tree. You have served me well and now I would like to serve you."

Tulsidas had only one desire in his heart. "Please give me a boon that I can get darshan of Sri Rama. That is my only desire."

The ghost chuckled merrily. He said, "If I could grant you a spiritual boon, why would I still be a ghost? Please ask for a material boon."

"I have no material desires," replied Tulsidas, dejected at his desire left unfulfilled.

But the shadow said, "I will feel I have been ungrateful if I do not help you. So I will share something important with you. Hear me carefully. Every day, there is Rama katha at Prahlad ghat in Kashi. You will find a leper there who is always present, covered in a blanket. He never misses it. No one knows who he is. Except me. He is, in fact, Pavanputra Hanuman. Go and fall at his feet. Do not let go till he promises to take you to Rama. He's your only hope."

Tulsidas had goose bumps when he heard this. He could not believe the mercy showered upon him. That very day he reached early for the Rama katha and saw the leper was already sitting in the last row, trying to be as discreet as possible. Rama katha began and ended but

Tulsidas had eyes only for the leper. He heard nothing, he saw nothing. When the leper was about to leave, Tulsidas ran and held his feet.

"Please leave me, I am a leper. Do not touch me!" cried the leper and pulled his feet away. But Tulsidas would not let him go. He had been instructed well.

"I recognize who you are and you cannot trick me. Please, I beg of you, please take me to your Lord. Till then I will not leave your feet."

Hanuman was touched by the devotee's intense desire to see the Lord. He knew it was Tulsidas holding his feet, Lord Rama's sincere devotee. He did not see any advantage in continuing the charade. He appeared in front of him in his original form. He said, "I cannot guarantee you a meeting but I can make a suggestion. You go to Chitrakuta and spend your time in doing bhajan. I will try to bring my master there. He usually does not refuse my requests."

Happily, Tulsidas did what he was told to do. Hanuman's assurance was more than enough. He did not expect any more than that.

Hanuman soon returned with Rama's heart-warming message that Rama would visit Tulsidas not once but twice, but the test was if Tulsidas could recognize him. The critical test for any spiritualist was to recognize God.

After a few days, Tulsidas was sitting outside his hut and doing some work when the lord and his brother went by on a horse. When Hanuman asked him if he saw the Lord, Tulsidas was surprised. "Where was He?" and when he heard that Rama had gone past him on a horse, he began to wail and lament. He had assumed some princes were going hunting. He fell at Hanuman's feet again. Hanuman assured him that Rama will come again and he also promised to be around when He came.

The next time Rama came, it was on a festive occasion. Many sadhus had gathered in the vicinity to participate. Tulsidas wanted to apply sandalwood on all the sadhus, so he was scraping sandalwood day and night. That's when Rama came as a child and said, "Baba, please give me some chandan."

Tulsidas failed to recognize the two brothers yet again. The Lord was applying tilak on himself. But this time Hanuman was nearby. He turned himself into a parrot and perched on a nearby tree singing,

'On the ghat of Chitrakoot, there is crowd of sadhu
Tulsidas is scraping chandan and tilak is put by Raghu'

Tulsidas heard this and fell at the Lord's feet. He had finally had darshan of his God. He was so grateful to Hanuman that from that day he never stopped singing glories of Hanuman. In all his writings and speaking, he constantly glorified Hanuman. And that kept Rama safe in his heart. *tulasīdāsa sadā hari cherā । kījai nātha hridaya maha derā*

Doha 41

pavantanaya sankata harana mangala mūrati rūpa।
rāma lakhan sītā sahita hridaya basahu sura bhūpa॥

*The son of Pavan or the wind-god, who is the remover
of all obstacles, is an abode of auspiciousness.
O best of the deities, please reside in our heart
along with Lord Rama Lakshmana, and Sita.*

Tulsidas ends the Hanuman Chalisa with a request to his
worshippable deity Lord Hanuman. His request is to come
and reside in his heart. It's a very clever request because
he knows very well that Lord Rama, Sita, and Lakshmana
eternally reside in the heart of Hanuman. Which means that
if Hanuman comes to reside in his heart, then along with
him, Lord Rama, Sita, and Lakshmana will automatically
reside in his heart too. One must end the recitation of the
Hanuman Chalisa with this final meditation of Hanuman
seated in one's heart and within the heart of Hanuman
is seated Lord Rama, Sita and Lakshmana. In technical
words, this is worship in the mood of dasanudasanudas.
The great acharyas explain that one should not aspire to

serve the Lord directly but should aspire to serve the Lord by serving the servant of the Lord. Instead of aspiring to serve Lord Rama directly, one should aspire to serve the servant of Lord Rama, who is Hanuman.

At present, our heart may not be a conducive place to invite the Supreme Lord directly. So Tulsidas cleverly invites a great devotee of the Lord to reside in it. By addressing Hanuman by four different names, Tulsidas actually reveals to us the levels of cleansing Hanuman does by residing in our hearts. Ramabhadracharya explains that Tulsidas is referring to the four levels of cleansing Hanuman performs. By calling him Pavanatanaya or son of the wind god, Tulsidas alludes to his ability to cleanse our mind (manas). By calling him Sankata-harana or the remover of obstacles, Tulsidas focuses on his ability to cleanse our intellect (buddhi). By calling him mangala-murati-rupa or one who is an embodiment of auspiciousness, Tulsidas points to his ability to cleanse our ego (ahankara). By calling him sura-bhupa or the king of deities, Tulsidas states his ability to cleanse the memory (citta). One whose mind, intellect, ego, and memory are purified by the grace of Hanuman, will one day become qualified to welcome the Supreme Lord within the heart.

With this mood of complete surrender to the lotus feet of the greatest devotee Hanuman, Tulsidas prays that he gets shelter of Lord Rama, Sita, and Lakshmana.

Acknowledgments

Walking through life, I have always seen myself as a student—surrounded by teachers who have touched and enhanced my life immensely. I would like to express my heartfelt gratitude for all that I have been fortunate enough to learn from them.

To name all of them here would be impossible; however, some of the most prominent teachers in my life have been: H.D.G. A.C. Bhaktivedanta Swami Srila Prabhupada, the founder Acarya of the Hare Krsna Movement, and H.H. Radhanath Swami, the author of the international bestseller *The Journey Home: Autobiography of an American Swami.*

I am indebted to Valmiki muni, the author of the Ramayana and to Tulsidasji, whose analogies bring out the deeper aspects of this epic. I have learnt a lot about the intricacies of the Ramayana from Sri Velukkudi Krishnan Swami and K.S. Narayanacharya, Shri Ramkumar Kinkarji, C. Sita Ramamurti, and Sri S. Appalacharyulu. I would also like to appreciate all those who have worked on the website—www.valmikiramayan.net—to make the epic accessible to the world.

My primary reference to the translation of the Hanuman Chalisa has been the commentaries of Swami Rambhadracharya ji, who is simultaneously a scholar and a great devotee. His work has been translated and expanded by Shri Nityananda Mishra ji. If anyone wants to read a scholarly and an accurate version of the Hanuman Chalisa translations, they should surely read the book entitled *Mahaviri* by Nityananda Mishra ji.

And of course, my warm thanks to the entire team of Fingerprint! Publishing, especially Shikha Sabharwal and Gaurav Sabharwal. My gratitude goes out to Pooja Dadwal for her editorial inputs and Neeraj Chawla and his team for putting in their best efforts in marketing.

Dr Shubha Vilas is a lifestyle coach, storyteller and author. He studied patent law after completing his engineering degree but finally chose the path of a spiritual seeker. He has just completed his PhD in leadership from Valmiki Ramayana and his thesis is considered path breaking in the field of leadership studies from ancient texts.

Ramayana: The Game of Life is his bestselling series. He's also the author of Open-Eyed Meditations, Mystical Tales for a Magical Life and Perfect Love: 5.5 Ways to a Lasting Relationship. He has authored more than 30 thought-provoking books. The focus of his work is the application of scriptural wisdom in day-to-day life and addressing the needs of corporates and the youth through power-packed seminars.

He has delivered more than 6000 talks, inspiring more than 5,25,000 people, across twenty countries in the last ten years. He is also a visiting faculty at several premiere business management schools in India including the Indian Institute of Management (IIM) and Narsee Monjee Institute of Management Studies (NMIMS), Mumbai. He has also been a guest speaker at the prestigious Massachusetts Institute of Technology (MIT), Boston; Dresden International University, Germany; WITS, Johannesburg; and several centres of Indian Institute of Technology in India. He is on the advisory board of MIT Pune's online education system.

He has also spoken at Google, Microsoft, Amazon and Samsung at their world headquarters in the USA.

To know more about him, visit www.shubhavilas.com